Date Due

Mar 24'66			
	PRINTED	IN U. S. A.	

North of Monadnock

NEWTON F. TOLMAN

North
of
Monadnock

An Atlantic Monthly Press Book
BOSTON · Little, Brown and Company · TORONTO

Six pieces in this book first appeared in *Atlantic Monthly* and eleven pieces first appeared in the *Boston Globe* and *Berkshire Eagle*.

ATLANTIC–LITTLE, BROWN BOOKS
ARE PUBLISHED BY
LITTLE, BROWN AND COMPANY
IN ASSOCIATION WITH
THE ATLANTIC MONTHLY PRESS

*Published simultaneously in Canada
by Little, Brown & Company (Canada) Limited*

PRINTED IN THE UNITED STATES OF AMERICA

To
N.H. Licensed Guide No. 147
(*My Wife*)

Contents

vii

North of Monadnock

1

A Great Place to Work

THERE must be something wrong with all those advertisements explaining how to save your money and retire in luxury. Those young-looking aging couples with beautifully waved white hair, playing shuffleboard on a cruise ship or sitting on the beach in front of a bungalow, wondering what the hell to do with themselves. . . .

Most people don't want that kind of life at all. What they really crave is insecurity. They must, because everybody who comes to visit us sooner or later exclaims, "Gosh, I sure do envy you people, living up here like this!"

Living up here "like this" means what? Nothing remotely resembling security, at any rate. And far from loafing around the deck of a Caribbean luxury ship, we haven't had a week's vacation in three years.

However, if we mention this to one of our vacationing visitors we get no shred of sympathy. "Vacation? What would you people need a vacation for? Why, your way of life is a vacation the year round!"

People talk this way who don't even know us, people who just happened to take the wrong road down by the pond and were looking for a place to turn around. For all they know our phone may be cut off because we haven't paid the bill, and the bank may be going to foreclose tomorrow. They would have a hard time trying to fry an egg in our unmodernized kitchen. Most of them would be far happier living in Leavittown, not here, where you have to walk a mile through the mud to get in or out every spring. So what are they envying?

Last fly-fishing season a very attractive young English couple, Mary and Nigel Steele, were spending a few days with us on their first visit to the United States. They insisted on helping us clean up the dinner dishes, and when Nigel saw the kitchen his eye lighted up and he began, "I say, d'you know this reminds me exactly —" and then stopped short. He had caught a sharp look from his wife.

We could guess what he had been about to be reminded of — probably some ancient kitchen in the Cotswolds where the cooking arrangements had not been altered since the reign of George III.

Ten years ago my wife and I said good-by to the old homestead down by the pond, where I had always lived, and moved up here to begin life anew. We moved exactly a mile and a quarter.

The way it happened was, we had a chance to buy this big old summer house up on a mountain, with several hundred acres of forest sloping steeply down to the shores of a wild lake. It took all we could beg, borrow and steal, and we planned to rent the house and develop the land.

We took possession on a hot day in August, and sat down on the front porch to cool off and admire the view. "I guess I'll retire and move up here," I remarked facetiously.

"You retired the year we were married," my wife said, "from the ski business. And you've retired from several other things since. What are you retiring from this time? And what do you expect to live on?"

These were questions I was not prepared to answer. But it was my wife who proposed we spend the night up here, and then the next night. And we never did go back to the other house.

As for making a living, anything is grist for our mill, somewhat in the manner of a bearded young painter who stopped here the other day looking for odd jobs — he left a card on which was printed: STRONG HANDS AND WILLING HEART FOR HIRE.

Our year is divided and subdivided into many seasons, each with its major contribution to good spirits and a flat, hard waistline. In the summer there's tennis and swimming and sailing and bass-fishing. In the autumn, training the dogs, bird-shooting, and deer-hunting. Winter, skiing. Spring, trout and salmon. It is necessary to find methods of earning a more or less honest dollar without cutting deeply into any of these activities.

You can't be choosy. Any job that doesn't take long

and has no future in it is all right. Keep an open mind and remember experience is the best teacher. If somebody hires you to fix a stranded automobile or a fireplace that won't draw, grab a few tools and go at it. If you know little about the thing, it follows the owner must know even less or you wouldn't get the job.

A reputation grows naturally. Once people get to saying, "Ask Tolman — he doesn't seem to be doing much these days," security is just around the corner. (And we let it stay there.)

There is always the danger that an odd job may lead to something bigger. Once, after helping a few neighbors with small building projects, we made a serious mistake. A friend got us to help him find a location, and we ended up by designing and building a twenty-five-thousand-dollar house for him. It was a bad year. Hardly any fishing or hunting, and only Sundays were anywhere near normal.

Real estate, too, has its pitfalls. We know people who spend all their time chasing customers for anything they can lay hands on. We don't operate that way. A few years ago we sold a house, and some day we'll sell another. In the meantime, the business doesn't keep us at the beck and call of every character who thinks he ought to own a place around here.

We also run an agency for supplying odd materials used in swank store window displays. Now there's a job we can really get our teeth into. Once or twice a year we get an order, say, for five old stumps. They must be a certain size and weight, with a little lichen on them, and just the right shade of weathered gray. This is easy; we're well acquainted with all the stumps for miles around, having at one time or another tripped over most of them.

It's inevitable that some individuals, even among those who never miss a chance to come up and share our wholesome way of life, should at times raise the question of whether we're Getting Anywhere.

A way out of this dilemma has gradually shaped up. It is well known that to get anywhere, you have to have a profession. Mine is that of an unsuccessful writer, and my wife is an unsuccessful painter. Whenever somebody comes along with that getting-somewhere gleam in his eye and asks what I'm doing these days, I say, "Oh, I'm working on a novel." It takes the wind out of his sails. Besides, it's true; I started writing it years ago.

My wife digs out the paintbox once in a while, but something usually interrupts her before she gets a picture finished. She didn't become an unsuccessful painter until after we were married and she got into the swing of things up here. Before that she used to sell pictures, worried about the future, and was a little underweight. Now she looks ten years younger than her age.

Opportunity may not knock often at most people's doors, but with us it is practically a weekly occurrence. We have learned to parry it with the practiced ease of long training.

Janet is a licensed guide, boards and trains dogs, about a dozen, and usually holds some local political job or other; and she paints a portrait once in a while. For my part, when nothing more urgent needs doing, like fixing the tractor or hauling wood, I have taken to writing. It is much less arduous than cutting timber or repairing somebody's plumbing.

It also makes it more convenient for all our good neighbors who so often drop in. They always know where to find me. I use the good-neighbor term in the international sense. During the past year we have been visited by old friends and new — bird-watchers, mushroom-hunters, explorers and various other pilgrims — not only from most of the States but also from just about everywhere else except Red China.

And as nearly all of these people, before leaving, have suggested topics I should write about, there should be no lack of material. Their combined ideas would fill more books than the entire output of Upton Sinclair.

Around nine this morning all the dogs out in the kennels, joined by three inside the house, announced with their usual enthusiams that somebody was approaching. I left my desk and went outside to greet a casual dropper-in who, camera in hand, just wanted to take a look at the view.

At least a whole hour later, as I strolled rather obviously toward his car, he said, "You sure have a great place to work, here at the end of the road . . . cool . . . quiet . . . no interruptions."

8

Perhaps others can manage to live in the country without attracting more visitors than Yellowstone Park. But not us. In winter, when there is four feet of snow and even the jeep can't buck it, they hike up on skis or snowshoes, just to see if it is true that we can keep warm on this mountaintop. (We usually can, with plenty of exercise by day and an electric blanket by night.)

Last spring I didn't get around to do much work on the road, but it hasn't discouraged the flow of visitors. Little foreign cars crawl nimbly between the rocks, and the big new American ones ride so super-luxuriously the passengers can't feel the crankcase biting into the granite. A conjecture on my part, since we cannot afford either.

We are land-poor, as my father always said of anybody who owned a lot of land and little else. More strictly speaking, we are land- and dog-poor. Janet's idea of how to run a kennel business is to keep five or six dogs of our own, so the food bills will look almost as impressive as the gross income.

Besides a couple of bird dogs that are good for something, there are two liabilities, Sissy and Red Ears. Sissy is a handsome but wild setter we were given when she was young by a friend who could do nothing with her. And she is still so wild we can do nothing with her either.

Red Ears looks like a cross between a fox and a jack rabbit and is deathly afraid of guns and birds, preferring to hunt chipmunks. When you blow a whistle for him he runs full speed in the other direction.

We got stuck for a fancy price when we bought Red Ears from a breeder in Pennsylvania. But Janet said let's not complain, the man who sold him to us was such a nice, hard-working chap, and nobody knows better than we do how tough it is to make a dollar in the dog business. Two or three years later we heard that this nice man owns all the stock in a runner-up to the Coca-Cola company. I like to think the profit he made on Red Ears paid for the gas in his private plane the next time he took a week off for a good rest.

In the house there is old Sandy, a golden retriever, The Man Who Came to Dinner. He was to board here for three weeks, but his owner, an elderly lady, didn't get around to collect him for three years. Then she decided he was too big, and generously gave him to Janet. All his life he has watched, from the front windows, the bird dogs being trained on pigeons; and he must have committed the whole routine to memory. One day we put a bell around his neck and took him shooting, just for fun, and got three grouse with him in half an hour. Instead of pointing he wags his tail, but it seems to work about as well.

I used to be quite satisfied when we lived in our modest-sized house on a little corner of the parental farm, but not Janet. She is small herself, but she hates everything small. Small houses and small plots of land. Small men, dogs, paintings, parties, drinks, small anything you can think of. She even objects to our son's small mustache. Her idea of a little walk is ten miles cross-country. And she would rather sell the last family jewel, if there were one left, than part with an acre of our domain.

This explains why we struggle along with a swampy water system that usually gives out altogether along in August. (There's nothing harmful about the water, it's just a little brownish, but it startles people to see it turn bright green when you add whiskey to it.)

It also explains why we get along with the old jeep, and why the taxes are never paid up, and why the roof needs shingling and the front porch is falling down. And to go back to the plumbing for a moment, our kitchen sink is an ancient trough where dishes are automatically washed by hand, and our bathroom fixtures function erratically at best.

Still, people are always coming to see us because of our view, or to find out if they can navigate our road, or because they have nothing else to do. And they invariably come if they are thinking of getting a divorce.

Apparently they think our own indestructible romance makes us eternally sympathetic to all marital troubles. This faith might waver somewhat if they could see us in the bird covers, on the verge of shooting at each other with twenty-gauge shotguns after heated words about who was supposed to be handling the dog.

In any event, we have decided to post a new set of rules on the bulletin board at the foot of the stairs:

VISITORS WITH ESTRANGED MATES ARE REQUESTED
TO COME ONLY ON ALTERNATE DAYS, LEAVING
THE ODD DAYS FREE FOR THE OTHER PARTY TO
THE PROCEEDINGS. ALL DISCUSSION OF WHO DID
WHAT AND TO WHOM IS DISCOURAGED BEFORE
8 A.M. AND AFTER 11 P.M.

One Sunday last summer we were visited by, among many other sight-seers, the proprietress of my wife's favorite beauty parlor down in the county seat. After duly admiring the view, Steffie discovered we had no television. This, she declared, would be bad enough anywhere; but up on this wild hilltop, snowed in for much of the winter, it was unthinkable. We said we had always managed pretty well without one, but it was plain Steffie thought we had been lucky to survive.

A couple of weeks later Steffie came again, accompanied by her husband, a chiropractor with shoulders like Ingemar Johannsen's. He came striding across the lawn with a large television set tucked under his arm as though it were a box of cornflakes, and deposited it in the living room.

"I just couldn't sleep, thinking about you folks away up here with no TV," Steffie said apologetically. "We had this old set, an extra one, and Ernie was going to turn it in. But you may as well use it until spring."

For the next ten days I didn't get to bed before three in the morning. Janet was a little slow to appreciate some of the programs, but she took to the prize fights right away. Soon we were both addicted, and of course it has revolutionized our life up here. One stormy Sunday I saw nine Westerns between five and nine-thirty, with a total of a hundred and thirty-three men slain.

This spring we bought the set for fifteen dollars. Sometimes the picture comes from one station and the sound from another, but this doesn't matter much with most programs anyway.

Newcomers up here take Janet for a dyed-in-the-wool native like myself, but the fact is she was gently reared in Philadelphia, studied painting in Paris, and was living in New York before we were married.

For generations all the men in my family have gone forth to seek wives from points south. New Hampshire girls were out of the question. I know they have improved in modern times, but when I was young they had not exactly emerged, at least up in these hills.

This is not to imply that we are too choosy about our wives. We just like them to be good-looking and keep their figures until they are seventy or so; to be superb cooks and good athletes; to hold their liquor well and work hard; and to be well educated and artistically talented. My present wife has a violent temper at times, she can't sing, and is not much good at mechanical jobs like overhauling motors.

Offhand I can think of nothing else she can't do if she puts her back to it. And it just occurs to me, this may be one reason my rich and successful city friends are always so envious. It must be difficult, if not impossible, to keep a city wife in very good shape. Women need to get out for a good run every day in the year, on rough ground. This is especially important as they get older.

Janet, raised as she was in city and suburb, has not entirely adjusted to the unquiet country life even after more than twenty years of it. Now and then, when our summer visitors are piling up in a traffic jam in the driveway, she takes a couple of dogs and sneaks down the trail to the lake half a mile below. There she can spend the night in her tent; the only callers will be a couple of loons offshore and perhaps an otter passing by.

Someday, if I ever lay hands on a few dollars, we are going to go down to New York and spend a week or two in a hotel, taking it easy. The first thing I shall do is drop in on that chap who came to see me this morning. Camera slung over my shoulder, I will scale the upper levels of the Empire State Building and stroll into his office at about 10 A.M. and make myself at home.

"You sure have a wonderful view," I will begin. And as they are throwing me out an hour later, "Great place to work up here . . . cool . . . quiet . . . no interruptions."

2
Birth Certificate

Who begat who and who he begat, otherwise known as genealogy, was always even less beguiling to me than the financial section of a New York paper. I didn't even know how to spell it.

But as we grow older our interests branch out, or at least they should. The other day I went to see a man who bought a place a few miles south of us. We do not like people to get the idea we are not neighborly up here in the country; even though he has only been settled seven or eight years, I had decided to drop over and say hello.

My new acquaintance, a retired clergyman, turned out to be a top-ranking genealogist. In no time at all he had me spellbound, and before the afternoon was over he had worked his way back to the eleventh century, when it was just becoming the style for families to use last names. (Upham is one of the earliest in England, in case you happen to be an Upham.)

I had such a good time I would probably still be there

if my wife hadn't called to see what was keeping me. And when I finally broke away, under my arm was a handsome gift of three autographed books by my host.

Genealogists, like architects or psychiatrists, usually begin by being their own clients. This one had traced his ancestry back almost to the last ice age, and has all sorts of awards and certificates to prove it. Both he and his charming wife are members in good standing of a select society called something like The Descendants of Illegitimate Children of English Monarchs.

There in that comfortable library, sitting in the shade of an indoor orange tree that had been in the genealogist's family for one hundred and sixty-two years — growing happily in a wooden tub — and surrounded by thousands of rare old books and manuscripts stacked on chairs and even on the floor, it struck me how few people know much at all about their forebears, even some of us who have been around these hills a long time.

An aunt once claimed to have traced our clan back a few centuries through England and Germany, but the oldest ancestor I can name is several-greats-grandfather Ebenezer. At the close of the Revolution, Ebenezer settled here, where we've been ever since. He had just got back from a Quebec prison with the remnants of Benedict Arnold's little army. He was a sergeant and left a journal of the terribly ill-fated expedition; it supplied Kenneth Roberts with material for a novel. But old Ebenezer never mentioned that beautiful girl who slogged along with the men the whole way. Roberts must have heard about her from somebody else.

Ebenezer had to be a first-class soldier to survive that ordeal, but as a farmer he was hopeless. The land he chose is so rocky, steep or swampy, his descendants have never yet managed to make it pay, and we have tried everything from goats to muskrat farming. Each generation, right up to the present, has had to live by its wits — marrying smart women, swindling the summer people, anything that came to hand.

Next to come to mind, after Ebenezer, is great-great-grandfather Allen. He was famous only for feats of strength. To deliver a greatly feared and savage bull to a neighboring farm, he rode it cross-country, tail in one hand and a horn in the other. He ate himself to death before he was thirty.

Then there was the old man, some relative or other, up on the very top of the mountain about a thousand feet above us. All trace of the house and even the road has been gone for well over a century, but the cellar hole can still be found. Like most of my ancestors, this one is also remembered for the manner in which he met his end.

It was on a clear moonlit night in midwinter, 25° below zero. The old man, near eighty, had been working on a barrel of very hard cider, and suddenly he was seized with some sort of vision. Clad only in a split nightshirt, he rushed out in his bare feet and started running toward Spoonwood Lake, a lonely body of water three miles east. There was a smooth, hard crust on the snow, and his wife couldn't catch him. Neighbors found him next morning out on the ice of Spoonwood, frozen stiff.

A famous California poet tells in verse how he awaits the end — on a couch in his ivory tower overlooking the Pacific, listening for the Voice to say, "Come, Jeffers . . ." For my part, I shall emulate my ancestor; when the time draws nigh, just skip out of bed some winter night and head for Spoonwood in the moonlight.

Grampa French was my favorite. He left me a ten-gauge Lefevre shotgun and a love for Irish novelists. Gramp was a freethinker, a disciple of Robert Ingersoll, Henry George and even wilder prophets. Stocky and bull-necked and minus one eye, he once defied death by diving under the thundering falls of the river in March, rescuing a drunk who had tumbled off the bridge. And when partridge season was closed, he used to shoot pigeons over the rooftops of irate neighbors.

Gramp was always too busy living to find time for any steady occupation. When not fishing or hunting, he wrote long and vitriolic pieces for the newspaper exposing local politicians. He spent a good deal of time over in "the Acre," a tough Irish settlement in the manufacturing town where he lived. He claimed that only in the Acre, in these United States, was free speech really tolerated. Even there his views sometimes got him in trouble, and he was said to return home at times in a considerably disheveled condition. The Acre had a thriving illicit saloon, and it was Gramp's forum.

Gramp finally so goaded the town fathers, they put him in jail. From the lockup he continued to send out furious attacks on them. Finally they agreed to release him if he would leave town. Gramp sold out, foreswore New Hampshire forever, and went into volunteer exile on Cape Cod. There, to his delight, he found he could live entirely on sea food of his own gathering; beat gardening all hollow, he declared; a much healthier diet. Steamed clams for breakfast!

When it came to my own personal twig on the family tree, I was able to help things along a little. Years ago I went over to get old Fred, our town clerk, to look up my birth certificate in order to apply for a passport. Fred took a lantern out to the barn, where he kept the records hidden under the hay. The best he could find was an old book stating that my parents had produced a child in 1908. There was no exact date, no place of birth, no sex — male, female, or neuter. I persuaded Fred to lend me a blank and filled in whatever it seemed might be appropriate.

Who knows? Perhaps by making out my own birth certificate, I have removed a bad snag from the path of some genealogist yet to be born centuries hence.

3

Something on a Dirt Road

AMERICA is a land of varied and violent fads. Admittedly, we have gone in for an odd notion now and again; and one of the strangest began around the turn of the century. Families of means were suddenly seized with an urge to return, voluntarily, to New England — back to the rigorous clime from which they had long been escaping in droves — bent on rehabilitating and occupying old farmhouses.

Heretofore no outsiders had ever come up to our country except in the heat of July or August. Their summer homes ranged from flimsy cottages encased in green latticework to the huge Italian villas, Spanish haciendas, and English manor houses of Bar Harbor and Dublin Lake. Now the *avant-garde* of the summer folk started moving into the farmhouses.

The new farmhouse aristocrats were ranked in order of age of dwelling; climbers soon learned to forge 1760 over doorways of newly acquired old homesteads. One very rich Dublin summer resident, determined to corner the market, bought up twelve old farms, extensively added to the buildings, and installed a resident farmer in each. The amount of money that this amphictyony managed to lose was too much even for a multimillionaire, and the places were soon sold off.

Some of the wealthier recruits to the cult found adjustment to farmhouse living difficult. An industrialist who bought an old house on a hilltop to the south of us remodeled it so extensively that the original house was lost to view somewhere inside. He moved up whole chunks of the rococo family mansion from Worcester and grafted them on all around. There were three-story bay windows, a variety of dormers with stained glass, and, towering over all, two red water tanks large enough to supply the Hotel Wentworth. When the place was finished, the owner ended up a speech at Town Picnic, ". . . and I hope the day is not far off, my friends, when every hilltop in New Hampshire will be crowned by a home as beautiful as my own."

Now, fifty years later, there are still quite a few uncrowned hills left, but the search for old houses is hotter than ever. In the beginning we shrewd, dour natives figured the thing must surely be a passing fashion. It is a notion we have clung to over the years, thus losing countless chances to make a fortune in real estate. As a result we are dourer than ever.

What has happened to "the country," meaning a background for living as distinguished from that of city or suburb? Even here in the hills it is as extinct as *The*

Country Gentleman, that weekly thriller we used to fight for by the light of the softly hissing mantle lamp. Lately, the only real farmers' magazine we've seen is a quarterly, slicker and more sophisticated than *Esquire,* called *The Farm.*

Our native-born Ethan Frome types are about all dead now, their mores and tenets, their very accent all but forgotten. Nor are their ways especially mourned by the handful of us, their descendants, who still live on the Old Place. It is the newcomers from Boston and New York and Indianapolis who keep their memory green. And these people are always insisting they see in us all the homely and quaint traits of our forebears. "Real characters, these neighbors of ours — lived right on the same spot for generations . . ."

Our upland township is one of the more sparsely inhabited in the state, yet it now depends on a suburban routine for its existence. Only two or three men still make a living in the vicinity of their homes. The rest, and some of the women too, commute to town jobs anywhere from ten to forty miles distant. School buses must navigate the most obscure cow path to its end, ensuring that our "country" children, if they ever get any exercise, must get it some other way than walking.

A few of us, far out in one end of the township, still put up a fight every year to stop the spreading tar roads from creeping our way. Not for purely aesthetic reasons, but to protect our hunting and fishing from the increasing tide of beer-bottle heavers. But more and more of our neighbors are coming to the conclusion that we are insane — fanatics throwing ourselves across the asphalt path of progress.

This matter of roads is becoming ever more important to immigrants landing in our region from points south. We know a man who, though he has lived in New Hampshire only two or three years, is urging us to find him a place just like ours. At first we couldn't believe he was serious. "Why, your house is one of the show places of the state, Bill," I said to him. "It must have had over a hundred and fifty thousand sunk on it at one time or another. Why on earth would you want to move?"

"The damn road," he replied. "Black top. Tourists, deer-hunters, riffraff! Cans and bottles all along the edge. Driving us crazy. We've just got to find something on a dirt road."

What he meant was a gravel road. Most of our country roads today that are not metaled (as they would say in England) are heavily surfaced with gravel. At least they are supposed to be, and that is why at town meeting there is always a great deal of talking, one might even say fighting, about Class 5 roads. The best of these roads are good the year round. But too often the gravel is only fine sand, or it has washed away, or there is not enough calcium chloride added to lay the dust. The result is a washboard guaranteed to shake loose from your chassis every bolt not firmly welded in place.

The drive leading to our house is *really* an old dirt road. Experts say it is one of the finest examples extant.

Part of it was used by my ancestors (*circa* 1770); the remainder was built only fifty years ago. (As was our house, the family farm being a mile away.) The more recent part of the road is a fine reproduction, hardly distinguishable from the original. Nowhere has a shovelful of gravel ever been added to the authentic dirt.

In summer a dirt road has a soft, moist center with patches of grass, dandelions, and daisies. The wheel tracks are glassy smooth and have a pleasantly cool texture. For walking barefoot there is no surface as good.

All winter long the dirt resembles nice smooth concrete. But when it unfreezes in the spring it becomes liquid. While this lasts, we either mount the farm tractor or walk. The six-foot rear wheels of the tractor disappear at times, but they can usually keep on slogging forward. Every day we go out and dig little canals here and there to drain off the excess soup and argue endlessly about how many weeks it will be before we can try it with the jeep.

We are taxed a bit higher for owning such a lovely dirt road than would be the case if we lived on a gravel or asphalt highway, but it is well worth it. Nowhere else in the world could we be so sure of a whole month of peaceful solitude every year.

Suburban though we have so largely become, our once silent skies roaring day and night with jets, 'copters, and quaint old props, there is a curious half-world all around us peopled with characters out of the last century. This illusory world-within-a-world began when I was a boy, long before Alexander Woollcott bought his old Vermont farm and called it Bellyacres.

It is the country as the city dweller sees it. It is the country of conservatively romantic novels, plays, and movies — and endless nonfiction accounts of how "we got tired of the tensions and struggles of city life, the daily hours wasted on commuter trains, the sham and glitter, the false standards, high taxes . . ." (My real-estate tax last year came to $840.67.)

The man who moves to the country, unlike the proverbial Englishman who always dresses for dinner in the remote jungle, feels impelled to go in for clothes that reflect his altered way of life. The only jacket-and-tie men in rural New Hampshire are native-born farmers or lumbermen.

All this is fortunate for the photographers from the national picture weeklies who every year do the features on town meeting, "Where Democracy Really Functions." In the front of the hall sits a broad-shouldered, jolly-looking fellow in the obvious garb of the woodsman. His round face, fresh in from the cutting March wind, is browned as though from the hot sun of the West Indies.

And indeed, he and his wife have just returned from there. Originally from New York, they moved up here some ten years ago. Usually they take a Southern cruise to relieve the tedium of our winter chores — the shoveling out of paths, over and over, the daily mixing of Martinis.

Many of our rural customs, neglected for two or three generations, have been brought back to life by the professional country dwellers. They have introduced us to every beverage known to history, including champagne cider, dandelion wine, elderberry cordial, maple-sap beer, and blackberry grub (or is it shrub?).

We were also introduced to something that almost killed us. It was an afternoon in the dead of winter, and the roads were so drifted that no car could move. A neighbor phoned in some excitement to tell us we had better come down right away to see what he had discovered. He would say no more.

We got down there as fast as the tractor would go and were ushered into the kitchen to face an amazing spectacle: about forty full liquor bottles lined up on the kitchen table. After generously sampling several we found out the story. Our host had ordered some wooden barrels from a wholesale liquor firm in which to age his cider. On arrival, the barrels were found each to contain some dregs from their former service, amounting to several gallons of cloudy, powerful, uncut whiskey. He had strained it off through a dish towel and filled all the old bottles he could find.

When we regained consciousness, it was forty-eight hours later and we were safe in our own home. We never knew how we got there, but our faithful tractor was standing in the barn.

Some time ago we drove across the river to visit Ruth Smith, who has written some good things, among them an inspired book called *White Man's Burden*. Ruth is a real old Vermonter, having moved there from Kansas twelve years ago. We were talking about the number of writers who had settled in the Green Mountain country since Kipling's ill-starred sojourn near Brattleboro from 1896 to 1898. We concluded that about half of what we had read lately must have been written in Vermont.

Even Ruth could not tell us why so many colleges have been springing up in Vermont, one to almost every village. It may be that in trying to elude mass-production education, the famed individualism of the region seems like the right environment.

In earliest days, the more adventurous and foot-loose of our hill-country farm youths used to run away to sea. In my time we also ran away, but we headed instead for Greenwich Village. When it came to glamour, with a high flavor of Bohemianism, even Paris could not compete with the Village. Only there could Max Bodenheim have written his classic, *Naked on Roller Skates*, and the area from MacDougal Alley to Tenth Street, lined with sculpture and painting studios, was the undisputed capital of the art world.

Today the painter or musician or writer who has arrived immediately buys an old farm in New England.

(Those who haven't try to land a free summer at the MacDowell Colony, one building of which was the old farm of composer Edward MacDowell, who died there in 1908. His half-smoked cigar lies in the ash tray on the piano exactly as he left it; at least it was there the last time I was over that way.) One of our neighbors is a woman who has recently scored a resounding success as a painter. She now has a winter studio in New York, but it is in the East Seventies, and she remarked the other day that she had never set foot in Greenwich Village.

Another neighbor, for a time, was a poet. He later went to England, where he soon became a great favorite of the Oxford crowd. Before he left, in exchange for a few cords of wood I chopped for him, he gave me the manuscript of this verse, written in his own angular scrawl:

EARLY SPRING LANDSCAPE

To old Ephraim Clapham and his wife, Sarah-Jane,
Spring had been long in coming; almost too long,
So it seemed, for their old frames had been unequal
To the task of keeping things dug out from blizzard
After blizzard. But when at last the final thaw began,
Cutting down the wind-carved hills of white
That had for months near buried the weathered homestead,
Old Eph took hope, and to his wife he said,
"Sarah-Jane, come to the south window with me here,
And look out toward the road — under the apple tree,
There, see? That's the cab of the old Reo;
Clutch went out in nineteen-seventeen, remember?
And just beyond, the Franklin, and the Dodge sedan.

SOMETHING ON A DIRT ROAD

For years I aimed to get a new transmission for that Dodge.
But when the tires rotted I figured, what's the use?
Can't see much of the Overland yet, guess the top collapsed
With all the snow we had . . . looks kind o' spring-like,
Don't it, though, to see them all again!"

For years I about to get a new transmission for the Dodge
that when the tires wore out I figured, rather, the way
Carol was using it . . . Over and past, past the top—before I
it had shifted that way by . . . . snake had a spring—like,
Dodge it though; to see there in the path.

4

The Curious Effects
of Gasoline

EAST of us there is a great wooded valley with a lake.
On the other side, about four miles around by road, is
Old Bert's farm. Farmhouse rather, for the farm part has
long since grown to forest. Not very long ago there was
an east wind and I could hear what sounded like somebody practicing with a shotgun.

The continued, irregular booming was coming from
the exhaust of Old Bert's wood-sawing engine. This reminded me it is now about thirty years since the day I
was working for Bert and the spark plug blew out,
whizzed past his ear, and passed cleanly through a two-
inch-thick barn door. About thirty years before that,
Bert had inherited the engine from his father.

If this machine is not someday placed up in Concord
at the Historical Society headquarters, or perhaps the
Smithsonian itself, it will be a significant loss to poster-
ity. And it could be housed outdoors, as Old Bert would

say, because it has proved more impervious to ravages of weather than the Civil War cannon balls around the village monument.

When I was small the engine was still operated by Bert's father. It was the only power saw rig in the town, and he hauled it from farm to farm sawing wood for a dollar a cord. It was always called what to me sounded like "the Abner-Q"; this was local pronunciation of Abenaque, a French Canadian version of Abenakee, generic Indian name for tribes of this region.

Old Bert's Abenaque came from a New Hampshire factory that looked like an old barn, where the engines were built one at a time. The place was closed up earlier than I can remember, and later tumbled down, but its product is perhaps the longest-lived mechanism ever devised by man. The Abenaque, towering seven feet high on its iron-wheeled cart, has one enormous cylinder surmounted by a square tank serving as a radiator. The massive flywheels look like the drivers of a steam locomotive. Altogether its metal would easily make two modern cars.

One day when Old Bert was "all used up" with the grippe, I went over to help Young Bert saw a few cords of wood. As the more experienced of the crew, I was picked to be the sawyer, while Young Bert "passed on" and the hired man "took away." The Abenaque was started after we had poured several pails of hot water into the tank, the rusty saw was whining eagerly, and then I found that the saw carriage would not return when pushed past the saw. The spring had disappeared some years earlier.

This difficulty, it was explained, was gotten around by means of a stout length of iron stake chain attached to the carriage. I had merely to pass the free end of the chain between my legs, drive a spike into the carriage bed, and then bend the spike over the end link.

I never sawed wood quite as carefully. Old Bert hadn't wasted any chopping and the logs ran from ten to thirty feet in length. It would have been easy to jam the saw, and with my thigh securely chained to the carriage, there was no chance to duck a deadly flying chunk of wood if one should come my way.

All went well for an hour or so. Then the Abenaque's booming suddenly died and the flywheels began to slow and finally stopped. Young Bert, an expert mechanic who had studied gas engines in a trade school, went to work. In the next hour he thoroughly overhauled the late Bronze Age equivalents of carburetor, magneto and valves. But no amount of wrestling with the huge flywheels would elicit even one boom.

We were ready to give up, and then Old Bert came out. He had been watching from the kitchen window. He picked up a can of gasoline and dumped a couple of gallons all over the engine. Then calling, "Stand back," he tossed a lighted match. With a great roar and whosh, flames and smoke rose toward the sky. When the last of the fire had flickered out, Old Bert gave the flywheels a gentle turn. The Abenaque started at once and ran steadily the rest of the day.

It is a strange fact that while this early engine was as efficient as anything we have today for wood-sawing, gasoline long proved disastrous for all other farm purposes. In the country at large, gasoline is supposed to have revolutionized agriculture. Up here it was the reverse. Up here, until very recent years, gasoline was just an excuse for the farmer to let his run-down farm run the rest of the way.

Those who could afford farm tractors found them too compact for our steep, rocky slopes. They would rear over backward, often with the driver underneath. Those who could not buy tractors built them.

Will Dunn's farm was reasonably productive until he got the idea horses didn't pay. After that he spent most of his time happily building and rebuilding his homemade tractor. Two old truck transmissions spliced together gave him something like thirty speeds forward and eight backward. He was never sure which gear he was getting into, and had to be prepared to take off in either direction whenever he released the clutch — sometimes at a considerable speed. Driving was further complicated because the shifting handles soon broke off and he had to reach down with a wrench to get in or out of gear.

Will and another old neighbor of ours were starting

to plow a field one day. They had to work together because Will's plow was designed to be pulled by a horse; someone had to walk behind, holding the handles and guiding the plowshare.

When everything was ready Will got his machine started and it leaped ahead. The pace soon proved much too hot for the old man clinging desperately to the handles, galloping along in the wavering furrow. Cursing and shouting at Will to slow down, he finally lost his grip and fell flat.

At the end of the field Will made a wild turn and came charging back, much too occupied with his bucking machine to look behind. The plow was bouncing about, and every time it hit the ground right side up it would tear out great masses of sod, scattering them helter-skelter.

When Will realized his helper could not catch up to him, he started going around and around in a tight circle. Still he could not stop, because he could not get the tractor out of gear. The ignition switch was not working and he would have had to dismount and get at some wiring on the motor to shut it off.

Meanwhile Young Bert had been driving by, and decided to see what was going on. He had parked his car and stood leaning against a tree, vastly entertained at Will's continuing circular progress.

As Will came roaring around on about the tenth lap, he happened to look up. By this time Young Bert was doubled over with mirth. "Go ahead and laugh, you damn fool!" Will yelled as he went past. "You ain't got brains enough to see that the clutch has stuck, have ye?"

To quote the great poet Robert Frost, who once lived in New Hampshire (some of us think the miniature poem "Fire and Ice" his best):

I think I know enough of hate
To say that for destruction ice
Is also great
And would suffice.

Our ice used to be put to other purposes now almost forgotten. But this age of scientific progress seems to have given up on finding a use for a most abundant natural resource. Given up completely. Long ago we had to burn a substantial number of our trees every year to keep warm, and now we do it with oil; still, trees are used more than ever — for paper, chemicals, and goodness knows what, besides lumber.

We pay as much for a refrigerator as we used to pay for a new Ford in 1920, and we keep on paying for the power it eats up. Yet the men who are trying to land on the moon can't think of a darn thing to do with the enormous energy of the thick layers that cover our lakes every winter. In a way it seems we were smarter when every pond and lake had a large black square hole cut out of its white surface in January. At least we didn't have to pay the Public Service Company for the ice. I guess it was the last free commodity in the United States.

One April in the 'twenties an odd item appeared in the local newspaper, written by our village correspondent, an elderly spinster cousin of mine. The main scoop that week seemed to be the ice "going out" of the pond. As our reporter had it, it was a beautiful and spring-like sight — growing patches of shimmering blue water, and the wind breaking up the islands of ice that drifted out into the middle of the pond and sank. The good lady wrote with true feeling, but her physics was a little foggy.

No doubt a greater loss to society than the ability to utilize a harvest of ice is the loss of the character-molding such a foot and hand-freezing, back-breaking trade inevitably produced.

Another of my relatives, a contemporary of my grandfather, was an unsuccessful forerunner of Mr. Frost. While he composed poetry nobody would read (a family failing I've inherited) his fields grew up to brush and his barns fell into the ground. Every ice-cutting season I used to hear the same story: How Old Wash met his end (his first name was Washington).

Old Wash and his son were down on the pond sawing ice one zero day. While concentrating on a new poem, Wash stood on a projecting ledge of ice and sawed himself off into the pond. His son pulled him out and, so as not to lose time, hauled a stove down on the ice and tried to dry the old man out while he worked. But Yankee ingenuity failed this time. Old Wash caught the pneumony and died.

In the early 'thirties, for a few years just before the electric wires reached the back country, we had a renaissance of ice-cutting. Somebody discovered that a wood-sawing engine with circular saw, mounted on a sled, could cut in a couple of hours what used to take us several days. We froze to death getting the cranky engine started, we got plastered with ice-sawdust, and we worked like horses to pull the machine around. But it was fine to leave those long, heavy iron saws with their great teeth and worn wooden handles hanging in the barn gathering rust. And we used a truck instead of slow, shivering horses, and nobody cared how many cakes we smashed loading and unloading.

In the old days, we used to catch the devil for breaking a laboriously hand-sawn hundred-pound cube of ice by carelessly letting it slide down the chute with too much force. (How many people today know that ice a few degrees below freezing is quite tough, but will shatter as easily as delicate glass when it gets down well below zero?)

Efficient ice-cutting, before the power saw, was a highly skilled art. My father always hired Harry Jefts to help us. Out on the lake, using his own carefully sharpened saw, Harry could cut a string of ten cakes while anybody else cut six. Then he would neatly crack off the separate cakes with sure strokes of his chisel. He never wore gloves in his life, and I can still see those great, muscular, horny hands. Shaking hands with him was like taking hold of a wood rasp. Father said he was so full of home brew his hands couldn't freeze.

It was true that most of the year Harry did little except manufacture and consume a powerful beer made of malt, brown sugar and raisins. But during the ice season he took great pride in his work. It was said that in his youth he had been an accomplished figure skater, and doubtless ice had a special meaning for him. Anyway, in the icehouse — he always did the packing — he could trim a lopsided cake with his sharp axe in seconds and fit it into place so tightly you couldn't get a piece of sawdust into the cracks between cakes. We couldn't chute them in too fast to suit him. He always jumped clear, light as a cat, just in time to save getting a leg broken.

When no more ice-cutting was done in these parts, Harry spent most of the winters devoting himself to the home brew. There came a day when this occupation caught up with him, and the woman who kept house for him called for help. Harry had barricaded himself in the parlor with a loaded Winchester and threatened to shoot anybody who came near. He said he was going to finish the current batch of brew and then kill himself.

By this time I had reached my majority and, being about the only young able-bodied male left in this run-out farming hill-country, had been elected constable. So I went over to Harry's place and finally persuaded him to let me in.

With a lot of argument and a little physical persuasion I finally got the rifle. But I had to sit up all night with him. Toward morning he was still pretty wild, and hadn't shown the slightest sign of knowing who I was. I began to get tired of my job and decided to take him to town and lock him up.

Just as I got him to the door, he straightened suddenly and looked me right in the eye. "Why, you no-good blank blank so-and-so!" he yelled. "I used to cut ice for your father, year after year, long before you were born. And when you were a few months old, and you had the colic, and your ma was sick, I walked the floor with you in my arms all night long — and now you'd treat me like this, you ————!" I thought it over, and I stayed there with him until he sobered up.

Now the lake is smooth and white all winter. There are no tall monuments of blue ice blocks marking the corners of the hole, the way we used to leave them so teams or skaters wouldn't get onto thin ice where we had cut.

But if we had small children growing up on the farm, I would be tempted to get out the old saws and sharpen them up, put a few layers in the icehouse and cover them with three or four feet of the coarse, damp, fragrant, clean sawdust from the lumber mill down the road.

Then on a hot day next summer the kids would be sent on a special errand. In the dark icehouse they would dig a deep hole down into the sawdust, barefoot so their shoes wouldn't get filled. They would pry out a big square chunk of ice and wash off the sawdust until the sides were glassy-clean, and each cold snap and thaw and snowstorm of the last winter would show clearly in the opaqueness of certain layers between the clear, prismatic ones. And as though still alive, a brilliant green sprig of delicate pond grass would be encased in the crystal here and there.

Then we would put the whole chunk into a burlap feed bag and pound it with an iron pipe until it was a mass of ice chips and snow. Then we'd pack the freezer and take turns grinding the handle for half an hour or so. And then we would have all the maple ice cream we could eat.

And so, until someone thinks up a brand-new use for ice, this will suff . . . I mean, this will have to do.

5

Monadnock

COMPARED with many higher peaks a hundred miles north, our own Monadnock is distinguished only because it leads the field in drawing attention to itself. An endless succession of writers, well known and unknown, have sung its praises.

I have always loved to climb mountains, especially on skis, but books about them I find extremely dull. At least until you get into the top strata — something like Everest or the Matterhorn. And Monadnock's summit is, after all, only a few hundred feet higher than my front porch.

The lofty ledge may have inspired eminent talents from Hawthorne to Mark Twain, but if anything very exciting about it was ever written it has escaped my memory. Otherwise I would hesitate to add these modest notes to the vast accumulation of sentimental effusions re The Grand Monadnock already gathering dust.

Twain, by the way, spent his last summers at the north base of the mountain, in Dublin — something the people over there never let you forget. Dublin in those days was a smaller edition of Bar Harbor or Newport and loaded with Proper Bostonians. I have always thought his wife got the great humorist to live in New England so they could cultivate the right people — part of a plot to emasculate his style and make him into a genteel literary lion. He should have gone back to the banks of his beloved Mississippi, and perhaps he could have written another *Huck Finn* or *Tom Sawyer*. As it was, all his last works were a tragic anticlimax to his earlier masterpieces.

Over fifty years ago the ridge that tops our skyline to the south was already known in faraway Japan. There is a large tin box in my mother's kitchen, used for a flour bin. This was a wholesale tea container shipped from Tokyo to the Holbrook Grocery Company in Keene, New Hampshire. The label is a landscape of Oriental delicacy and color, inscribed with the faded legend, *Monadnock Brand*. A Japanese-looking Indian chief, slant-eyed and wearing a feathered kimono, gazes reflectively at a volcanic cone at least twelve thousand feet high with smoke wafting from its snow-capped peak.

Travelers from other parts of the world, unfamiliar with our geology, do sometimes mistake our long, double-ended mountain for an extinct volcano. And indeed among the tumbled boulders in its saddle there is a fine film of ash. But this is just the result of so many Monadnock worshipers, from the summer colonies around the base, having willed that their ashes be scattered from the summit. The prevailing west wind has done the rest.

Nowadays, on some of the shorter trails, midsummer weekend traffic still rivals the ramps of a subway at rush hour. But when I was small there were many more well-worn trails that are now grown to brush. "Climbing the mountain" was then the high spot of the summer for everybody living within twenty-five miles of the peak. Anybody who hadn't made the ascent was ostracized, like a Moslem who lived within sight of the minarets of Mecca and had never entered the city.

Mountain Day was even more exciting than July Fourth at the farm. Many of the summer people around the Pond at that time had come here by train, and there were never enough cars. So a crowd of younger men and boys would start early and hike the nine miles of dirt road to the mountain. We all carried canteens and other paraphernalia, as though we were heading for the back country of the Himalayas.

The climb itself, straight up the north slope, was somewhat longer than the Jaffrey trail, which began at the old Halfway House. Still, we could do it in an hour flat if we hustled, and the whole party of all ages might take a bit over two hours.

The big thrill was getting above the timber line, where for the first time the vast panorama of lakes and hills and villages below could begin to be seen.

The other day, flying past the mountain after leaving

the Keene airport on my way to New York, I thought back somewhat sadly to those days when so many of us had never been higher in our lives than the small peak below. And I remembered the couple, summering near the mountain, who recently told us they had not been able to persuade their teen-age children to make the climb. When I was young nobody with two legs ever needed to be persuaded to climb Monadnock. Further reflection led me to conclude that if I had the custody of those teen-agers, I would personally prod them from behind, every step of the way up the longest trail, with the well-sharpened point of a ski pole.

Wherever a single mountain stands alone, like this one, there is always a good deal of legend and superstition surrounding it. The story goes that a great forest once covered the barren upper section, sheltering a pack of timber wolves. Some early settler, aroused by losses of sheep, burned the forest.

But biologists say that whatever forest may have ever managed a foothold on those naked rocks was done away with by the creep. This was not the chap who set the fire — geologically, a creep means a downward movement on the surface of a high place due to wind, frost and rain working with gravity. On Monadnock this has now been offset by an annual upward movement of several million Kleenex tissues, tons of bottles and picnic remains, and other assorted items.

Yet another sort of creep is the pilgrim from Ohio or perhaps Medford, Massachusetts, who lugs a pail of

paint or a hammer and chisel to decorate the summit
with his immortal initials. Some of the ledges up there
have more lettering on them than a whole train of
freight cars.

Despite the anguished protests of nature lovers, the
millions of broken bottles have added a unique touch to
our mountain. To appreciate this you have to see the last
rays of the setting sun slanting across the summit. The
first primitive man to stumble onto the Kimberley diamond fields probably beheld nothing so impressive.

Practically everybody looking for a building site in
this region demands a view of the mountain. In Marlboro
they seek east slopes, in Peterborough they face west;
in Jaffrey they resolutely square their windows toward
the north, while nobody in Harrisville or Nelson would
dream of facing any quarter but due south. (Except my
sister-in-law, a rebel from New Jersey, who insisted on
a spot where there was no chance of even catching a
glimpse of "that old thing.")

Most of these people today merely want to look at
the mountain, not to climb it, and they are unaware of
the subtle change they have collectively wrought in the
view from the mountain itself. In the past, the most
striking impression from the summit came from the
many ponds and lakes glinting among the wild hills below. But now we have an added effect — myriads of
picture windows winking back at the mountain from all
directions.

A view of Monadnock was not always prized. Our

ancestors who cleared the farms were an austere, pious breed. They took no chances. Wherever a house had a fine outlook, invariably a huge barn was built squarely in front of it. Plainly, the builders figured the going would be hard enough in this stony wilderness, without their womenfolk getting starry-eyed from gazing at Monadnock.

By the early part of this century the climb had become so popular that British mountaineer Frank S. Smythe wrote, ". . . when I saw that the summit was black all over I thought it was some queer geological formation. Then I realized that the black was moving; it was people."

On a winter night in the mid-'twenties my brother and I skied up the south side by moonlight. It was about twenty-five below zero, but we were cheered by the company of two pretty nurses who were having a night off from the Keene hospital. It was their first try at skiing, but somehow we got them down alive. Even then we had met some people at the top, around midnight — a party of Appalachian Club snowshoers.

The north side is a potential skiers' paradise, but there are still no ski trails on its wooded slopes. People are always asking why. It seems odd that in a state where millions have been spent to create a little Switzerland, the only real mountain in the southern part is entirely neglected.

The answer was a subject of some bitterness when we were younger. We had envisioned a winter playground for all the youth of the region, and a vast amount of winter business brought into towns around the mountain.

But wealthy Dublin summer residents determined that no unsightly trails should mar their view. Vast tracts of land on the mountain were bought up, ending apparently forever any hope of a winter resort in the area. It seemed to me a sort of retribution when, a few years ago, the sawfly killed most of the big spruce forest on the north slope — a far greater devastation than ten ski trails could have caused.

In Scotland with Dr. Johnson, Boswell once pointed out "yonder immense mountain." "No, sir," said Johnson. "It is merely a considerable protuberance of the earth." Visitors coming here from Austria or Colorado may be even less impressed with our solitary mountain. But there are always plenty of tourists from places like Florida and Kansas, and even Boston, to keep old Monadnock from getting an inferiority complex.

And after all, Monadnock is a few feet higher than Skiddaw, in England, about which Wordsworth went quite off the deep end:

> *What was the great Parnassus' self to thee,*
> *Mount Skiddaw? In his natural sovereignty*
> *Our British hill is nobler far . . .*

Of course the Greeks who live in the neighborhood of Parnassus may take a slightly different view. Their mount-of-the-poets is better than eight thousand feet high. (Olympus is over ten thousand.)

47

I suppose I have seen enough canvas used up in painting Monadnock to build a tent that would cover the whole mountain. Some seven hundred oils of the blue profile were turned out by a single painter — all terrible. Most southern New Hampshire artists keep a stock on hand, and we know one who sells them by the square yard, like linoleum.

Present-day artists have taken to depicting well-known earlier ones painting Monadnock, as in the murals of a Keene bank. Future painters will doubtless paint these painters painting earlier painters painting Monadnock.

Our mountain is a comfortable little mountain, in spite of the impassioned attempts by so many New England writers to endow it with the awesome majesty of an alp. In all my life I remember hearing of only one fatality among its millions of climbers. And that one occurred in winter, when a lost hiker died of exhaustion and exposure. Emerson used to stroll up the south side dressed as though he were walking up Beacon Street.

But any mountain grows in stature when you get a few miles away from it. From our house we look directly at Monadnock to the south, and due east at Mount Crotched, which is only a little over two thousand feet high. Even Crotched, on dim days when its blue silhouette has lost its top in low-hanging clouds, can look unbelievably soaring and majestic.

Some of us who have, like our forefathers, looked at The Mountain every day of our lives are not quite so sentimental about it as the summer people. Still, as I turn around in my chair and see the familiar high twin-humped ridge beyond the lake, I'm glad earth-movers and bulldozers probably will never get big enough to endanger it. At least not in my lifetime.

6

Schussing a Few Decades

BY 1920 we had begun to use skis fairly consistently instead of snowshoes at Tolman Pond. A Norwegian family who visited at the farm introduced us to bindings that stayed put reasonably well, and to ski wax and proper poles, and soon we were exploring the magical mysteries of the Christiania turn. My brother and I improvised homemade equipment for many school friends who came up for winter weekends.

But it was all strictly for fun and nobody dreamed a business might be made out of it. In fact the older generation did its best to discourage us from such a dangerous and silly waste of time.

A few years later tractor plows began to keep our roads open. People from Boston and points south, who in summer had stayed at the farmhouse or in our summer cottages, started besieging us for winter reservations.

Almost before we knew what was happening we were running a ski school — one of the first in the country.

And for the next twenty years my winters were wholly occupied with various aspects of teaching people how to ski.

They were golden years when there were still almost no ski trails in the White Mountains and Vermont had not even been discovered. Ski enthusiasts came to the farm from all over the United States and even from abroad. Then, in 1937-1938, there was a winter spent on hills a little higher than I had been accustomed to at home; I had been engaged to make a sort of survey of methods in the best Austrian alpine resorts.

A little later, as middle age began to close in on us, we finally abandoned our skiing interests except as a casual sport, or as a means of getting down the hill when the road was drifted deep. And now there are good-sized trees growing on the old practice slope where hundreds of fledgling skiers once mastered their first stem turns.

It took centuries for skiing to spread from Finland to the Alps; over here events began to happen in the late 'twenties at a clip no chronicler could follow. Imagine, for example, a downhill race in Newport, New Hampshire, on a very hot day in August. And this was no dream.

The ski madness had infected a lot of people in New England. It had hit them hard; like firewater and the red man. Skiers just couldn't wait for next winter to come, and some misguided fanatic had discovered that pine needles were slippery. Being in the ski business, we felt obliged to go along with the idea. As I remember it, a couple of us outstripped the field, having cheated by gluing celluloid to our ski bottoms.

All known technique was useless. The only way to turn was to jump. You had to fend off the pine trees with your poles. We ended up not only bleeding and bruised, but completely black. Dives into pine needles encrusted everything but our eyeballs with dirt, pitch, and sweat. It really combined two sports — skiing and tar-and-feathering.

Out-of-season skiing — on pine slopes, sand dunes, and indoor death traps lined with borax — was just one of many odd results of the sudden craze. "Dry-skiing" classes in city gyms were mobbed by eager novices. (Memories of lining up a hundred women in the Y.W.C.A., all in their skiing gear, and putting them through kick turns and stem bogens — what a clatter!) A smart shoe manufacturer made a fortune out of "ladies' " ski boots; the things had pointed toes and couldn't be fitted to any kind of binding.

Many optimists, showing up for lessons in downhill running, were outfitted with Finnish *langlauf* skis about ten feet long and two inches wide. One chap went around trying to sell a binding of his own invention we called "the bear trap." It gripped the whole leg up to the knee in an arrangement of ratchets, levers, toggles, and springs, and must have weighed twenty-five pounds.

Among my own modest contributions were metal edges made out of bronze clock springs, a patented ski with a stepped bottom, and a technique known as "figure skiing." It required eight-foot double-ended skis, and it enabled the skier to approximate, somewhat loosely, much of the repertoire of Sonja Henie.

We even had the temerity to try figure skiing in Austria, where it was received with something less than enthusiasm. I went out alone for a limbering-up of spins and outer edges on a vast Arlberg slope one afternoon. Coming back to the village I met Herr Direktor of the ski school; he was a sort of regional dictator of everything pertaining to the sport. He stopped. I stopped. He peered at the upturned points of the rear ends of my long skis. Then he said, "Shees for dancing, hey?" roared with laughter, and went on his way. "Very funny, you old goat," I muttered at his departing back. Afterward I took a feeble revenge by doing Telemarks around his classes and inviting the instructors to try them. It was strictly *verboten* to be seen skiing in any other style than that ordained by the master. But some of our American innovations were destined to develop the sport considerably and were later adopted in Europe.

In the early days we had to import all our equipment. A ski was made of one solid piece of wood and could be broken by a bad spill. As a result, we had hundreds of skis smashed for every leg that was broken. Then we started to mass-produce laminated skis, and soon after, metal ones. These are so superior that now we have hundreds of legs smashed for every broken ski.

In the early years we were at great pains to sell the public our belief that skiing was a safe sport. We must have overdone it, because we were besieged by many specimens who would have caused veteran European instructors to throw in the sponge. There were retired bankers in their late seventies who had even given up golf. One large Boston matron, insisting on lessons, probably hadn't taken so much as a short walk in years. With such formidable girth and battlements, when she caught an edge it was like a mighty pine toppling. We would have to round up all hands to get her back on her feet again.

In New Hampshire a few of us took up skiing because the most glamourous alternative winter occupation was the cutting of cordwood. We learned the Norwegian system, which emphasized a graceful, upright posture. The technique was well explained in a book by an Englishman published around 1920. There were many photos of the author in action. He wore knickerbockers, white gaiters, tweed jacket, and square-visored cap, and sported a luxuriant mustache. In every maneuver the straight briar pipe in his mouth lent him an air of calm nonchalance. And his posture was always very upright and graceful. This posture came in handy much later. After some fifteen years of sliding about the slopes all doubled up in a most uncomfortable squat known as the Arlberg crouch, it again became fashionable to stand erect.

There have been, of course, many refinements of the three main systems (Scandinavian, Austrian, and French or parallel) that succeeded each other in American skiing. Some of these refinements were: weighting the outer ski; weighting the inner ski; weighting both skis; unweighting both skis; going "down-up-down"; going "up-down-up"; rotating with the shoulders; counter-rotating with the shoulders; and just whizzing down the trail and the heck with all of it.

A point fervently stressed in all the newer systems is the forward lean. For several years some new maestro would come along every winter claiming his method enabled one to lean a degree or so further forward. When the Austrians started infiltrating the Laurentians, bringing this fetish with them, my friend (whom I'll call Pierre) was annoyed.

Pierre, a superbly graceful skier who all his life had been teaching people to run the gentle Laurentian slopes, saw no reason to lean further forward. But all he heard from morn till night was a shouting of *"Vorlage! More vorlage!"* One day he had an idea. Behind the heelplates of his skis he fastened metal rings; from these he passed stout straps around his ankles. He then went out and took up a prominent position on the Austrian-staffed school slope. Slowly he bent his lithe form forward until his nose actually touched the points of his skis; then he straightened up and skied victoriously down the slope.

Pierre it was who advocated, with no success, a ski event I would dearly love to see someday. He was sure it would prove more popular than hockey or football. And indeed the idea not only combined some aspects of hockey and football with skiing; boxing and dueling were also thrown in. Two teams were to race six times up and down a rope-tow slope, all at the same time. They would be allowed to shake each other off the rope on the way up, body-check and trip on the way down, generally mixing things up with no holds barred. I'm still hoping some farsighted promoter will get hold of this.

In the 'twenties most of the winter fraternity who had risen above the barrel-stave and toe-strap phases could call each other by their first names. Then a Norwegian trader named Hambro ran a cargo of ski equipment into the port of Boston. Oscar Hambro touched off a social revolution in New England equal to the shake-up Admiral Perry gave to old Japan. In no time every New Hampshire hay field was a potential ski school. The Era of Glamour had dawned. Dodging debutantes was the only serious hazard of the "ski pro." It remains a sociological mystery why so many girls so suddenly wanted to propose marriage, or at least propose to any male eking out a living on skis. The trouble was, there weren't enough ski teachers to go around — about four, all told, in the East. They had to spread themselves a bit thin until we started importing Swiss and Austrians.

For a while I had a partner who had grown up in North Africa and claimed to be part Arabian. (We used to introduce him as "the only Arab skier in the world" and send him down the slope wearing a headdress like Ibn-Saud's.) He was small, skinny, and the homeliest man I ever saw. Yet so many girls were always fighting for his attentions, he almost had a nervous breakdown trying to decide between the richest and the prettiest. He finally went to Alaska and married an Eskimo.

In these days of resort skiing en masse, one doesn't worry about having to crawl down a trail dragging a broken leg. The nation-wide ski patrol is ever alert. But some of the publicity given these people — and I hasten to offer them my sincere tribute — might imply that in earlier times we often left the dead and wounded on the field.

This was not the case. I remember running a narrow trail with an experienced group when we came upon an unconscious skier. He had ventured far above his fellow novices and run into a large maple tree. The damage included concussion, a broken back, and some cracked ribs. With great presence of mind we rushed over to a nearby cottage, ripped off a screen door, and used it for a stretcher. We got him down in fine shape except that near the bottom the screen broke and he dropped right through the door. Anyway, we heard later that he recovered.

In the whole history of skiing, the largest class ever to be taught by one instructor was not at Sun Valley, as one might imagine, or even in the Alps. It was in Connecticut. When the boom began spreading southward, a certain large and select girls' school decided to initiate skiing. A young man who had done some professional teaching was found up in New Hampshire. For what looked to him like a Hollywood salary, he agreed to drive down once a week.

The young pro arrived for his first workout expecting to teach a couple of sessions with perhaps ten or fifteen girls. He found two hundred, each issued a brand-new outfit, all out on the slope and eager to begin. Desperately trying to figure a way out of this dilemma, he told them all to line up at the top of the open hillside. To make matters worse, there was a breakable window-glass crust on two feet of unbroken snow.

When the whole two hundred were spaced out in line, the poor pro could hardly see to the ends. Hardly any, including some six teachers deployed to keep order in the ranks, had ever before seen a pair of skis.

"All right, come ahead!" the pro yelled, intending to add, "One at a time," but it was too late. On that icy crust the whole line was bearing down on him. With the same technique used to escape an avalanche, the pro turned downhill and raced for his life. And when the last flying figure had piled up, about half the girls and five of the six teachers were out of action for the rest of that day at least.

Somewhere around that time we were suddenly jerked into an era of rope tows. They sprang up everywhere, and if the country was flat the optimistic proprietors seemed to think the demand would cause hills to sprout.

Occasionally some debonair skier would get caught by the rope and emerge like a heap of laundry spewed

out of an electric wringer — and be quite as lifeless —
but this only added to the fun. Even today you can
easily spot a veteran of the early tows. Just look for a
man with arms about six inches longer than normal and
subject to bursitis.

Those of us who survived were rewarded by entering
the Golden Age of Non-Climbers. Comfortably relaxed
and swaying gently in our seats, we were wafted aloft
by the chair lift. Big business, technology, and sport
combined at last. Now all we had to do was stuff our
pockets with wads of dollar bills, stand in line for an
hour or so, and presently we would arrive at the summit
so numbed with cold we wouldn't care how we got
down.

One day my wife and I were skiing on a crowded
slope when the lift stopped for repairs. We kept right on,
making a round trip up and down in little more time
than we had been doing via the lift. The idle waiting
crowd stared at us as though we were defying the laws
not only of gravity but of decent propriety as well.
Only then did I realize that a generation of skiers had
grown up as ignorant of climbing as we had been when
we first saw an uphill ski track. (When we were children
a wandering Finn had climbed the hill past our farm; for
years we marveled at how he had managed it.)

I remember two trips to Canada. On the first we met
thousands of happy, frolicking skiers, all strung out
along the Maple Leaf Trail. This trail runs from village
to village all across the Laurentians, and we loved it. A

couple of years later we found the Maple Leaf deserted. Not a single track marked the perfect powder. But in every village five or six tows were doing a land-office business.

The period of Frechette had begun. Who was Frechette? Well, we were on a large tow-slope at Ste. Adele, or maybe it was St. Sauveur. About every half-hour a great shout would go up, *"Make way for Frechette! Make way for Frechette!"* Several hundred skiers would scurry toward the edge of the slope. And presently down would come Frechette, scornful of any sissy attempt at turns to right or left. Crouched so low he could just peer over his knees, poles outstretched like the wings of an eagle, straight down he would sail. Somewhere short of the bottom there would be sudden wild pinwheel of arms and legs and skis and snow. Then Frechette would gather himself up and start back for another exhibition.

I don't know if it was the late Harvey Gibson or the late Joseph Ryan who first found that it was easier to remove a forest than to ski through one. And I've forgotten which one of them spent the most millions of dollars. In any case, Gibson scraped and polished a knoll in the White Hills, as they were known in pre-Chamber of Commerce days. Ryan did his job on a hirsute height in Canada. Thus was started a new and strange trend.

Formerly the heir to unusual riches, seeking an exclusive setting for social shivarees, bought an ocean-going yacht, or built a castle, or picked up a defunct

Scottish earldom. Now if your family owns a few railroads or a diamond mine, you buy a mountain. Bulldoze it off, run up some lifts, build a chalet village and a couple of hotels, and there you are. (Note for lesser millionaires: Secondhand mountains can now be bought at half price in the spring, and at even less after a light winter.)

Meanwhile, I think I'll just ski over to the old field on the hill half a mile from where we live. I just want to practice my Telemarks where the virgin snow is unmarred and there is plenty of room.

7

How to Catch
the Really Large Ones

CERTAIN upland birds and animals have become so adjusted to traffic, as every hunter knows, that they take fright only when a car stops and the motor is shut off. Here in New Hampshire the fish are learning a few tricks too.

Around 1918 a summer visitor arrived at one of our ponds with what he called an "outboard engine." It would have discouraged Ole Evinrude himself; the best its owner could do that season was to coax it into running about ten minutes. But the local anglers all rose up in arms, sure every fish would be scared out of the pond. They gave the power pioneer such a hard time he never came back.

Some thirty years later we went over to the same water one spring day to try the trout. The pond had been "cleaned" and stocked with rainbows; it was becoming a favorite with the car-top and boat-trailer crowd from far and wide. (The state hatchery sends down a truckload of trout every Friday after starving them a couple of days.) We took merely a canoe, not wanting to bother with a motor. Fish were rising, at a distance; but all day long we couldn't get a strike, and we exhausted the tackle box. At the same time we noticed the outboard people were able to take fish, some of them on trolling lines fairly glittering with assorted hardware. Finally light dawned — we realized these fish had never seen a craft in their lives without the familiar rumbling and rattling outboard, and they would have nothing to do with us.

Now the traffic at that pond follows a set routine on weekends. A line of cars creeps toward the landing, while those ahead unload their trailers and roof racks. When you finally get water-borne, you ease out into a parade all going clockwise around and around the pond, with a low blue haze of gasoline fumes close to the surface. And when the evening rise begins, you see that even the trout are all swimming in a clockwise direction. Every once in a while some novice tries to run his boat counterclockwise and quickly gets rammed and sunk. Fishing has always been a friendly and sociable pastime, and this is the most sociable place to fish north of the Jersey Turnpike.

One aspect of the New Hampshire stocking program known as the "put and take" method is seldom understood. Every spring we hear, "Say, your fish-and-game people up here aren't very bright, are they? Why, last weekend we saw some chaps dumping a whole load of trout into a stream right beside the state highway, in broad daylight!" We try to explain that the department is supported, to a large extent, by license fees of fishermen who follow the hatchery trucks; but we can see the point isn't getting across. The average American fisherman instinctively feels that game wardens are always on the side of the fish. When he gets a big catch he puts one over on the man with the badge. This attitude is a historical hangover from Europe, where the eagle-eyed English bailiff or the German Herr Einforgotnvatissdertitle still patrols the majority of the streams.

Now many of our states are transforming their wardens into something more friendly sounding, such as Game Protectors, Wildlife Agents, and New Hampshire's Conservation Officers. "Contact your Friendly Fish-and-Game Distributor, and let him plan your vacation for you. . . . Nabbed with too many trout, or without a license? We will show you how you can pay your fine in easy installments."

Actually our officers are fish salesmen. It is one of their jobs to see that as many as possible of their hand-fed hatchery pets are promptly hooked, because fish escaping downstream will for the most part fall victim to predators, lack of food, or the turbines.

Out-of-state deer-hunters buy expensive licenses every year whether or not they ever kill a deer. They never really expect to get one anyway; and they're so thankful if they end the season without getting shot themselves that they feel the money was well spent. Most fishermen are different. If a fisherman doesn't catch something, pretty soon he'll go somewhere else.

But New Hampshire doesn't overlook the hardy minority: anglers who love to back-pack folding boats into remote ponds where they can listen to the beaver slap his tail, and the kind who spurn spinning rigs or bait. There's the chap who will tramp all day to catch two or three small trout he thinks are "native." One patron of our guide service not only used nothing but the driest of dry flies, but refused to make the slightest attempt at hooking a fish when it rose. Said he was accustomed to fish that hooked themselves, and all he had to do was reel them in.

I guess this man had fished "up north." You have to get up into the north country to find real trout fishing. We're told about it every season. Northern part of the state, the squaretails run two, three pounds; Laurentians — three, four pounds; Hudson's Bay country — five, six pounds. I suppose up near the North Pole you would need a tuna rod and a swivel chair to land them.

When we have heard enough about the fishing up north, we tell them about our brook. This is a wild stream that rises on our place and is well hidden along its entire run to the lake by dense undergrowth. There is no road or trail. It is never fished by anyone except ourselves. The cold, crystal-clear spring water is teeming with *native* trout. They are darker than is common, brilliantly speckled, and full of fight. And they can be taken easily any time. We may also explain — at our discretion — that the brook is about a foot wide and the maximum length of the trout is five inches.

Once a year or so we do indeed fish this Lilliputian rill. It is the only place where we stoop to bait. A fly rod could never be managed in the tangled jungle, and a can of worms is the only way. (As Charles Dudley Warner remarked in the 1870s, a real sportsman never uses anything but flies, except when he's alone.) On a warm June afternoon, when the pokeweeds are up so you can hide behind them, there is no pleasanter way of obtaining the main dish for supper. Especially if there is a very small niece or nephew along, to keep those delicious four- or five-inch trout in proper scale.

(Note from Conservation Department: Small trout indigenous to small streams do not move along to larger waters, as we formerly assumed. If you put these little fish into Lake Winnipesaukee and gave them all they could eat, they wouldn't grow an inch.)

Our larger streams, wide enough for comfortable fly-casting, become too warm in summer for any trout except the recently imported browns. We prefer the shores of our favorite lake when stalking the wily brook trout, that is, squaretail or charr. The latter not to be confused with parr, a name for young salmon, also known at various stages of growth as smolts, grilse, and springers, by anglers with Abercrombie & Fitch vocabularies.

We do have a few landlocked salmon in our lake too. They are descendants of the Atlantic salmon. Generations ago they must have run up from the sea and become trapped back here in the hills. (Our own ancestors did the same thing, and now we too are so well adapted to our environment we would soon sicken and die if returned to the outside world.)

Whenever a fly fisherman insists on trying for these salmon, about all we can do, as guides, is to help him keep his courage up. Pass the time (and the flask perhaps), point out the fire tower on Pitcher Mountain, the eight-hooter owl's nest in the old hemlock, and other sights of interest. Tell him the family history, and the town history, and why no Indians ever lived up here. (Fish were too hard to catch.)

In the meantime, before our man's arm gives out and we go home, there is always a chance he may get a look at one of the big fellows, hauled up by some passing outboard troller using the copper-cable and gang-hook method. If he does not, he is apt to conclude our salmon are just a local version of the Loch Ness monster.

Last summer, down near the public landing, we were hailed by a party of tourists making their way along the rocky shore. They were carrying salt-water rods thick as baseball bats, with double grips and huge star-drag reels and lines designed to hold anything from tarpon to sharks. "Are there any blues or stripers along here?" they wanted to know. We answered that we hadn't caught a single one all day. We never learned whether they thought they had struck the Maine coast, a hundred miles to the eastward, or heard, maybe, that blues and stripers were following in the footsteps of the eels and landlocked salmon.

Until the last decade or two, biologists had come up with very little about our fresh-water fish that was much use to the angler. We learned that our eels are all born in the Sargasso Sea. We knew that suckers eat fish eggs, but we did not know what to do about it. And that Mother Hornpout shepherds her young until they are big enough to fend for themselves with their own little horns — something of a feat of motherhood, considering an average brood runs around a hundred thousand.

The states are now pooling their conservation knowledge, with happy results. Today you hear more talk around the hatcheries of enzymes, genes, protozoa, and plankton than you do of poachers. It wouldn't surprise us if they should come up any day now with a line of trout bred to subsist entirely on artificial lures.

In our lake (up here the nearest one is always "ours," though the state owns all waters of more than ten acres) it was found that "natives" of the lake proper had almost no chance to run up the inlet brooks to spawn. The lake is mainly spring-fed, and the inlets run largely underground. And as mentioned earlier, the pygmy trout inhabiting the brooks were not helping to stock the lake at all. A few hours with a bulldozer cleared a jeep trail. Then a few thousand fat cousins imported from the hatchery gave the population a shot in the arm that bids fair to last indefinitely. For the new recruits, differently conditioned, don't seem to mind spawning right in the shallows of the lake itself. Riding around the country in a jeep seems to give a trout a broader point of view.

The newcomer to these waters may always pick up some tips from an Old Expert. Every New Hampshire lake has one. Ours can be found out in the middle on any fine day, still-fishing with a mysterious array of lines over the side of his flat-bottomed scow. The Old Expert is almost as broad-beamed as his craft, and he has removed the stern seat in favor of a large armchair. When you get within hailing distance of this floating oracle he greets you with the reminder he has fished right here for fifty years, and his Ancient Mariner's voice echoes from shore to shore. Then follows the announcement that the squaretails are all but extinct.

"What's happened to them?" you ask, and the old man intones mournfully, "It's the togue! The togue has et them all. I've been telling 'em for years they'd ought to screen the pond, but nobody does anything." He shakes his head. "There's only a few little ones left. Why, I used to take my limit of three- and four-pound trout, even five-pound, up in the channel every spring. Dry flies, five-ounce rod. Prob'ly I caught the last big squares there was in the whole pond. Now I just fish for togue, don't even wet a fly no more."

We mutter something sympathetic and move along, still rigging up our fly rods in spite of the prophet's words. For we've heard the story before, and still the squaretails always seem to show up when the fly hatch starts, along in May. And there will come a certain day, if you happen to be there . . .

It was a cloudy afternoon, warm and just breezy enough to keep the black flies away. Buzz Williams was with us. He is a retired scientific man and thinks nothing of taking ten minutes to debate about what fly he'll start off with. But this time he got his rod rigged up in ten seconds flat. For as far as we could see up the shore, perhaps half a mile, thousands upon thousands of black sticks were being thrust up into the air from beneath the rippled surface by unseen hands. And when we got out on the rocks, we could see that the sticks were squaretail trout.

It made no difference at all what flies we used, wet or dry, large or small. There would be a savage strike at every cast, often by two or three fish at once. There were rises aimed at a knot in the line, the line itself, and the leader. We took up stations about a line's length apart, and the shallows between us looked like feeding time at the rearing pools. Trout swarmed up from below, pushing the ones on the surface half out of water. When you laid out your line it rested across the backs of half a dozen, and if you weren't careful you would foul-hook one.

We decided to avoid taking our limit until we had each hooked a "big one." After a time I heard a sound over near Buzz, like a wet hand slapping a rubber boot.

"What's going on over there?" I yelled, above the churning and splashing of hundreds of trout all around.

"I was retrieving my fly, right at my feet," Buzz said, "when a trout — maybe two pounds — made a jump at it. From the opposite direction another big one came up, and they met head on — smack! Knocked one of them out cold for a minute, but I was too surprised to net him before he recovered."

Even as Buzz was talking, as though to accent his story, close by my fly a twelve-incher shot out of water and struck the back of a three- or four-pounder rolling on the surface. The smaller fish ricocheted in a fifteen-foot arc, flipping end over end, before regaining the water.

And so, although we don't have anything to compare with that north-country fishing, when the ice starts breaking up in the spring we begin to think again about certain old names: Parmachene Belle, Silver Doctor, Brown Hackle, Jock Scott, Queen-o'-the-Waters. Guess I'll start off with a Black Gnat, dry — what's your choice?

8

Good Hermit Country

MOST people think New Hampshire became a tourist state because of the scenery. Actually you could put all the scenery we have into New York State about five times. No, our lakes and hills were a secondary attraction. Boston people started coming up our way in the 'nineties to see our hermits, much the way the English once went to the Holy Land, long before New England was discovered, to visit some famous anchorite or other.

It was lucky for Thoreau (pronounced *thorough*), the recluse of Walden Pond, that he settled down in a thicket so near Boston. Had he lived only fifty or seventy-five miles north, he would have been just one of the boys — there was a Thoreau-like character living on about one farm out of three up here in those days.

For some mysterious reason there seems to be no detailed definition of the word hermit. Last fall three of us were bird-shooting in a cover we call the Hermit's Run, and we got into a pretty hot argument about

72

whether or not a true hermit can have a wife around somewhere on the premises. None of the dictionaries we later consulted could even clarify this point.

Having lived in very good hermit country most of my life, I can state from scientific observation that hermits fall into three basic types. First, there is the true or lifelong variety; these must become practicing hermits in youth or early adulthood. Crazy Ben was a typical example.

Ben's brothers and sisters went away to the city to seek their fortunes, as all young people around here are still expected to do unless they are feeble-minded. And when Ben was about eighteen, his father hanged himself from the high scaffold in the hay barn. When Ben found him, he cut the rope, dropping the old man thirty feet and landing him on a spike-tooth harrow. Some of the neighbors said Ben wanted to be sure the job was finished.

Whether or not this incident shaped the course of his life, it was the sort of thing that often got somebody started toward becoming a career hermit. By the time Ben was thirty, when I was attending the village school, he was no longer on speaking terms with anybody in town. He was a big, handsome, clean-shaven man with enormous shoulders from a life of dawn-to-dark wood-chopping. His long black hair was cropped but once a year; he held that forty cents was too much for a hair-cut.

When he went striding through the village, head

very erect and looking never to right or left, we would yell, "Hello, Ben! How are you today, Ben? Why don't you answer us, Ben, is it because you're crazy?" Then we would run inside the schoolhouse and lock the door, for he had once caught the Carroll boy and nearly shaken the teeth out of him.

Around that time, Ben worked for George Hall a few days, building a barn. George tried to pay him four dollars a day, but Ben refused, saying three dollars was all any man was worth. They had a row about it, and Ben would never again work for anyone during the rest of his life.

This strange man was puritanically devout; his sole social activity was tending the church stove in winter. Suddenly, in mid-service, he would vault right over the high back of his pew with a great thump, and stamp across the church. Then would come a loud crash-bang and whacking of the iron poker, and the old preacher would have to wait patiently in mid-sentence until Ben's noisy ritual was finally ended.

Ben lived in a cottage. He had boarded up the big, beautiful family farmhouse, and over the years we watched it fall into ruin and finally collapse. But Ben took care of his money and his woodlands. When he died not long ago he left a substantial estate, and one of his timber lots was sold for some thirty thousand dollars. The hermit's life up here often proves more profitable than any occupations the rest of us can manage to find.

Old Ed Shedd was another of the many true, life-long hermits who used to live around here. In his youth he had been one of the last overland cattle drovers, walking his herds all the way from the Stoddard hills to the Boston markets. He was said to have amassed a good deal of money, but he was a miser.

When I was riding to high school on the "stage," we would sometimes overtake the ragged, dirty old man walking to Keene, a distance of some twenty miles from his tumble-down farmhouse. In warm weather he would walk in his bare feet to save shoeleather. Horace, the stage driver, would offer Ed a lift, and the old man would always ask, "How much?"

And Horace would say, "That's all right, Ed, get in."

"Nope, I'll pay, and then if suthin' should happen to me, you'll be liable — how much?"

"Well, if you want to pay, it's fifty cents," Horace would tell him.

"Too much! I'll give ye a quarter."

And Horace, with a chuckle, would accept it.

When they built the new county hospital a young man from the fund-raising firm asked the Stoddard storekeeper for directions how to find the Shedd place. The storekeeper told him it was no use driving all the way up there. The old man would not talk to strangers, and had never given away so much as a nickel in his life.

The young man went up anyway and began to tell old Ed about the hospital drive. Before he could finish his appeal Ed went into the house, came out a moment later and, handing over a check for a thousand dollars, said, "That be enough for ye, will it?"

The startled canvasser began to mumble his thanks, but Ed was already turning back into the house, calling over his shoulder, "Might want to go there myself some day."

A few years afterward somebody found the old man lying on the floor with a broken hip, half dead. They took him down to the hospital and after many months he made a complete recovery. But when the doctors told him he could leave, he said he had decided against it. He liked the young student nurses and he liked the food and he liked to sit out on the sun porch. He would just keep on paying his twelve dollars a day and stay right there.

So he stayed, and when he died two or three years later his whole estate had been left to the hospital. It turned out to be something over half a million dollars. His nearest relatives, some cousins, tried to break the will, but he had sewed it up airtight.

The second type of hermit is the man who starts out in ordinary circumstances and drifts by chance into the solitary life. We have had many of these, and one of our best examples, Charlie Flagg, is still with us. He lives at the end of a nearly impassable road, with a couple of hundred goats, in a house which has seen no paint or other visible repairs for at least a century.

A number of years back, before Charlie had adjusted

to the hermit's way of life, he got himself a mail-order wife. She was a grasping, ambitious type, and when she found Charlie had put away some money she was determined to get hold of it. They fought bitterly from the very beginning, and were soon separated.

The court awarded the wife a small amount of money for support, but Charlie refused to pay a cent of it, claiming he had been swindled. When all persuasions had failed, the judge finally sent him off to the County Farm, where our minor criminals are incarcerated.

He stayed there two or three years, though he could have gotten ten thousand dollars or more for any one of several timber lots he owned. Then one day the sheriff called on Charlie and announced, with the proper note of sympathy and sadness in his tone, that the wife had been taken ill and passed away.

Charlie promptly jumped up and began to dance a jig, shouting, "Glory be to God, the damned old bitch is dead!" They let him go home, and he has lived a happy hermit's life ever since.

Third, we have temporary, or amateur, hermits. And though they may only stick at it a few years, like a now famous college professor who once practiced hermitry here in his youth, they can often outdo the professionals in performance.

Bill, the professor, spent four years in a ten-by-fifteen chopper's shanty heated by a rusty cookstove. He shared bed and meals with old Nellie, a coon hound with three legs. Each week he would work a day or two for some farmer, earning enough to buy a sack of groceries. The rest of the time he would play chess with himself.

Before coming here Bill had acted for a time in stock theaters, and on winter evenings he gave me a thorough education in Shakespeare. In summer he would go down and sit on the landing at the lake and wait for tourists. With his old overalls, straw hat, bushy beard and bare feet, he gave a fine impression of bucolic indolence.

If someone chanced to ask him if it got very cold up here in the winter, Bill would reply along these lines: "Wal, it gits a mite chilly, sometimes. Had a spell last January, thirty, forty below. Went down one mornin' to milk the cow, and she was still layin' down. Found she was froze right to the floor." Long pause.

"Goodness! What did you do?"

"Why, I just had to pour a teakettle full of hot water over her, then take the crowbar and pry her loose."

There are those who think it is no longer possible to become a true hermit, except perhaps on one of the polar icecaps. State welfare agencies, income tax collectors, zoning laws, and the Board of Health do indeed make it more difficult. But then, life in other fields is equally complicated; and there are ways of getting around these factors, if one has the right temperament and a determination to make good.

Many a young man of today would do well to consider the unusual opportunities still left in this field. We are always glad to point out suitable locations in our own neighborhood, and will give such advice and help as we can to anybody wishing to make a start.

9

A Country Store

When I was small, a summer cottage next to our farm was owned by a couple who had never endeared themselves to us by any great show of generosity. One day the lady next door (she would approve the term *lady* because she really worked at it) brought my mother a handsome box of chocolates. When Mother, startled by this sudden largesse, thanked her profusely, she exclaimed, "My husband gave these to me, and as soon as I unwrapped them I could smell cigars. You know that dirty old storekeeper in the village has tobacco and candy all together under the counter! But I thought *you* probably wouldn't mind, and anyway you could give them to the children."

It seems unlikely that the aroma of Mr. Canavan's stogies could actually have pierced the sealed wrappings and stout cardboard of a box of Page & Shaw's. But it is true that the country grocery stores of those days were pretty unsanitary, and their proprietors usually even more so.

A COUNTRY STORE

In late years we've all grown accustomed to nostalgic, sentimental accounts of the old Village Store — the delightful smells of horehound and licorice, mingled with emanations from the vinegar barrels and the molasses jugs.

The way I remember it, those pleasant odors never had a chance. There were rat holes in every corner of the dirt-encrusted floor; the overworked cats could never subdue the well-fed grocery store rodent population. Only fresh-ground coffee could win out momentarily over the felt boots drying around the stove, spilt kerosene, rancid cheese, sticky flypapers, clouds of dust from the grain bins at the rear, and sundry other pungent olfactory competition.

Keeping store at the crossroads had not yet been recognized as a glamourous and picturesque profession. In fact my father always took for granted only a shiftless, lazy character would stoop to such a life. "That Harry What's-his-name has taken over the store down in East Harrisville. He never did amount to anything . . ."

I think it was this same Harry who was seldom if ever strictly sober. My aunt, a militant Temperance evangelist, once asked him for five pounds of sugar. Harry set a bag on the scales and walked unsteadily to the far end of the counter and reached into the sugar barrel. He got hold of a large funnel instead of a scoop, and when he got back to the scales the sugar had all run out the small end of the funnel onto the floor. After he had made three or four trips and succeeded only in building a sugary path the length of the store, my aunt took the scoop and filled the bag herself.

In those days the more affluent summer people were not seen in the local store unless they were facing starvation. Boston families had large crates expressed from S. S. Pierce; New Yorkers, from Charles & Company. One of my boyhood jobs was to deliver these crates to cottages over at the lake. It was great fun to pry out a large bottle of ginger ale, drink about half, refill it with pond water and carefully seal it up again.

Running a country store is a highly personal sort of business. Now, as in the past, success rests entirely on diplomacy — mainly in the matter of extending credit.

Old Will Partridge was one of our wealthier farmers, but not given to needless extravagances. When his wife died he went down to the store and bought a pair of rubbers to wear to the burial. Next day he was back with the rubbers. He had carefully washed off the mud and wrapped them like new in the tissue-lined carton. "Mite too small," he explained. "Ought to have tried 'em on before I took 'em home — have to get my two dollars back."

Today's rural storekeeper may dress the part, but the part he dresses is merely rustic rather than authentic. The old-timer always wore a very dirty white apron, woven-straw sleeve protectors, and a hard-topped straw hat the year round.

If we go over to the "state road" and head north, we come to one crossroads store after another all the way to Concord. The first three are fairly typical. Jack's place is a quaint little building dug into a side-hill, so jammed with merchandise three or four customers can barely squeeze between towering stacks of Ball Band overshoes and nail kegs. Jack probably hasn't penetrated back under some of those stacks for years. On top is a mouth-watering array of practically the entire line of S. S. Pierce delicacies, for Jack is an epicure.

Almost completely buried between precarious mountains of groceries and buzzing freezers is the little cubicle where the storekeeper also acts as postmaster. When he's in there you can't see him, but you can hear him humming. Jack is always humming happily because he loves the life of a country storekeeper. That's what he came up here from New York to do.

And if it seems like a confining occupation, it may be added that Jack takes to the road in a green Jaguar on Sundays, and usually come spring is off to Europe for a month or two.

Up the road a few miles we come to Joe's. He too gets a real kick out of his little store, but with the added diversions of running a motel and acting as fire chief. A huge and genial man, Joe has an accent that originated in Arizona and took on overtones from Brooklyn, Boston, and Florida. He pitched in the major leagues for twenty years. Joe was a great hurler in his day, but always in the back of his mind was the dream of buying his country store.

Going on north from Joe's, in the next village the

store is kept by Charlie — or at least it was until he got into politics. Now his wife is on duty there while Charlie stirs things up in the state senate. The store-keeper-senator was once a teacher in Yonkers, but soon gave it up in favor of life in a country village.

So, thank heaven, you can still drop into any of these convenient places on a winter afternoon and pass the time with the boys gathered around the heater, as of old. Except that Charlie is more interested in talking about his latest conference with the governor than in village gossip. Joe will pass along some inside baseball dope he just picked up from his old pal Ted Williams. And Jack will tell you about the choicer spots in Italy or Norway.

Twenty-five years ago everybody said the little one-man store was doomed. But in spite of all the new grocery cathedrals down at the county seat, with their airport-sized parking lots, their soft music and magic-eye doors and assembly line checkout counters, our country stores survive. We even know of one, a few towns north of here, still run by a native New Hampshire storekeeper — rats, cats, white apron, accent and all.

10

Rum, Pneumonia and Doc Burke

GLANCING at one of those Unforgettable Character type stories about a kindly old rural sawbones, I was inevitably reminded of our local practitioner of past years, Doc Burke.

Today, up in these hills, you could be bleeding to death or wheezing your last pneumonic breath, and a phone call to the doctor would only elicit a crisp answer in a girlish voice, "Dr. Smith will see you at the clinic at four this afternoon." All you have to do is drive fifteen miles and wait until five-thirty after you get there.

In other words, the country doctor is no more. But his passing is not regretted too much by those of us who remember the ministrations of Doc Burke.

Burke's bedside manner was somewhat lacking in the suave evasiveness we now take for granted. When he was going the rounds of a temporary ward set up in the boardinghouse during a flu epidemic, one of the patients asked feebly, "How am I doing, Doc?" The man was a

85

burly millworker who had once knocked Burke flat in a fight down at Brown's saloon. Burke examined the sufferer briefly, straightened up and announced, "There'll be just one more white shirt for you, you s———!"

My first intimate sight of the doctor was during my grandfather's last illness. He arrived in a livery stable rig, and you could smell the whiskey as soon as he got into the house. He never took off his old black overcoat with its muskrat collar, nor his moldy-looking derby hat. I thought he had the most evil face I had ever seen — round and bloated, eyes squinting redly, yellow mustache straggling above thick lips which he kept puffing out with grunting sounds while he rummaged for medicines in his valise.

It was decided by the family that Burke had been too drunk to attend my grandfather properly. As he left they told him not to come back, and they sent to the city for another doctor. Down at Brown's saloon afterward, Burke said he was well out of it, as the old man didn't have a chance anyway — he'd had but one sound lung to start with and was too feeble to withstand virulent pneumonia. And of the city doctor he remarked, "When that fellow went to Europe, he forgot all he had learned at home; and on the way back, he forgot whatever they taught him over there."

In spite of such frank comments, other doctors often called Burke for consultation. He was recognized as having no equal in saving bad pneumonia cases. And though this is hearsay, the story goes that even Dr. Purdy, head of the county seat hospital, himself once called Burke on a tough pneumonia case. "You'll probably find him in Brown's saloon," Dr. Purdy told the man who was sent to fetch Burke from the village where he lived. "Look him over, and if he isn't more than two-thirds drunk, bring him along."

His colleagues generally conceded that had he left the drink alone, Burke might have become a truly great physician. It was rumored that some secret tragedy had driven him to a life of squalor and poverty. He had an office next to his unheated room over Brown's saloon, but it was so filthy nobody ever went into the place except in direst emergency. His main business there was pulling teeth, which he did without even water to wash his instruments. Whiskey was his only sterilizing agent.

As our own family practitioner used to tell it, one day the Doc drove up to the saloon and found a man with a badly swollen jaw waiting for him. "Can you pull a tooth for me, Doc?" the man asked.

"Sit right down here on the doorstep," Doc Burke said, opening his bag and hauling out a very rusty pair of forceps, "I'm in a hurry."

The sufferer began to back away. "Say, Doc, ain't you even goin' to wash them things?"

"They're no dirtier than your mouth," Doc snapped. "Open it up!"

An extraordinary number of people on the back-country farms never lost faith in Burke. Charlie Betts, the stage driver, came down with pneumonia one winter and his wife called a city doctor. But when this man told her there was little hope, she decided to send for Burke. When the city doctor left, Burke put his horse in the barn and went to work on the patient. He kept at it without eating or sleeping for thirty-six hours and he pulled Charlie through.

The Bettses were pretty slack about paying their bills, and a year later Burke was still trying to collect. One day he stopped Charlie at the post office and demanded at least a small payment.

"Can't do a thing for you today, Doc," Charlie said as usual. "Haven't got any money with me."

"Well, let me tell you something, then," Burke shouted at him. "If you ever give me another chance to pump the needle into your tight old hide, you won't need any!"

A woodchopper who lived near our farm, Pete Dubois, had a bad case of flu and was being treated by Burke. The doctor stopped by to see the patient and asked how he was feeling. "I'm terrible seek man, Doc," Pete moaned. "Never feel so bad!"

Burke renewed the medicine he had selected, measuring out a spoonful of something into a glass of water, and started to leave. Then he eyed Pete's huge, powerful frame tossing on the bed. He took out the medicine

88

bottle again and dumped about half the contents into the glass. "Can't shoot a bear with a charge of bird shot," he remarked. "Put that into you as directed. If you're still alive when I come back tomorrow, I'll give you some more."

It was the doctor's habit to try to collect overdue fees by accosting his debtors in public, shaming them into paying. A long-time delinquent was a notoriously lazy little man whose wife had borne him about ten children. The family standard of living was not high and the children were put to work as soon as they could walk.

When Burke applied his usual tactics to this man, hoping to extract a little money, the request was met with righteous indignation. "I'll pay when I get around to it, and not before! Besides, Billy wouldn't have been so sick if he'd had proper care."

"Why, you weazened-up little runt," Burke roared. "Has it taken you twenty years to figure that out?"

Ed Wilson, who used to be road agent, was about the roughest and toughest old character who ever lived in our town. He was also thoroughly unprincipled and never paid a bill if he could squirm out of it. Ed's method of dealing with Doc Burke was to outcuss and outbluster him.

One day, before Ed saw him coming, Doc Burke collared him on the street in Keene, intending to demand something on a long-owed bill. But before he could begin Ed started shouting at him, telling him what a no-good doctor he was, and recounting a long history of grievances, ending with, "And when you said my wife had eg-zeema, it turned out she only had the itch!" The Doc by this time was laughing so much at Ed he never did get around to the matter of the bill, and Ed got away as usual.

For all his rough ways, Burke's devotion to patients he liked or thought worth the trouble knew no bounds. Over north of the mountain, five miles from nowhere, an old Civil War veteran and his wife lived in contented solitude. When his wife fell seriously ill, the old man walked to the village and sent for Burke. At that time the doctor's drunkenness had lost him even his lifelong adherents, but the old man would not hear of anyone else.

Burke cleaned himself up and tackled the case. It was said he never touched a drink for more than two months, until the old lady was finally out of danger. But that case was his last. He had suffered a stroke and one arm was paralyzed, and not long afterward he died.

It's a wonderful world and many of us are still in it only because our modern medical wizards keep us so well patched up. But no one of them is likely to leave such vivid and lasting memories in the minds of his patients as Doc Burke. It is now many years since he downed the last bottle of his favorite personal prescription, and still the stories about him live on.

11

Saturday Night Bath

By lovers of New England lore, at least, no custom is more taken for granted than Saturday night bathing. Perhaps our town of Nelson, New Hampshire, has always been different.

Careful research shows that the habit was never prevalent hereabouts. In fact, a surprising percentage of our population, in years past, did not bathe at all.

On the next farm there was a sociable old man who lived alone, and I used to visit with him on my way home from school.

He had moved from one room to another as the floors fell into the cellar, and was at that time established in the last still-intact corner of the crumbling old house.

To my certain knowledge there wasn't so much as a washbasin in the place. There was a lean-to just outside for the horse, which would put its head in through a window so the old man could feed it oats without getting out of bed.

Stove, dishes, walls, ceiling and bed sheets were all

equally black, and the old man's face and hands not much lighter.

Another neighbor, patriarch of a large family, lived to be ninety-odd; he swore water gave him the itch, and he hadn't bathed in fifty years. Nobody who knew him at all intimately saw any reason to doubt his word.

One thing he would do on Saturday as long as he lived — get happily intoxicated. As he would express it himself, "I was cocked-er'n a mink!"

Yet another patriarch of less than regular bathing habits had lost a hand in the sawmill; he used to stir his pig swill with the stump. Though Rob McColl, the blacksmith, always called him the dirtiest man in the country, he was not without a certain sense of neatness.

In cold winter weather the chickens stayed in the living room, and before going to bed he would always turn around those which roosted on the back of the sofa, so they faced front, tails toward the wall.

In contrast to our non-bathing neighbors, there were also many whose concern for cleanliness amounted to fanaticism. Far from bathing only on Saturday nights, even once daily was not enough for some.

One old chap, a hermit of sorts, had such a fear of germs he was forever scrubbing everything. Once in a while relatives would come to spend a day with him. After they left, he always gathered up all the dishes and glasses they had used and broke them on a rock outside the kitchen door.

In this region of lakes and ponds everywhere, for two

hundred years most natives steadfastly refused to make use of them for bathing. Until recently many farm children grew up without even learning to swim.

One spring at the close of school the annual picnic was held on the beach of a nearby lake. The Wardwell children, all six of them, appeared with rings of lampblack painted around their legs. On the smallest one the rings were well down on the ankles, on the next halfway to the knees, and so on, with the tallest one ringed somewhere above the knees.

These rings were a sort of built-in depth gauge invented by the Wardwell parents. There could be no doubt about just how far each child would be allowed to wade into the water.

In the early 1900's plumbing began to be installed in some of the better farmhouses. Like all radical innovations, it was not always at once successful.

I remember one housewife proudly showing the neighbors a new bathroom. It was not extravagant to the point of including a tub, but it did have a flush toilet. Before long something went wrong with the piping, and twenty years went by before somebody figured out how to make it work.

Old Sam Wilson, an ingenious tinkerer, bought an early model water closet at an auction. Probably he had never seen one in operation, and he installed it with no pipe leading down from the overhead tank; he merely aligned it so that when the chain was pulled, an open column of water cascaded straight down into the bowl.

When his sister went up to the farm to care for him during some illness, she tried it out and nearly got drowned.

When we were young we had a wonderful summer-time diversion which is now, alas, no longer possible. There were then many large sawdust piles here and there in the deep woods, left by portable steam mills. These piles remained damp except for a few inches on the surface, and soon began to heat from spontaneous combustion far inside. Some were known to smoke for several years, though fire never reached the outside.

Sawdust is inherently clean; wood alcohol from fermentation repels insects and plant growth.

We used to take sawdust baths, tumbling and rolling down the steep sides of the pile, and covering ourselves with the steaming stuff as though it were sand on a beach.

The result was a delightful combination of massage and alcohol rub. We would emerge looking like breaded veal cutlets, but after a moment the sawdust would dry and brush off, leaving us clean.

For about fifty years now, since the coming of many Finns to the region, we have had a *sauna*, or steam-bathing establishment, in the village.

It might be argued that since the place is open only on Saturdays, it follows the New England tradition. But the fact is, the Finnish people brought the Saturday habit with them from the old country. Very few of us with a strictly Yankee background have adopted the healthful relaxing joys of the *sauna*.

Many even cling to the old, prejudiced notion that such an outlandish way of bathing could only be relished by furriners and is no doubt an immodest, if not immoral practice.

In the midst of these ruminations I had a visitor, a friend who operates one of the largest combination dairy and apple farms in the state. Better than anyone else of our acquaintance, he knows the thinking and the habits of his fellow Yankees — a knowledge that enables him to beat them invariably on any kind of trade or deal.

"Walt," I asked him, "would you say that folks around here generally take their baths on Saturday nights?"

He looked right through me a moment with his shrewd squinting eyes to see if he was stepping into a trap.

Then he replied, "No, I wouldn't say so. If they ever did, it was before my time. Seems to me most folks around here take their baths — them that takes baths, that is — whenever they need 'em, Saturday or not."

Then he added, "But I'll tell you something you can count on — if they thought it was customary to take baths on Saturday, they'd be darn sure to take 'em on Wednesday!"

95

12

When Babies Came So Naturally

OFTEN some visitor asks what has done most to change the character of our life in this rather remote section of New Hampshire. Since I haven't heard of an illegitimate child being born around here in years, my answer is: The coming of respectability. The Age of Conformity has at last reached back into these hills. In my still-not-too-long lifetime, I haven't quite got used to it yet.

I couldn't be more thankful, looking back to school days, that the school bus — that very expensive and dangerous contraption — had not then been invented. Walking along country roads was education, good exercise, and great fun, we thought in our ignorance. And as children, those of us who were even half bright picked up an acute knowledge of, and love for, all our birds and animals, even insects; we knew every tree and shrub and wildflower that grew; and we knew about snow conditions, and how to protect ourselves in bad weather.

To get to high school I still had to walk two miles, then ride another fifteen with Horace, a wonderful man who "drove the mail." (Horace, now well over eighty, is still driving the mail every day with an occasional passenger, just as in 1915, when he took over from his father.) One day Horace introduced me to an elderly, pleasant lady who got aboard the old Maxwell at a village along the route. A Miss Somebody-or-other.

Later I asked Horace about this passenger. "Why, she's Jeff Willard's mother, and Charlie Brown's mother, and Harry West's — Frank Parker's wife is one of her daughters. . . ." And he went on, naming eight middle-aged people around the neighborhood. Some of them I knew well, and they were all solid and respected citizens. "But I thought you called her Miss . . ." I said, and Horace explained, "That's right. She never married. Just gave each child the father's last name. That's why they're all different, of course."

Today, when a girl is expecting, she gets married promptly. At least several weeks before having a child. And even those who may be only fourteen or fifteen. It used to be that girls were not considered old enough to marry before they were eighteen or so. If one happened to have a child, her parents just took care of things until she reached a proper marriageable age.

The Lukes family lived far back in the hills at the end of a road that now has trees a foot thick growing in it. I remember old Lukes at town meeting, a gaunt man with a shaggy black beard and hair down to his shoulders, always chewing tobacco. When a daughter of old

97

Lukes's had a baby one spring, he walked down to the village north of the mountain, where Fred Carey kept store.

Old Lukes bought a few groceries, and then hung around awhile. Finally Fred, who was a nervous, impatient man and the wealthiest in the village, called out, "Is there something else I can do for you?"

"One o' my girls, she had a baby yesterday," Lukes finally allowed.

Fred wanted to know how that concerned him, and was told that one of his boys was responsible.

"All right," Fred snapped. "How much d'you want?" Old Lukes bit off a large chunk of cut-plug and chewed for some time, pondering. Then he said, "Well, we figured it ought to be worth fifteen dollars."

Fred handed him the money, and the incident was closed.

At town meeting our selectmen always hand out a stack of town reports and each voter takes a copy. On one such occasion, glancing as usual at the "Vital Statistics" page — two or three births, two or three deaths, a couple of marriages — we found the following: Under "Births" there was a child listed, with Miss So-and-so, the schoolteacher, named as mother. The father listed was none other than the chairman of the board of selectmen. His name also appeared in the latter capacity in the front of the booklet, the compiling of which was one of his duties. There was no question he had done his job well; everything properly recorded and in order.

Today such an incident would cause some discussion, at least among many self-appointed guardians of social and civic responsibility. But at the time not an eyebrow was raised.

In the matter of drinking, respectability is also now the rule of the day. Almost everybody "drinks a little." But some chap who hasn't drawn a sober breath in years would shudder at the thought of appearing boisterously happy in public. Even one of our neighbors who recently drank himself to death was well-dressed, quiet, and extremely polite to the end.

We had no such conformism in the old days. We had a hard core of abstainers who wouldn't touch "sody" if it came out of a bottle. We had some who would sip a little cider or elderberry now and then. And we had the old-timers, hard-working and respected farmers or lumbermen who might not indulge for months, but when they did it would be a rip-roaring two or three days.

One Memorial Day some of the village boys heard that two Civil War veterans, old Dan and old Jerry, were whooping it up at Dan's cider mill. The boys promptly got busy.

Just before the usual march to the cemetery to decorate the soldiers' graves was to start, Dan and Jerry made a noisy and spectacular entry into the assemblage. Dan was wearing a pointed dunce cap; hanging from his neck was a tin drum which he was beating vigorously. After Dan came Jerry, wearing a red wig in contrast to his white whiskers and blowing on a toy bugle; a string tied to his coattail trailed a dead rat behind him. In the ensuing confusion Dan and Jerry got into a fight and had to be forcibly taken home.

There was nothing more exciting to us, as children, than seeing Peter Harrington appear at some gathering after he had been sampling Dan's hard cider. Peter was a big man, but quick and graceful as a cat. He had been a wrestler and something of an acrobat in his youth, and it was said he had never been beaten in a fight. At an auction I saw him stand a sixteen-foot ladder upright in the crowd, ostensibly to examine it, and suddenly run up to the top. People scrambled away in all directions while he balanced up there for minutes, the auctioneer begging him to come down before he broke his neck.

Another of his performances I remember was at a box-social square dance. During supper he pretended to faint, falling straight over backward with a mighty crash and smashing the plate he was holding. Then he snapped himself erect and, with his great whooping laugh, started turning cartwheels and somersaults in the air. The ladies turned their heads away, and Pete's wife pretended she was horribly embarrassed.

Later, when the orchestra played a waltz, Pete swept the prompter into his arms and started waltzing him wildly out onto the floor. The prompter, a pompous and dignified little man, struggled desperately, but his feet never touched the boards. Pete whirled him around the hall about three times, then out through the door, finally heaving him head downward into a deep snowbank.

Getting back to Sex, and such associated matters as weddings, sleeping arrangements, etc., there is no doubt we are now living in a very romantic and standardized period as compared to such a recent time as my own boyhood. Lately we have had a good many weddings in town, and often church weddings at that. It used to be that often as not a couple would just go to the nearest justice; and sometimes they didn't even bother to do that, just sort of settled down together. After a few years nobody would remember whether they had ever actually got married or not.

Cal Plummer, who was not noted for his industry, for some years courted a widow who lived in a shanty near his ramshackle farmhouse. She held out for only one condition — that Cal agree to cutting his winter's wood supply ahead of time. One fall Cal got around the situation by ordering ten cords of dry wood from a neighbor.

Everybody was pretty surprised to see so much wood piled in Cal's front yard. A few weeks later the widow married him, confident that at least she would be provided with a warm house.

But when Cal and his bride returned from a two-day honeymoon, the woodpile was gone. The man who had sold the wood had decided that Cal, with a new wife to support, would never pay him. So he had hauled all the wood back home.

When there were still many old farmers living on remote places around here, if one were widowed or had never married he was apt to get hold of a housekeeper. The status of a housekeeper might mean almost anything.

A small incident that had people chuckling concerned old man Hutchinson and his housekeeper. He had obtained her through a newspaper ad some years before, and she had turned out to be a young woman with a small baby.

One day several of us were walking home from school together, and the Smith kids got to talking about where they all slept. One of them said to the housekeeper's boy, who was then around nine or so, "Where do you sleep, Billy?"

"Oh, I sleep up in the attic, and Mama sleeps with old Hutch in the downstairs bedroom."

The Smith kids told their father, and he told it all over town — said he'd been wondering about it for years.

If something like that should happen today, I suppose the selectmen or somebody would look into the situation right away.

Even my Aunt Agnes was not worried about the conventions when it came to her private life, though she was always quick enough to jump on any of the rest of us for any fancied misdeed. She once tried to organize a sort of family boycott of her cousin Belle when the latter took up Christian Science, which she said was a heathen faith. (She herself was above any sort of church affiliation.) Aunt Agnes was a schoolteacher and had a summer cottage near the old family farm.

Aunt Agnes had been teaching a few years and it began to look as though she would never marry — she was a large, plain woman with an autocratic nature and about as much femininity as a drill sergeant — when romance finally came to her doorstep.

A young man named Egbert DeWolfe Bumpus arrived to spend the summer, and pitched a tent near Aunt Agnes's cottage. He claimed to have had some illness or other, and was going to camp out in the fresh air to recuperate. He had all sorts of gear, a big tent with a folding bed, and he wore a sort of Teddy Roosevelt khaki uniform with gaiters and a felt scout hat — a costume he affected for the rest of his life.

Aunt Agnes struck up an acquaintance with Egbert, and before he had been in residence in the tent for more than a week or so, there was a rainy spell and she insisted he move into the cottage. The dampness would be bad for his health, she said.

Egbert never went back to the tent, and Aunt Agnes never went back to teaching. They just stayed on in the cottage together. Egbert had means, as my mother used to say, so they had no worries about the necessities of life.

After three or four years, a young minister and his wife came to town. They called on Egbert and Aunt

Agnes a few times and the two couples became quite friendly.

Before long the minister and his wife figured out that their neighbors were, so to speak, living in sin. Though my Uncle Charlie, who was fond of referring to Egbert as "the eunuch," would have disagreed — he said the minister had jumped to conclusions on this point.

In any event, the minister's wife tactfully hinted that her husband would be glad to offer his professional services. And one day they all took a trip somewhere together, and when they returned Aunt Agnes had officially become Mrs. Egbert DeWolfe Bumpus.

Newcomers around here could hardly imagine the straight-laced ways of some of our neighbors of a few short years ago. There were families who never let their houses be desecrated by tobacco or playing cards, and disapproved of sody-pop because it came out of a bottle. Their children were not allowed out by themselves after nine P.M. until they were twenty-one. And this was not back in the last century, but during the age of jazz and Scott Fitzgerald.

At the same time we had such nonconformists as socialists and spiritualists and various forms of freethinking. We also had some pretty crude characters, and they were not always woodchoppers or run-out families on the poorest farms. I remember, for example, old Deacon Randall. One of the local sagas about him concerned the time he took over the mortgage on a farm owned by a young couple, and soon afterward called on the wife.

He timed his visit so that the husband would be away at work. The Deacon said he had come to see about payments on the mortgage, and the woman asked him inside to talk it over. When she explained that they just did not have the money, the Deacon came right to the point. Using homely but explicit phrases that might be described as the barnyard sort, he suggested exactly how she could square things with no money needed. And she could make the first payment right then and there.

Unfortunately the husband had not gone to work that day. He overheard these generous financial proposals from the next room. He came out and gave the Deacon quite a pounding before the old man could escape.

The Deacon told his wife his injuries had been caused by a kicking horse. But the real story got around, and he was excommunicated from the church. He had, however, been excommunicated a couple of times before, and after a while they let him back in again.

All this has not been offered in the attempt to minimize our social progress of recent years, as evidenced by the degree of respectability we have reached. But along the way we seem to have lost a certain tolerance we took for granted in an earlier time. A time which was somewhat less conformist.

13

Tree and Underbrush

WHEN Uncle Bill was too old to run a dairy farm of his own any more he came to live with us. One morning he took an axe and started whacking away at a big old spreading oak beside the road. My wife ran out with an anguished cry. "Uncle Bill! What are you doing to that tree?"

"Cuttin' it down, by Gol Rye!"

"But you just can't do it! Why, that's one of our loveliest trees . . ."

"Don't give a damn if 'tis," the old man yelled without slackening his strokes. "Keeps the sun off the garden. Can't grow beans in the shade."

From the eternal war Uncle Bill waged on all forest encroachments into field and pasture ("Got to git rid o' them vipers under the soil," meaning fibers, or roots), you would have thought he was a fanatical tree-hater. Yet he knew how to take care of a good stand of spruce or a sugarbush. And it was Uncle Bill who set out the shiny willows along the shore of the pond, remembering the graceful beauty of the native ones killed many years before by the blight.

For some time now we have seen more and more TREE FARM signs around the countryside. Not so many on the old native places. But often the newcomer who buys thirty acres of underbrush will hang up one of these signboards before he gets his cellar dug.

Since our own "farm," except for the lawn and a thirty-foot square of vegetables, grows nothing but trees — about a thousand acres of them — we probably ought to have one of those signs. But we never seem to get around to it. They are put out by some government agency, the Department of Agriculture I guess, to encourage silviculture.

One time, having paid for our groceries for several years by thinning our forest and selling wood and timber, I tried to call myself a silviculturist when making out an income tax return. But the tax experts said there was no such thing in their book. And they didn't care a hang if the Department of Agriculture spent millions to promote such an occupation. They just insisted I had to be something else.

After that I lost interest in being a silviculturist. They can call me what they like. The trees keep on growing just as well, which is all we care about. And sign or no, almost any plot of land in New Hampshire automatically starts to become a tree farm, if you just don't cut any brush for three or four years.

At the moment I can hear a chain saw, which was what got me onto this track, up on the mountain where we were still picking blueberries about twenty-five years ago. They are cutting some pretty good spruce up there in what used to be an open pasture of some two hundred acres.

From our living room windows, a few years ago, we could see a number of large open pastures and fields. Now, looking off across the rolling hills for fifty miles — all the way around, from the southwest toward the Berkshires to the northeast toward the Unconoonuks — we can hardly find a bare spot in the unbroken forest. And all this growth has taken place unaided by the Yale Forestry School or the Society for the Protection of New Hampshire Forests.

This is quite a different sight than I would have anticipated in the 'twenties, when we first became indoctrinated by trained foresters and the SPNHF. These people convinced my young and impressionable mind that our fair state would soon resemble the loess country of central China, where the last tree was cut for fuel a thousand years ago. I could almost see our topsoil blowing away (if we had had any), and our skins turning yellow, and our women starting to bind their feet.

The SPNHF was founded by wealthy Bostonians. Vacationing in New Hampshire, and seeing a farmer here or there cutting his year's wood supply, they jumped to the conclusion that our entire forest was being decimated rapidly. They raised money, hired foresters, bought up some choice spots of woodland, and preached forest conservation.

Gifford Pinchot, establishing forestry schools, and Theodore Roosevelt, with his vast program of national parks and forests, together awakened the United States to the concept that our timber was being horribly slaughtered. But up here in New Hampshire we didn't pay much attention until the trained foresters began to arrive. Like Uncle Bill, the average farmer was much too busy keeping trees out of the pastures to worry about raising more of them.

Why so many Yale forestry graduates headed for our part of the world is a mystery, because they would seldom find any jobs here. Lumbermen figured it was hard enough to market the trees that grew naturally. Hiring a forester to plan crops for future generations seemed to them a needless extravagance.

Still the Yale boys kept coming. Over the years a few did get jobs with the state or the larger lumber concerns. And the common term for a piece of ground where all the trees have been cut clean and the brush windrowed — a "slashing" — became a dirty word around here. (Later we learned that slashings are really not so bad after all. In fact, if not too extensive, they make invaluable cover for birds and sanctuaries for all sorts of game. In the well-regulated forest, free of underbrush and weed trees and blackberry clearings, most wildlife would soon starve to death.)

Most of the Yale graduates would polish off their training with a year or two in Scandinavia, returning with Swedish or Norwegian wives. Forestry attracts a highly intelligent type of man, and the foresters were quick to discover that the best wives to be found anywhere in the world occur in Sweden and Norway. They are also decorative. The dark ones all resemble Garbo or Viveca Lindfors, the light ones Ingrid Bergman.

We knew one forester who made the mistake of not bringing back a bride, and on returning he married a standard American wife. Right after the honeymoon, a Swedish girl he had known abroad arrived for a visit and was established in the spare bedroom. Our friend's wife could not speak a word of Swedish and the fair guest knew no English. For a while at least this gave the advantage to the husband, who could interpret all conversation between the two. But as the weeks went by we began to sense a little coolness on the wife's part. She could not find out when, if ever, their guest intended to leave. Her husband kept assuring her he had been so lavishly and hospitably entertained in Sweden, it would never do for him to ask. At the end of six months things were reaching a point where the husband no longer dared to speak Swedish and his wife wasn't speaking to him in any language; but further crises were averted when the Swedish girl finally left.

Nowadays, in this enlightened age, our foresters have become established. They are considered almost as respectable as lawyers or psychiatrists. And the wise tree farmer consults his forester at the first sign of anything amiss among his saplings.

We have found tree farming to be a very restful occupation, free from the tensions and strain that beset people in other walks of life. We don't know a single tree farmer with ulcers. Even when the trees are ripe for harvest, there is no great rush. If you don't like getting up early, you can sleep until noon. And while any other kind of farmer gets himself in a lather about how to manage a day off, you can propose casually to your wife some morning, "I think it's about time we took two or three years off, dear — what do you say?"

Whenever somebody moves up here or builds a summer cottage nearby, we'll soon be hearing that stock question, "Say, what do you do about all this underbrush that keeps growing up everywhere?"

I don't know why they always ask me, because I gave up the fight on reaching middle age. My family had been waging constant warfare against invasions of brush since the American Revolution, and brush always won out in the end. Spending a beautiful weekend in fly-fishing season — or bird-shooting season — hacking away at the encircling forest is not my idea of how to spend the declining years. And in the summer it's too hot.

We still have a little lawn left and a clearing through which we can see a slice of our broad view. Fortunately we have a young neighbor who (for three-fifty an hour) enjoys brandishing a seven-horsepower chain saw in one hand, the way we used to do with a light swamping axe. So far he still has both his feet. And he is perhaps the only one of his generation who can operate an old-fashioned bush scythe, having learned the art from Old Joe Damboise, last of the Master Brushcutters.

However, neither of these weapons is much use in the hands of one who has not grown up amid timber and woodcutting operations. Of late many homesteaders here have succumbed to the only alternative, hiring a big bulldozer.

There is no question that the bulldozing method is most effective. But it also removes the sod and most of the topsoil, and it is hard to entice grass back into a landscape that looks like the floor of a granite quarry. Also bulldozer drivers have an ingrained hatred of trees. Ask one of them to spare a tree here or there and he is likely to go into a sulk, take his machine home, and double the amount of his bill.

In clearing a nice building site on an old grown-up hilltop farm, bulldozing does have one great advantage. It is a perfect insurance against attack from the rear or flanks by hunters, berry-pickers, or other denizens of the forest. You are left surrounded by a barrier that combines the best features of a tank trap and a castle wall. This impregnable outer rampart is a tangled mass of twisted trees and stumps, boulders and brush and dirt. It would take forty laborers forty years to reduce

any portion of it to a passable condition even for pe-
destrians.

The thing about underbrush that eludes newcomers
to the country is that all their lovely trees — if they
still have any left after clearing their building site — began life as underbrush. Hence if you keep on cutting
all the brush, you're never going to have any more
trees. This always seemed simple enough to me, having
grown up along with the underbrush and under about
the same conditions.

But it seems that all city folk are determined to take
much too literally the immortal verse (was it Kilmer's?)
ending with the lines, "Poems are made by fools like
me/ But only God can make a tree." Who makes the
brush?

Well, in any case, people have queer ways of dealing
with it. A typical example is the immaculate summer
residence of Jimmie Twinfire.

We simple natives have always called the owner Jimmie Twinfire because he is an unfiery, timid little retired
banker whose first name is James; and the name of his
place, as proclaimed on a large rustic sign at the en-
trance gate, is Twin Stacks. (The house has two brick
chimneys.)

Jimmie Twinfire built his luxurious chalet, complete
with picture windows and extensive flagstone terraces,
on a forty-acre plot at the top of a wooded hill. The first
thing he did was to hire a crew to cut all the brush,

saving anything that looked to him like a real tree. The
result was a grove in which half the trees were scrubby
old poplars, gray birches, and worthless swamp maples.
A lovely grove perhaps, but one which in the natural
course of time will be decimated by ice storms, high
winds and old age — and there will be no replacements
at all coming along, because there is no brush anywhere.

For the next twenty years Jimmie Twinfire hired old
Joe with his bush scythe, every spring, to mow down
every offending sprout. Jimmie never knew that among
underbrush there are such things as thorn apple, a beautiful shrub beloved of the grouse. Or our flowering
dogwood, which never gets very tall. Or June pinks
with an indescribably lovely perfume. Or all the other
flowering semi-trees like moosewood and wild pear.

The result is that the ground, beneath widely spaced
trees, has become one vast forty-acre fern garden. Now
there is nothing finer than ferns, in the right places.
They are about the oldest plants on our planet still
growing in their original forms. Up here we have over a
hundred varieties, many of them rare and beautiful. But
these damn things on Jimmie's place are what we call
"brakes." They are the coarsest and ugliest of ferns, and
if you try to pick one it will cut your finger half off.
There is nothing that more effectively chokes out every
vestige of grass, wildflowers, berries — everything.

It has been years since a songbird or even a squirrel
had occasion to go near that house. Deer, foxes and
rabbits, whenever they are passing that way, take a wide

detour around the whole forty acres. If you don't believe it, go up there any time in winter, when there is
snow on the ground, and you'll never see a track.

As in most things, the whole answer to the underbrush problem is a little knowledge. At least, short of
moving to some place like the sand dune country on
Cape Cod or the desert of Arizona.

Anybody who buys a piece of woodland up here
should compare it to a garden full of weeds into which
has been dumped a bushel of mixed vegetables and
flower seeds, helter-skelter. The first thing to do is to
hire a consulting forester to tell you which seedlings
are worth saving and which ones should be cut out.
Then, because we don't have much in the way of wild-
life-cover consultants, get a couple of books and learn
something about shrubs and plants and game habitat.

Every year countless people go out and burn some
brush piles, convinced that they are doing something
really worthwhile, like getting rid of empty beer bottles.
Actually it would be hard to find a more futile waste of
energy. It just leaves burned patches where for a long
time nothing will grow except thistles and juniper.

Burning may be sensible from a landscaping viewpoint, when there is no other handy way to get rid of
brush where it is an eyesore. But back in the woods is
another matter. There brush piles provide hotel accom-
modations for just about every kind of wildlife. We cut
some wood last fall in an area where there were never
any rabbits, for example. This spring a whole family

had taken up residence under a brush pile (yellow birch and maple), and no doubt had a feast on the bark and twig-tips all winter. Young spruce will grow right up through rotting brush, the ground being kept moist and covered with humus from the decay.

As for the popular notion that every brush pile is a fire hazard, it is sheer nonsense. I have been a forest fire warden for a long time, and I think the idea comes from the fact that windrowed brush, in a clean-cut soft wood slashing, does make a hot fire. But this situation has no similarity to piles of brush and top-wood left here and there in a standing forest or on sprout land.

But perhaps we are a little prejudiced in all this. Anybody who dearly loves woodcocks is apt to be. For that crazy little bird is an expert on underbrush, especially thick poplar whips, side-hill black alder runs, and sumac laced with tall blackberry vines. You just can't be a real bird-lover, whether it's gamebirds or songbirds, without being something of a brush-lover too.

14

All Those in Favor Say "Aye"

"THE most democratic form of government in the world . . . where everybody takes part . . ." We have been discovered. And every March we are discovered all over again, by Sunday papers, picture magazines, radio and TV, foreign exchange students and others.

Most of what is written about town meetings in little country townships like ours is definitely on the idyllic side. We manage our affairs with Yankee thrift and shrewdness and no nonsense, and everybody goes home happy. Maybe it happens that way in some towns, but in all those I know around here the facts are somewhat different.

For sheer inefficiency and mismanagement little towns like ours have often rivaled, and sometimes surpassed, anything that is done in Concord or even Washington. We knew one selectman who dominated a board continuously for over forty years. This long and distinguished public service was directed to one main objective — keeping his own assessment at a subterranean level. (The New Hampshire selectmen's most important duty is to assess all property yearly.) He owned a piece of property — one of several such listed under his name — worth at least ten thousand dollars, and from which he had derived more than that amount by selling only part of the timber. Year after year this two-hundred-acre tract always carried the same valuation — two hundred dollars.

There are some ghost towns in New Hampshire where misrule won out, apparently for keeps. Sometimes the three selectmen get into so many fights or other difficulties the whole board will resign. But in our town we never had anything of that sort, at least in my time. Nothing worse than frequent threats to resign. A few years back a selectman did knock one of the others down on the floor of the kitchen, where they were having a monthly meeting. The third member called the constable, not knowing that under New Hampshire statute he himself outranked the arm of the law.

The constable, who had held that office for years because he was the most peace-loving man in town, wanted no part of the battle. Finally the town fathers simmered down, and all served out their terms without further bloodshed.

I have no doubt that the tale of the little college town whose selectmen decided to cash in on students' poll taxes is based on fact. The way we first heard it, long ago, the town fathers figured they might as well collect from several hundred college boys of voting age. The town would rake in a pretty penny, while few students would bother to attend town meeting.

But the students did attend — and in such numbers that they outvoted the natives. The meeting was thrown into complete confusion, climaxed by the passing of a motion to have the town build a covered sidewalk for a hundred miles cross-country to the nearest women's college.

At one town meeting when I was small, a long argument developed over how much money should be raised for highways and bridges. Crazy Ben in those days was not yet so very crazy, and still liked to be heard on town affairs. When he managed to get recognized he stood up and shouted, "Mr. Moderator, I move we raise the sum of one million dollars for highways and bridges." Just behind him an old Civil War veteran reached forward, gave a tremendous jerk to Ben's coattail, and said, "Sit down, you damn fool!"

Ben sat, and never again opened his mouth.

That was back in the time when town meeting was attended only by the men. The women would all be busy over in the schoolhouse setting up long tables piled high with pots of baked beans — at least fifteen varieties — salads and mashed potatoes and scalloped potatoes, huge bowls of creamy coleslaw garnished with winter parsley and paprika, all kinds of home put-up relishes and jellies, loaves of home-baked bread and mountains of hot rolls, and one whole table loaded with fancy pies each one of which was designed to outdo the rest for sheer perfection. We used to identify the best ones by the plates they were cooked in. And there was always one sad, burned-looking specimen brought by poor crazy Flossie. Somebody would cut several pieces out of it when Flossie wasn't looking and shove them out of sight so she wouldn't be offended.

In all the years since women got to vote, their participation in town government has produced only two results. First, there are no more wonderful dinners in the schoolhouse. We eat sandwiches and store doughnuts with coffee right in the town hall, so the girls won't miss anything. A messy system, for which it can only be said that it does prevent actual starvation. And second, the hall is no longer filled with the aromas of pipes, cigars, and tobacco juice. It is now filled with cigarette smoke.

A neighbor from a nearby town told us that a big issue over there last year concerned a state highway which was slated to bypass the village. It was decided to take a vote so that an opinion could be registered with the state road people as to which side of the village was favored for the bypass.

Half the town held out for one side, and half for the other. Everybody wanted to be heard and the discussion grew warmer and warmer. It looked as though the whole meeting might be stalled for the rest of the day. Finally some rugged character in the back of the hall jumped up and yelled, "Mr. Moderator, I move we lay out this bypass so it leads straight to hell, and that ought to accommodate everybody here!"

The bane of town meetings, and for all I know any other legislative or political body, is usually a lawyer. Nobody but a lawyer, especially a newcomer from the city, can waste so much time, provide such lengthy misinterpretations of state laws pertaining to town affairs, quibble so much over every minor misprint in the warrant, and so scramble some simple "motion before the house" that the clerk is reduced to tearful frustration. (The year my wife was up in the legislature somebody actually tried to get a bill enacted to bar lawyers from the House.)

Some years ago in a larger town than ours an old Yankee named, we'll say, Bert Wheeler was chairman of selectmen. Bert was a professional politician — not that he ever made even the barest living out of it, but his hobby was town, county and state government, in all of which he was active. Army service had ended his scanty schooling, but in time he had become a walking compendium of just about every parliamentary rule, statute and statistic that had ever been heard of.

In Bert's town there was a wealthy summer colony. Many summer residents had become year-rounders, and hence voters, and among them a certain very famous lawyer. He was internationally known for his interest in the World Court or some such activity, and I will call him Mr. Hague.

Now, Mr. Hague, like all lawyers who have recently retired to the country, felt it his duty to take a serious interest in town affairs. And when he learned that Bert Wheeler had spent some four thousand dollars on repairs to some town building or other, he investigated. Evidently he thought little of Bert as a town official and suspected some skulduggery of the sort he had seen in Tammany Hall when he still lived in New York. As a result of his sleuthing, Mr. Hague became convinced Bert had acted without proper authority, mishandled the public funds and so on. Bert meanwhile remained mum — doubtless feeling that as a token-salaried public servant he was not bound to explain every action to some erstwhile summer resident poking his nose into town business.

Bert's attitude fanned the fires of Mr. Hague's worst suspicions. The eminent lawyer pressed his case, and Bert was hauled down to the county seat to answer for his misdeeds. And there began the long and very intricate maneuvers of masters' hearings and endless legal hocus-pocus that precedes court action in such affairs.

Many of us felt pretty concerned about old Bert. Here he was, without a dime, a strictly self-educated country politician, fighting for his life against a world-prominent lawyer with untold wealth and legal talent at his disposal. And as if that were not bad enough on the face of it, Bert insisted he would plead for himself without even local legal assistance.

The record of the case is an immortal chapter in our

local lore. In his calm and deliberate way, with no show of emotion whatever, Bert made hay of every point the great lawyer had raised. When all the evidence had been heard and duly evaluated, Bert was completely in the clear, the crusading lawyer left without a leg to stand on. An overwhelming, crushing victory — but Bert just went back to his town duties as though it had all been in the day's work, and we never heard him mention it afterward.

It is unlikely that every little town in New Hampshire has a Washington lawyer on the checklist, but a visitor to this region might get that impression. We happen to know of five towns in our vicinity where it is true.

In one of them, a native son with a Washington legal practice always attended town meeting, and always took an active part on every issue. Having been away most of the year, he was almost entirely uninformed on town affairs. Nevertheless, he seemed to feel it devolved upon him to question each article, however routine. And he would always offer some simple amendment, such as a regulation against throwing orange rinds on the town dump, in elaborate terms that would fill several pages. The poor clerk would have to read it all back to him three or four times before he could untangle his own legal phraseology.

One year a voter came to the meeting armed for a counterattack. He jumped up with a motion he had written in rhymed couplets. It described the lawyer's customary delaying action with more sarcasm than tact, and ended with the line, "And I move we limit lawyers to one minute on the floor!" No action was taken, but the resolution had the effect desired. The self-appointed legal counsel had little to say at meetings thereafter.

The popular conception that "everybody goes to town meeting" is a myth of the first water. The degree of apathy varies from town to town, but there are plenty of voters who, as our old town clerk used to say, "always turn up missing." I know of one town where a couple of hundred at town meeting is about par, out of nine hundred on the checklist.

Visitors at town meeting are generally tolerated and sometimes welcomed — reporters, non-resident taxpayers, road-equipment salesmen and others. However, the matter of allowing non-voters in the hall may be put to a vote, and the motion must be carried unanimously if it is to prevail.

In one of our neighboring towns a regional school official had been asked to speak on school appropriations, though a non-resident. Somebody called for a vote on allowing his presence at the meeting. When the moderator said, "All those in favor signify by saying 'Aye,'" there was a general response. But when he added, "Cont'ry minded?" some independent voter with no love for the official shouted a lone "No!" So the poor man just had to pack up and leave before the meeting could continue.

I suppose the greatest fun we ever had at any town meeting was back in the 'twenties, the year of the great snowplow demonstration. An article in the warrant called for some six thousand dollars to buy a large tractor for snowplowing. It was an unheard-of sum for those happy low-budget days when we got three dollars a day for "breaking roads" by hand with shovels. Everybody in town showed up to watch three rival salesmen fight it out with their monstrous new machines.

It was a dark, windy day, around zero, and the snow was deep and powdery from a long winter with no thaw. None of the salesmen had ever penetrated so far back into the hills before. They made the mistake of choosing the nearest unbroken road — leading up a steep hill just beyond the town hall — for their exhibition. All three were happily confident they could conquer it, not knowing the wind-packed surface was twelve feet above the roadbed itself. The spectators walked up ahead where they could watch the tractors plunging toward them and placed bets on their favorites.

There wasn't a tractor in the world half big enough to break through those drifts jammed between high banks on either side. Before long one driver, ramming full throttle time after time into the hard wall of snow, ran his tractor right through the plow, leaving scattered wreckage in his wake.

Of the two contestants left in the field, one was a hardy type who had been collecting backers by surreptitiously handing out paper cups of uncut grain alcohol. With a mouthful of snow you could swallow a little at a time and not quite burn the skin off your throat.

Well stimulated himself by this nectar, the dispenser of it finally ran his plow into the rear of the other machine, cutting an oil line. Under a ton of pressure black oil sprayed out over half an acre, dousing several of the spectators. Shortly afterward he got his own rig permanently stuck in the drifts. This left all three tractors out of action, hopelessly defeated, to the vast satisfaction of all the old-timers among the voters.

A year or two later we did vote to buy a large tractor plow, but it was not one of the makes we had seen in the great demonstration.

In little towns like ours nobody really cares much about who gets elected to such offices as selectman, town clerk, tax collector or constable. The big excitement is always about who will run for road agent.

When visitors from the West remark that they thought a road agent was a bandit who plundered people on the highways, we answer that the definition would do about as well here. A road agent is hardly ever a good fellow. If he is, he usually resigns after a few months, on the verge of a nervous breakdown, often leaving town to start life anew somewhere far away.

Everybody has it in for the road agent because he always fixes somebody else's road first. To be a success he must soon learn to parry all complaints and criticisms with a barrage of insults and excuses. "You say the rain's washin' out that culvet up on your hill, Dr. Cutler? Well, why in hell don't you go up there and hold an umbrella over it until I get the truck fixed?"

For some mysterious reason every time we elect a new road agent he soon discovers that his predecessor didn't make any ditches while scraping the roads. It is easy to see why no road agent is ever on speaking terms with anybody who has held the office before him. "Go ahead and holler to the selectmen about your road if you think it'll do you any good! The trouble is, when Fred was road agent last year, he never made no ditches. And of course, he never greased nothin', and he run the tractor without oil, and he never tightened nothin' up. You could pick up a bushel of nuts and bolts betwixt here and the town line. But the worst thing he done, he never made no ditches!"

Last year our town meeting was a disappointment. Nobody brought up zoning and there was little argument about the town dump; only a few sharp words passed between the new road agent and his defeated rival. The whole affair was peaceful and quiet as Old Home Day.

So before next March a few of us are going to get together and put a couple of articles in the warrant that ought to stir things up a little. We don't want to get a reputation for complacency up here.

15

The Beaver Who Came to Dinner

WE once attended a very dry lecture by a man who was
promoting a scheme to conserve our water resources.
The idea was to work on the small feeder streams, as
opposed to the government program of huge dams.
When a question-and-answer period finally came, I
asked, "How do the beavers feel about this? Have you
got them working for your group, or against you?" The
speaker looked blank and said he was sorry, but couldn't
recall having heard from anyone of that name.

Actually these organization-minded animals have accomplished much more, thus far, than our lecturer
friend. They skip the red tape and go to work wherever
water flows. They are not worried about water rights,
they don't wait for legislation or travel to Washington.
And they make fewer and less costly mistakes than the
army engineers.

There are probably good scientific sources to be
found, if you wish to go far into the ecology of beaver-

dom. My own reading on the subject consists solely of a passage in a boyhood favorite, *The Last of the Mohicans*.

According to my unreliable memory, Uncas hid out in a beaver lodge for some time, dressed in beaver skins and conversing in beaver language. The animals made this visiting cousin feel right at home until it was safe for him to go on his way.

Quoting from someone else's research, however, tends to sound unpalatably warmed over. Though limited, firsthand experience is more fun to relate.

In recent years we have become very familiar with some large colonies, on our own land and elsewhere, but before middle age I had never met a beaver face to face. Even now they don't receive me with anything like the warmth they accorded Uncas.

Driving home alone late one night, high up on the mountain road which ends at our house, I saw a very large porcupine waddling along ahead. Nobody loves the porcupine; least of all ourselves, with dogs, timber, and buildings to protect from his frequent deviltry. I jumped out and grabbed a heavy stick and gave chase. In almost total darkness off at the side of the road, the beast growled savagely and rushed at my feet. There was no time to think. I swung hard again and again until finally my attacker was laid out, thoroughly dead.

I left it there in the darkness and drove home, reflecting on the boundless surprises of nature. For in a lifetime of warfare with porcupines, never before had one been known to growl, let alone attack — they invariably run away, or if cornered turn tail and curl up with their vulnerable nose tucked underneath.

Next morning I went down to bury the carcass and received a great shock. It was almost like thinking you had shot a burglar and then discovering it was an old friend. Lying dead in the underbrush was a very large, handsome beaver.

My wife said there was no use crying over spilt milk. We would find out what beaver meat tasted like, and make a rug or fur piece from the hide. With advice and some help from Old Frank, our wise woodsman neighbor, we set to work. Even a novice, we discovered, can skin a beaver in a matter of eight or ten hours of hard work. The fat, streamlined body has its legs all inside somewhere, so you can only get a grip on the feet.

Then we roasted and roasted and roasted, until finally all the fat was melted away, and we had a few pounds of rather tough meat left. A good part of this was so bitter we had to throw it away, because we hadn't found the fifth musk gland in the back. The most hard-earned meal we have ever eaten!

After that we began on the hide. Soakings and rinsings in all kinds of solutions. Pounding, rubbing, scraping, and some rather heated family arguments. Several times I was for giving up the whole business. But weeks later the thing was finally more or less tanned. My earnest advice to anyone wishing to tan a beaver skin is to marry an Eskimo.

Surely we should protect these animals that feed only on worthless poplar. Our most valued asset has long been our lakes; many were caused by centuries of beaver work. Settlers trapped all the beaver for fur and drained many shallow ponds to make more land, keeping those they wanted for water power by erecting dams. The man-made dams were often made of wood and soon disappeared with the short-lived rural industries. Result — flood and drought conditions, and hard times for waterfowl and fish.

When beaver were reintroduced a few years ago nobody had any idea how fast they were to reclaim vast sections of country. They can make a good-sized lake in a few weeks. Once started, a dam is forever being improved, consolidated by weeds and trees, and enlarged from time to time.

When washed out, it takes only a day or so for beaver to completely repair a dam's holding capacity — as state road engineers have learned. Altogether we are very glad to welcome the beaver back; they have cost us very little and contributed a very great deal — more than we can say for all our human newcomers. And the beaver are easier, by far, to get along with.

A college biologist asked us for information about beaver, and I told him the following story: We know a certain woodcock cover far back in the hills where an old road ends at a marsh. For some years beaver have been enlarging a dam across the marsh, and they have created quite a pretty lake. Out in the water the unusually large dome of their lodge rises high above the surface, a clever tangle of logs, brush and mud.

Two or three years ago somebody who wanted a remote summer retreat built a log cabin a hundred feet from the water's edge. It was quite an elaborate affair, and facing the lake there was a picture window of perhaps five-by-eight dimensions.

Last year when we reached the cabin there was a great gaping hole in the wall; the window was gone. All around the hole the ends of the logs had been neatly gnawed away. A few minutes after we made this discovery someone happened to look out at the beaver lodge. And there, neatly framed in the south side of the lodge, the picture window had been installed.

Unfortunately, this story seems not to have been believed. But, as it always has been, the greatest reward of living close to nature is the odd or the unusual — that which sometimes must be seen to be believed.

16

Dog Days

THERE are those who hold that in the heat of summer bird dogs are better left in the kennel. What sane person would not prefer the cool shade of the side lawn to the green hell of a brambly, insect-ridden bird cover? Better for dog and man to wait for cooler weather.

We disagree with this theory. In fact, like most bird dog people, we disagree with all other bird dog people. Havilah Babcock, master storyteller of the southern quail country, writes about a sure-fire trick to make the hardest-jawed young dog give up a retrieved bird. Blowing in the dog's ear is the great secret — but we at once take exception. How about that Jack dog from Vermont? Why, you could blow at him till you were black in the face, he would just shut his eyes and clamp down harder.

Take the common opinion that pointers are "hardheaded," while setters are "gentle." With our dogs it is the other way around. Our big pointers come from a line just about the most sensitive in the world. We

hardly dare raise our voices during their whole education. But our little white setters? Wild and fearless. The
toughest, most intractable, stubborn, unmanageable, and
belligerent of bird dogs. Weimaraners are lap dogs by
comparison. Once I was bitten by three of these setters
at the same time. While I knew they were trying to bite
each other, not me, their mistake did not make their
fangs feel any less businesslike. After making sure her
sweet dogs were not injured, my wife finally turned her
attentions to me, and decided that all I needed was an
anti-tetanus shot. When I went into the clinic and the
girl at the desk said, "Sit right down here," I answered,
"Thank you very much — but I guess you don't know
where I've been bitten!"

We used to think summer training was a pretty tough
job. Thrashing around in briars and swampy jungles
with a wild dog on the end of a long rope, sweltering
and getting eaten alive by flies and mosquitoes, day after
day — while everybody else was swimming or sailing
or loafing around the tennis court.

But as years passed the work seemed to go out of it.
"Working the dogs" became a sport in itself, looked forward to with something of the enthusiasm we used to
feel only for shooting. As for the dogs, they get almost
as excited when we shoot the blank pistol as they do
when the real thing starts later on.

We learned not to take dogs for training that were
too old and hardheaded — the kind that would be sure to

jerk you flat on your face in every thornbush, and run away for an hour if you lost hold of the rope. We learned it doesn't pay to work on dogs that haven't first been taught to obey, above all to come in to whistle. And we got to know all the places where grouse or woodcock could be found quickly, within easy distance of the car, so that the dogs could be taught to point with a minimum of effort.

The most pleasant aspect of summer training is that there are always people who are glad to come along for the ride. Bird-watchers can have a fine time. Also mushroom-fanciers and orchid-hunters — anybody, in fact, who likes to roam the woods in summer. Provided they like dogs, of course. My favorite companion is a neighbor of recent years who always says, "If you ever put *me* in one of your stories, just call me "the Poet.""

The anonymous Poet must have done a good deal of shooting in younger days. You can tell by the way he moves through thick cover, watching the dog work. Now he comes up to his big house in the village only in summer, but he is always ready to explore the old covers he knows well or to prospect for new ones. And whenever I see him he usually pulls out a crumpled bit of paper and stuffs it in my pocket.

The paper will be a copy of his latest poem. I have quite a collection, but they don't take up much space. The Poet plans to publish his entire output sometime in a two-page book. Sample of one of his longer efforts:

WRITING VERSE

Genius
Is a myth.
I get four lines
From a fifth.

On days when my wife is busy at home and I am starting out alone, I drive past the Poet's house, and if his car is there I stop. There is a broad lawn with two beach chairs under an apple tree. Instead of going to the door — the Poet will have heard my car — I sit down and wait, watching some half-tame pheasants, two or three cats, a beagle, a sleek whippet and an ancient springer.

Presently the Poet appears. He is a small man, and his usual summer costume consists of rubber boots, baggy knickerbockers, a heavy flannel shirt and felt hat. But if it is very hot he wears nothing at all except shorts and a straw cap.

Without a word he trots down the stairs of the open cellar bulkhead, coming back with two opened cold beers. He hands one to me, sits down, we take a drink, and then the Poet is ready to open conversation.

One bright August morning the Poet and I were heading for a cover some distance to the north. Much of the way we could follow old abandoned roads, narrow and grass-grown, putting the jeep in low-low to get over ledgy places. Now and then the Poet would ask me to stop while he fixed his binocs on some rare warbler.

136

It always turned out to be just another myrtle or chestnut, but we saw some interesting hawks and other fauna. And the Poet told me again all about how his setter bitch, Belle Whitestone, beat them all in some field trial back in the 'twenties.

At the cover — a vast side-hill solidly grown-in to poplar whips and other brush, with a rocky little river along the bottom edge — we drove across a rickety wooden bridge and ran the jeep into a thicket. We let the dogs out for a drink and a good soaking. We had Buck, a very large thirteen-month-old pointer, and our little white female setter, Track. An oddly matched pair, but as it has since turned out, a rare combination of dog talent.

We worked Buck first. It was plain the Poet didn't expect much of him, because Buck looks like a show dog. But after several long, solidly held points, one after another, on some young partridge with no birds flushing wild — Buck keeping one eye on me the whole time for directions — the Poet was impressed.

"Here, take the pistol yourself," I said, knowing he always carried a whistle. "I'll keep back and you try handling him. Just point your finger where you want him to work." By the time we had circled back to the car the Poet was ecstatic.

All the way home he talked about Buck's performance. Some weeks later I happened to see the Poet in the village store, and as usual he shoved a piece of paper into my pocket. When I got home I took it out and read:

DOG DAY

*Newt and Buck
And a gun
Hunting birds
Having fun.*

In summer dogs need to drink and dunk themselves very often. Every cover should be close by a beaver pond, a stream, or at least a spring hole. It is also thirsty business for the handlers, and to maintain morale we appreciate something more invigorating than spring water. To this end, the Poet's well-stocked cellar is but one of many such ports of call. Our training covers for miles around have been carefully selected for their refreshment potential as well as for their bird population.

In fact Cousin Buzz, who often goes along with us, claims that whereas in the fall we move about a lot so that we won't "shoot out" our covers, in summer we move about so we won't drink them out.

But Buzz thought he was in for a pretty dry run one afternoon when we set off with the dogs and drove to a cover about thirty miles back of nowhere. My wife and I had agreed not to tell him a small cottage beside the cover happened to be the weekend retreat of an old friend. Or that this friend, whenever he saw our jeep pass by, knew from long custom about when to expect us back and would be prepared.

After a long, hot session in the underbrush, we finally emerged with our tongues hanging almost as far out as the dogs'. And when Buzz saw that tray loaded with tall iced glasses topped with mint, he was sure it must be a mirage if not a miracle.

To the public at large, the bird dog world is thoroughly confused. Distinctions are never clear between show dogs, field trial dogs, and gun dogs. Breeders, owners, handlers and trainers only add to the confusion.

Show dog people claim their dogs make the best hunters. The rest of us claim that show dogs are bred entirely for appearance and a disposition solely adapted to standing still endlessly, doing absolutely nothing, while being stared at.

The field trial crowd, on the other hand, care little for appearance. They drive all over the country with truckloads of dogs, and most of them look as though they have never had a bath or a haircombing in their lives. (You can take this to apply equally to the dogs and their handlers, though certain owners affect natty getups of high boots and riding pants, with wide sombreros.) The dogs are trained to take off like whippets and race madly to the end of the course. There the handlers shoot off their pistols, pretending their dogs have "pointed" while the judges were looking the other way.

Like the show people, field trial people also claim *their* dogs make the best gun dogs. And so they might, if the buyer intended to use them gunning for gazelles instead of grouse.

As for the dogs themselves, most of them are more confused than anybody about all this. And as we train only for shooting, we have learned to have nothing to do with any dogs at all which have had any previous training. We prefer to start from scratch, at well under a year old, from whatever lineage so long as the pup shows inherited brains and ability. Then, by the beginning of its first hunting season, the pup should have a pretty good idea of what is expected. But this is only because we have been out working every day through the spring and summer.

This first-year pup has been working in thick covers too, not out on the lawn with a bunch of feathers tied to a fishing pole. And for those who may be interested, a well-educated gun dog at two years of age is worth to-day, at the very least, upward of three thousand dollars. With rare exceptions, however, this class of dog just isn't bought and sold on the open market. There are not enough of them.

Even the most eminent of writers go off the deep end when they get inspired by their pets. Bromfield's book about his boxers, for example, seems to me a work that only the dogs themselves would have really enjoyed; and despite the author's sentimental estimates of their intelligence, I don't think they knew how to read.

T. S. Eliot's effort about cats sounds like something written by a precocious seven-year-old who had been experimenting with the contents of Papa's liquor closet. And there are several other conspicuous examples even in our own modest library. All of them, it may be noted, were published only after the writers had become so famous they could call their own shots.

With this warning in mind, I have said little about our own house dog, old Sandy. But one incident comes to mind which may not greatly strain the patience of those who are not ardent pet dog lovers.

A golden retriever is never happy unless carrying something. Long ago we got into the habit of letting Sandy carry a flashlight, held like a cigar with the lighted end pointing straight ahead. It is not only a useful trick at times, such as when bringing in firewood at night; it also makes a good gag when visitors arrive after dark — Sandy rushing out to meet them with his flash, his great plume tail wagging happily, and lighting their way to the door.

One August afternoon Janet set off for her usual swim at the lake, down the trail from the house, with Sandy and a couple of the kennel dogs. When she was ready to start home, at six o'clock, Sandy was absorbed in trying to dig his way into a muskrat burrow. He was having such a good time she didn't call him along with the other dogs, thinking he would follow her up the familiar trail when he tired of his digging.

That evening we were giving our Big Party of the season, and I was too busy to notice that Sandy was not around.

At about midnight some of the guests who had to leave early started looking for Janet, but she was not to be found. It was an hour or so later when she finally came back into the house, accompanied by Sandy with his beloved flashlight.

Janet had begun to worry when Sandy had not appeared all evening. So she sneaked off and clambered all the way down the steep, ledgy half-mile trail to the lake. And there she found Sandy, lying forlornly where she had left him. Darkness must have come on while he was busy with his muskrat hole. It was a pitch-black night, and he just had not dared to make his way home without his flashlight.

As we grow older there may be summers when, because of too much other work, we will take no young pups to train. For our own shooting we always seem to have more trained dogs around than we need. But when warm weather comes we will be back roaming the covers a good deal just the same. Because even for an old dog or an old hunter, from autumn to autumn is too long a time to wait.

I found a scrap of paper in my pocket just the other day:

AUGUST UPLANDS

There's nothing like those summer covers
For hunters, dogs, and secret lovers.

17

Plain Country Food

THERE may still be a few people up around here who think a good boiled dinner beats anything to be found in the restaurants of New York, New Orleans or Paris. The same people who still use kerosene lamps and outhouses and saw wood by hand.

When my mother supervises every step of the preparation — corning the beef under a large stone in the pickle crock, cubing and seasoning the home-grown turnips, and finally surrounding the platter with all the proper accessories — the result may satisfy a ravenous appetite on a winter day. Still, I have not eaten a boiled dinner for a long time. Years, I guess.

Our country eating habits have changed. Changed even more, perhaps, than any other aspect of country living. For example, last week at a neighbor's cottage we were treated to a steaming kettle of bouillabaisse the equal of anything you could find in France. Frozen sea foods, plus a hostess who had attended the Cordon Bleu, was the answer.

We still have our kitchen gardens, but they have to compete with the supermarkets when it comes to such delicacies as avocados and artichokes. I ate my first avocado here back in the 'thirties when a neighbor had some flown from California.

But only last year we introduced a summer visitor from Massachusetts to the artichoke. He was a college graduate, too — Dartmouth. When we showed him how to dip and nibble until the final prize at the center lay revealed, he said he had always thought artichokes were those tall plants with blossoms that looked like little sunflowers. (The kind we call Jerusalem artichokes and dig up in early spring to eat raw, sliced very thin, in vinegar.)

New Hampshire has long been a pretty cosmopolitan state compared to Vermont or Maine. Even back in these hill towns, when you run across a well-kept dairy farm or poultry ranch it is apt to be owned by people of French Canadian, Finnish, Greek or other non-Yankee background. All of thirty years ago I went to my first Greek barbecue and learned the delights of white goat's milk cheese and wine chased with a thimbleful of *oozo*. And from our Greek neighbors we learned how to fry sliced zucchini in olive oil with chopped nuts.

Our recent bouillabaisse feast reminded me of Bill, the part-time hermit who later became a college professor and great scholar in the field of ancient Semitic languages. When I was fourteen, and Bill was living on boiled potatoes in the chopper's shanty and tutoring me in chess and literature, one evening in his clear and eloquent actor's voice he began an impassioned recital of "The Ballad of Bouillabaisse." It was the first time I had heard of this regnant glory of all sea foods.

Some thirty years later Bill returned to his old haunts, no hermit this time but with a family, and built a large house high on the mountain, above the site of his former shanty. The other day I asked him if he could remember "The Ballad of Bouillabaisse."

"Of course," he said. "There are a hundred stanzas and I know them all," and he promptly delivered several to prove it, with a great smacking of lips and the sweeping gestures of Edwin Booth:

> *A street there is in Paris famous,*
> *For which no rhyme our language yields,*
> *Rue Neuve des Petits Champs its name is —*
> *The New Street of the Little Fields;*
> *And here's an inn, not rich and splendid,*
> *But still in comfortable case —*
> *The which in youth I oft attended,*
> *To eat a bowl of Bouillabaisse.*

> *This Bouillabaisse a noble dish is —*
> *A sort of soup, or broth, or brew,*
> *Or hotchpotch of all sorts of fishes,*
> *That Greenwich never could outdo;*
> *Green herbs, red peppers, mussels, saffron,*
> *Soles, onions, garlic, roach and dace:*
> *All these you eat at Terré's tavern,*
> *In that one dish of Bouillabaisse.*

And so on. After a good deal of digging deep into the bowels of the Keene library, I finally found a Thackeray edition containing the mouth-watering masterpiece. But it turned out to have only eleven stanzas. If Bill was right and there are actually a hundred, maybe they have been added over the years, the way good cooks have kept on adding new ingredients to the ancient dish itself.

Now Bill has become a master of ancient Near Eastern cooking techniques as well as languages. The high spot of our summer is one of his authentic Arab meat dishes roasted over charcoal in the open. We gorged, the last time, on a long cylinder of beef tightly bound with strings; Bill had lovingly inserted no less than thirteen different seasoning ingredients through hundreds of little incisions. Each succulent mouthful seemed to have a slightly different but highly harmonious flavor of its own.

It was also from Bill's encyclopedic mind that I first learned of the dish called dung-fish. According to Bill this is the favorite food of a certain eminent historian of Boston origin. It consists of codfish which has been given a long and complicated treatment including immersing it for a period of time in a manure pile.

Certain sentimental New England writers to the contrary, I suppose the average native cooking around here when I was young was about as unpalatable as it is possible to imagine. Boiled potatoes, salt pork and beans were the staples.

Uncle Will, a typical dairy farmer, never would eat a

green vegetable in his life. Standard Sunday supper consisted solely of "crackers 'n' milk." A huge bowl of
cold milk — strongly barn-flavored — into which were
dumped handfuls of dry crackers. I have not eaten a
bowl of crackers 'n' milk for forty years, and I sincerely
hope I shall not have to for another forty.

I remember the time Fred Blake and his wife decided
to try taking a few summer boarders. When I went over
to help Fred get in some hay he told me about it. "Queer
notions them summer folks get, don't they?" he said.
"Don't seem to want nothin' but coffee for breakfast.
Yesterday mornin' Alice set out a big dish of cold
macaroni and a can of sardines, but they wouldn't eat a
mouthful."

There were a few native items worthy of mention,
especially around hog-butchering time. Pork scraps
from trying out the lard (not to be confused with
scrapple) set out in a big bowl and eaten like candy for
two or three days. Headcheese, pressed and chilled in
bread pans. And home-cured hams and shoulders and
bacon smoked with corncobs or dry sugar maple. Then,
in spring, the first-run maple syrup provided endless
desserts, from ice cream to rye balls fried in deep fat and
served floating in syrup with heavy whipped cream on
top.

But we were unusually fortunate at home because
my mother, besides being naturally talented and inven-
tive in the kitchen, had been sent by a rich uncle to a
cooking school in Baltimore. She returned with a back-

ground of Southern cooking that got her off to a good start. From then on visitors to the farm from all parts of the world were seldom allowed to escape without divulging some recipe or other. And today, at ninety-odd, she is still collecting them. She must know at least a couple of hundred methods of making bread alone, all of them good.

My mother's basic tenet is that nothing should ever be wasted. Orange rinds are saved for marmalade, apple peelings for pots of jelly boiling down on the back of the stove, old meat bones and fish heads for soup stock, and so on. There are never less than a dozen odd tins and kettles warming on her wood stove, and many more in the "cold room." Cooking is a continual process of adding and mixing and setting aside, which the well-trained modern housewife would find hopelessly baffling.

But sometimes my mother's sense of thrift would lead her talents astray. We used to go around to the summer cottages every fall and Mother would collect all the left over staples. Sugar, flour, and anything else that might attract the mice and squirrels. Once we brought home an unmarked sack of flour and Mother used it to bake several loaves of bread. When they turned out hard as rocks she decided she must have got one of her exotic bread recipes confused some way. She threw the loaves out for the dogs and the old Airedale broke a tooth on one of them. I was building a stone foundation under the barn at the time, and after the dogs had given up I laid the loaves into the wall, and they are still there. Mother's bag of flour had turned out to be plaster.

Another time she found some corn meal and made a big pan of johnnycake. When she opened the oven door huge billowing cascades of golden suds poured out across the kitchen floor. On this occasion the corn meal proved to be soap powder.

Even back around the turn of the century, my mother and certain other outstanding native cooks around here had learned where to find good Italian olive oil and the hard bricks of Parmesan cheese we kept wrapped in vinegar-soaked cloth. There were the Leveroni and Vanni family shops in Keene and Peterborough. Scandinavian neighbors regaled us with smorgasbord and pastry and taught us how to fry eels properly. And from the Poles my mother learned of many varieties of wild mushrooms that forever spoiled her taste for the plebeian market type.

In return we introduced the immigrants to coon dinners, venison and rabbit, squirrel pies, snapping turtle soup, milkweed-shoot greens, brook-run smelts fried in deep fat, and many another dish that came neither from the garden nor the grocery store.

In recent years variety is the rule up in these parts. Real old-time New England cooking is now largely a myth, fortunately for our digestions. The other day I met a woman who claimed there was nothing finer for a salad than pokeweed sprouts. It is about the only thing

I haven't tried, from porcupine livers to salt-water mussels. Somebody brought a bushel of the latter from the Maine coast this summer, and after steaming them in white wine we found them delicious. The Maine natives used to tell me they were poisonous.

One of our mushroom-hunting neighbors, a specialist in French cooking, has been searching New England woods and pastures for truffles. He hasn't found any yet, except a tiny variety about the size of seed pearls, but he is hoping to establish some imported ones. And he is training a bird dog to point them.

Last night we took potluck at a neighbor's. Before dinner there were the usual odds and ends with drinks — chilled shrimps, smoked oysters, two or three cheeses for the crackers, hot miniature sausages, and that old New Hampshire favorite, a large bowl of creamy onion-flavored gunk to be scooped up with potato chips.

For dinner we had two-inch-thick individual steaks charcoal-grilled, stuffed eggplant, a tossed salad and sweet corn which had been growing in the garden an hour earlier, and hot rolls. There was a passable red wine from a French-labeled bottle that had been lying around in S. S. Pierce's cellar for about fifteen years. Then there were melons and ice cream and cake or, if we preferred, a pretty good Stilton cheese aged in wine. A spot of brandy or liqueur closed the deal.

Afterward, one of us made a complimentary remark about the dinner, and our hostess began explaining apologetically, "It was only a pick-up thing, you know

— I've been away for a few days and there just wasn't time for anything special."

Tomorrow night we are invited out again, and hope to have better luck. I understand somebody has just come back from down around Chesapeake Bay, bringing a bushel of oysters and a couple of live green terrapins.

18

The Mysterious Hedgehog

ONE September evening we were sitting around the fire down at Old Frank's. Henry Savage and some of his Boston fly-rod friends were there. Henry has a rather high opinion of himself in many respects, among them as an observer of nature in the wilds.

After we had chewed over the day's fishing, Henry began telling us about the remarkable things he had seen in the woods at one time or another. "You know, one of the cutest sights I ever saw was up on the Allagash. I'd been fishing all day and was coming back to camp around sunset. There was a log across the stream, and just as I got there I saw a big porcupine crossing on it. And right behind her six little ones —" He stopped at this point, looking at Old Frank.

After a minute Henry said, "Well, Frank, what's the matter?"

Old Frank took a puff on his pipe. "I didn't say there was anything the matter."

"Well, there is, I can tell by the look on your face. Come on, let's have it."

"Oh, I was just thinkin'," Old Frank said, "I've heard hedgehogs might have twins, oncet in a great while. But I never knew 'em to have more'n a single young one."

We have always kept on stubbornly calling our native porcupine a hedgehog, and Webster finally allowed the alternative definition in spite of naturalists' protests. So call it what you will, to us this unlovely beast is a hedgehog — usually referred to as "a damned hedgehog" or something worse whenever one of them starts gnawing on the front porch. Hardly anything that has been left outdoors around our house is free from those chiseled teeth marks, from tractor tires to furniture.

The proverbial goats are extremely fussy eaters compared to hedgehogs. We had a goat which died after swallowing a copy of *Time*, but hedgehogs thrive on all kinds of paper and would digest a Kerouac novel as happily as a row of tender lettuce from the garden. They also eat plastics, wood soaked in kerosene or creosote, even aluminum; and I have seen one trying to gnaw through a galvanized-iron sap bucket.

One summer I was rebuilding a half-collapsed barn for a New York man who had bought a place up here. Sills, joists and much of the flooring had been nearly eaten away. The owner could not understand why hedgehogs would consume dry century-old timbers in

preference to all the succulent plant life in the surrounding forest. After several of us had been unable to
give him any intelligent answer, he approached an old
woodsman who was cutting brush nearby. "John, what
is there in a dry old board that makes a porcupine want
to eat it?"

"Well, I'll tell ye," John said, after pondering the matter. "To you or me, an old board don't look quite so
nourishin' as a green popple shoot, or mebbe a handful o'
blueberries. But to a hedgehog, now — well, th' critters
just know whereof them things be!"

When it comes to the private lives of hedgehogs there
is still much mystery, attested to by many a ribald tale
and verse. Sometimes defined as nocturnal, they yet often
behave exactly the same in daytime as at night. (To
some of us who are well acquainted with their mentality,
it seems very likely they don't know the difference.)

You can follow one of their well-trodden paths for
mile on mile, all day long, and never discover their
destination or purpose. But still they are just about the
slowest-moving and most slothful animal next to the
sloth itself, and will sometimes sit in one tree for two
weeks at a stretch. Even biologists do not know as yet
whereof them things be.

The man who surely knows more about the subject
than anyone else in the world today, Dr. Parke H.
Struthers, happens to be one of our neighbors. A Syracuse University biologist, he is more or less a native, his
mother's side of the family having lived here since the

country was first settled. Some thirty years ago he bought the farm adjoining ours and began the first exhaustive long-range study of our prickly friends. He has explored the anatomy, reproductive processes, and digestive systems of hundreds of specimens, alive and dead. And he is the author of enough scientific papers and articles to fill several volumes, if they were ever gathered together.

Years ago Parke came back from one of his South American expeditions happier than if he had found a brand-new gold mine. He told us he had discovered a colony of porcupines, exactly like ours, about eighteen thousand feet up in the Andes. They got stranded there when the Isthmus of Panama sank, or whatever it was that divided the two continents. A hedgehog cannot stand much heat, so there was no question of their ever getting back north again — they have to stay up in the high altitudes down there to stay cool. Outside of maybe occasional trips down the mountain to sample a few bananas, they have lived pretty much the same as their New Hampshire relatives.

Along the upper Orinoco, Parke found some slightly different ones, with round tails instead of flat. And on another trip, in Haiti, he found a toy variety about the size of squirrels.

Several years ago I went out one spring morning and jumped in the car for a quick trip to town. It was very nearly my last trip on earth. When I started down the mountain the brake pedal went completely limp. After a good deal of double-clutching and slewing around I finally came to a stop.

Under the car I found all four hydraulic brake hoses missing. Rubber shock-bumpers were also gone, and even a section of wire cable to the headlights, copper and all. The tires still had air, but the treads looked as though they had been hacked off with a wood rasp.

That particular midnight snack of some hedgehog with an unusually epicurean turn of mind cost us well over a hundred dollars.

But this was not the only incentive for my wife's part, as a legislator a little later, in getting the fifty-cent bounty on hedgehogs restored. A certain number of our young dogs are bound to get quilled every year. Sometimes when they get a mouthful of several hundred it means a fifteen-mile rush trip to the vet's. And sometimes it means an operation months later to remove a quill we missed, working its way toward some vital spot.

[Note: Appropriately enough, while I was writing the above the phone rang. A woman eight miles away, alone and without a car, asked if we would hurry over there because her golden retriever had come home full of quills. I fully believe hedgehogs are psychic, and they don't like what I am writing about them. And I most certainly hope they don't after two hours of yanking quills out of that struggling golden.]

Many people who have lived in hedgehog country all their lives have never heard them utter a sound. And while they are almost always silent, I once heard a great chattering and chirping I couldn't identify, and on creeping toward the sound it turned out to be from a large hedgehog sitting on a stump. He went on at a great rate for half an hour, growling, grunting, squeaking and whining — every sort of animal sound you ever heard and some besides.

The question is, with such a vocal range, why are the beasts usually silent? My own answer may not be scientific, but it is my belief that most of them are so stupid they just never happen to discover they have a voice. And when one in a thousand does discover it — perhaps by sneezing or something — he is so delighted he just sits down and makes every sound he can think of, until he finally gets a sore throat or runs out of wind.

Not all our neighbors despise the hedgehog. Fifty years ago a Boston clergyman built a summer home on a hill near our farm. It was in hedgehog paradise, with several large dens nearby, and the house was all of wood — wooden porches and steps and latticework everywhere.

These people were all nature-lovers and wouldn't even kill a mouse. Once in a while a hedgehog would come up on the porch, and they would just throw a little kerosene at it and ask it politely to go away. To this day there is not a tooth mark on that house.

I have a theory about this. Remember, Parke has told us porcupines were here untold thousands of years before man, before even the most primitive of us. Not being very bright, to put it mildly, these animals have not yet learned to fear man exactly, but their defensive mechanism leads them to chew holes in anything man leaves around, from houses to aluminum canoes. However, in a situation where man does them no harm, there is nothing to start their defensive mechanism clicking. And if this is farfetched, I am open to any likelier suggestion why, in all these years, no hedgehog has ever touched the Reverend's buildings or belongings.

Newcomers to this region can never believe that for every old farm left there were dozens not so long ago. And when I mention that I have seen people living in houses that stood on some of the tree-grown cellar holes, they look at me as if I were Rip van Winkle.

The explanation is, in large part, hedgehog work. As humans moved out of the decaying houses, hedgehogs always moved in. Sometimes they started moving in even before the people moved out. Then, as roofs began to go and floors collapsed, the hedgehogs chewed up the remains, and the cellars were soon half filled with their droppings.

Hedgehogs also eliminate newer buildings with equal enthusiasm. Only twenty years ago choppers left a shanty up on the mountain, and for several seasons we took shelter in it when hunting up that way. Today there is nothing left except a few gnawed stumps of two-by-fours.

I have no intention here of dwelling unduly on the overworked subject of hedgehogs-and-outhouses. But an incident of my youth comes to mind, still remembered by some of the old-time visitors to the farm.

One of my summer jobs was to be on call to remove hedgehogs from the summer cottages whenever there was a complaint. Usually it was late at night. Some family would be awakened by a sound as though somebody were underneath the floor busily running a crosscut through the joists. I would have to crawl under the cottage with a flashlight and whack the hedgehog on the nose with a small stick.

I never used a gun because the bounty was only ten cents; wasting a cartridge would cut into the profits. Besides, the only way to kill a hedgehog is to strike one exactly on the end of the nose. Just shooting it full of any amount of lead will not kill it unless you hit the one vulnerable spot. (Biologists are still trying to figure out why this is true.)

One summer a Boston matron with several children occupied a cottage back in the woods where the hedgehogs frequently attacked. This lady was a determined, self-reliant type, and she didn't need any boy to defend her against hedgehogs. Just give her a gun and she would take care of them herself.

We loaned her a double-barreled twelve-gauge shotgun, and late one evening a booming fusillade began that soon aroused everybody around the lake and the farm. Our sharp-shooting tenant had found a large hedgehog gnawing inside the outhouse. And without thinking to chase it outside, she had grabbed the gun and opened fire.

The animal happened to be perched up on the seat. After about ten shots at close range it was thoroughly dead. But nobody was ever able to extract all the hundreds of quills embedded in that pine seat. And for rather obvious and painful reasons we finally had to replace it.

We know a young couple who delivered a live baby hedgehog, by caesarean, from a female some hunter had just killed. After unsuccessfully trying baby foods, they finally raised it on eggnogs (non-alcoholic). The baby is now six months old and even more domesticated than its playmates, the house cats. Last week we drove over to see how things were progressing.

What sort of person would raise a hedgehog for a pet? Well, these young people are certainly typical New Hampshire back-country folk. The husband, a designing engineer with a job in a nearby town, landed up here when his family moved from New York City. The wife is a golden-skinned blonde with a robust beauty that plainly bespeaks her Scandinavian ancestry.

Their rambling, comfortable one-story home looks something like a flat-roofed poultry house on the outside, due to the fact that it was once a flat-roofed poultry house both outside and inside. Now, however, the interior is most attractive, with a stone fireplace in the center and broad windows facing out toward the wooded valley below.

While we waited in the large room that constitutes

most of the house — the husband was out and the wife
busy with a small child — my wandering eye took in:
A studio corner jammed with drawings and oils highly
imaginative in subject, a large lunar telescope, several
musical instruments new and antique, an elaborate record player, radio installations, part of an airplane bomb
sight, a modern kitchen complete in another corner, a
table made from a long plank and a widened sewing-
machine base intricately guyed with piano wire, parts
of textile machinery, an astrolabe, barometer and other
scientific instruments and tools, furniture ranging from
Early American to modern Finnish, books everywhere,
plants growing in boxes and pots, two pairs of snowshoes, a fighting cock in a cage, and sundry other interesting items.

When Leni had got the child to sleep we asked what
had become of Nettles, the hedgehog. "Oh, he's fine,"
she told us. She has a soft, sweet voice and a way of
speaking that is slow, clear and completely unaccented.
"But you know, we have had to make him a house outdoors. He kept crawling into our bed and trying to sleep
with us. And when we locked him outside, he whined
miserably and scratched on the door and kept us awake.
Come along, I will let him out for you."

Leni led us to a cage on the back lawn and reached in
and produced Nettles, holding him dangling by one
front foot, like a handbag. She set him down and he
trotted along behind her, grunting. Then he grabbed
one of the cats and began to lick its ears, which were

pink and hairless from his ministrations. The cat purred contentedly.

We sat down on the grass, and presently Nettles climbed onto my lap to be petted — and I was careful to stroke him in the right direction. Then Leni told us about Yetta, a wild albino hedgehog they had caught only a week before, about the age of Nettles. She went over to the cage and came back with Yetta, snowy-white, perched on her bare arm. Yetta was already almost as tame as Nettles.

The high spot of the performance came when Leni hung both Yetta and Nettles on the clothesline. They swung back and forth happily, squeaking and grunting, and each held on easily with one foot alone.

Leni and her husband take a very dim view of the bounty on hedgehogs. And after watching her with her two pets it is easy to understand their point of view. But when I look at several thousand dollars' worth of timber destroyed in our woods, I am of two minds.

Anyone who knows hedgehogs will agree they are the most inconsistent of animals, not excepting even man. In all the years since they ruined our car, they have never molested one here again. They will despoil a corn patch in one night, but perhaps never again return to the same corn patch.

They appear to be entirely senseless, but they will keep a few hemlocks alive outside their dens for a century. These trees become three feet thick at the ground and taper up to a height of only twenty feet, but always provide a handy meal of green foliage. Trees further away from the dens will be girdled and killed indiscriminately.

According to Parke Struthers, hedgehogs — I guess I should switch to porcupines when quoting such an authority — live longer than any other North American mammal except ourselves. Probably an average of twenty years in a wild state, and upward of seventy-five on a controlled diet in captivity. So if you want to have a nice house pet that will stay with you a while . . .

Also, according to Parke, this animal is our earliest, having been climbing around here and chewing things up for more thousands of years than I can count. From my own firsthand experience at trying to get rid of the beasts, I think that if the worst happens and atomic blasts are ever let loose, hedgehogs are by far the most likely candidates for survival. When the dust settles they will just crawl unconcernedly out of their dens and start looking for some old boards to eat for breakfast.

19

The Biggest Liars of All

YEARS ago we used to run into old Tom Blodgett every bird season. On warm sunny days he would be sitting with his back against the stone wall at the south corner of the Blueberry Hill cover. He would sit there all day, waiting for "pa'tridges" to come out and feed. When they got within a few yards he would blast them on the ground with his rusty single-barreled ten-gauge.

Old Tom was the soul of honesty in most things, but he always told us, "The shots I like best are high and pretty near overhead, crossing. I set here and wait for 'em to break out o' them tall pines, and when they git just over the road, I knock 'em."

At their best the trite little exaggerations of fishermen, deerstalkers, and the like cannot stand up against the polished technique of bird-hunters. All bird-hunters are trained liars. Oh, we might except a few who shoot only pheasant; the pheasant is a first cousin of the Rhode Island Red, so there is no need for lying. The real experts are the upland grouse-shooters, the ones who use dogs alleged by their owners to hold points on the elusive grouse. These are the true artists.

They always give the dogs the benefit of the doubt and lie accordingly. They will tell you the dog was pointing beautifully when he only stopped to lift his leg. They will tell you a bird flushed wild when they know well the dog ran smack into it. And they will tell you the dog that ran off after a rabbit just couldn't hear the whistle because of the wind.

New Hampshire Fish and Game figures show that grouse killed in a two-month season, divided among the licensed hunters, would average three quarters of a bird per hunter. Let's say one fourth of the kill was unreported, giving one bird per hunter. Now, for every hunter who killed, for example, six grouse, there must be five who got none. Yet who ever heard a grouse-hunter admit to getting no birds in a whole season?

In defense of the upland gunner's fanatical devotion to the untruth, let it be said a truly honest one might well trade his gun for binoculars and take up songbird-watching. Find a good cover; then just forget to lie — just once — when someone asks where you've been. Next weekend you'll think they're holding a field trial there. Station wagons bumper to bumper, bushes swarming with setters and pointers, Brittanys and Weimaraners.

Safety is the first lesson the novice must learn. We start drilling him on it when he takes his first tottering steps into the cover. He is taken to no choice spots until his lies are natural and convincing. He must watch his footwork when referring to specific terrain, such as mountains, lakes, and streams. A gunner is safe only when, asked of an evening if he remembers the village where we stopped that day to buy some shells, he will at once name a place at least fifteen miles removed.

Our upland grouse is the hardest bird in the world to hit. Rarely does a foolish one sit on a limb waiting to be nipped off. It follows that many a gunner, because he is a novice, or too slow on his swing, or just unlucky at finding birds, ends the season with a borrowed feather in his hatband. These unfortunates always say, "Well, I didn't get quite as many birds as usual, but of course it was a poor year anyway." (We always agree solemnly about the poor year even if our logbook tallies up to an all-time high.)

Sportsmen often claim our bird-shooting has nothing in common with the British version. They overlook two main points — the same type of gun is used, and the same type of imagination.

A friend of ours casually mentions "that day a few years back when old Spot was in his prime and I killed five grouse over him," and we politely say we remember it well. We do remember well that he killed three.

His British counterpart will mention the day when, on Lord Somersby's grouse preserve, he killed "a hundred and two brace." And we can assume he did kill fifty.

If an English sportsman relates in the letters section of *The Field* the circumstances of how, in 1949, he accounted for three grouse on the wing with one shot,

the next issue will have a letter topping it. Major
T. S. R. Throke-Chillingham, Ret., will write that in
August of 1927, shooting from butts near Inverness,
Scotland, he brought down four grouse with one barrel
of his twelve-gauge — adding that it was raining, tem-
perature forty-six with a thirty-mile wind, time 11:30
A.M. This will bring still another letter, from an old
gentleman in Ireland; in 1902, near Killarney, he walked
up to a covey of grouse, and getting off but one shot,
picked up no less than five dead birds.

After that the editor will presumably have decided
to knock it off before they get back into the nineteenth
century. Some blighter may even have written him earlier on, displaying the bad taste to doubt the five-bird
story.

Our New England birds never fly bunched up
in great numbers; even our most skillful liars would
hardly attempt a claim of dropping several with one
shot. However, a neighbor told us the other day he fired
at seven partridge by the roadside and bagged the lot of
them. They were ringed round an apple, feeding on it,
and his shot got them all in the head. It makes him admittedly six times more guilty than the unsporting gunner who stoops to shooting one bird on the ground. My
own method of handling such a shot puts great emphasis
on hiding the bird quickly under my coat, sprinting
back to the car, and getting under way in a flash.

The veracity of our friend the Doctor is legendary

in medical circles. Outside his career, the love of his life is a lumbering, fat old pointer named Mercury. The Doctor is a delightful field companion and a fine shot. But he couldn't hunt the simplest cover without a guide, not if you gave him a relief map showing every thorn apple and hardhack bush. Still, he undertook the entire training of Mercury by himself.

Once we got softhearted and let the Doctor bring Mercury along on an all-day hunt. Pointers are noted for stanchness and Mercury is no exception; he is the stanchest ally of the Audubon Society. On his first cast he expertly chases all birds out of cover well ahead of the guns. Then he relaxes an hour or two, deaf to whistle, frolicking in hardwoods, hay fields, and highways.

While not bird-hungry, we do like to shoot at one now and then. The Doctor was firmly discouraged from ever bringing Mercury with us again, on the pretext that our own dogs needed work. This seemed to have an extraordinary effect on Mercury's behavior. Now every time the Doctor hunts with us we get another bulletin.

Mercury held a whole covey of grouse for half an hour. He pointed a bird sixty feet high in a spruce top. And the latest, "You know, Mercury gets smarter every year. I put him down the other day in that Haunted House cover — not the pines, just the open part. Well, Mercury didn't find anything, so he waited till I got out on the road. Then he ran into the pines, crept around a partridge, and put it straight out over my head. And of course, ordinarily, Mercury *never* flushes!"

Shooting is a tense business. Many a hot altercation, if not bloodshed, is averted by a little dissembling in the field. A gunner snaps a quick one at a bird swerving behind a clump of trees. He cries happily, "I hit it! It's down, just beyond these pines."

Meantime, from where we stand we can see the bird sail on, unruffled by a single pellet, over the hills and into the next county. But do we say so? Oh, no. We call back, "Good work! Keep a line on the spot — we'll get the dog in."

All hands converge and we start searching every likely thicket. After a decent interval one of us says to the weakening gunner, "You know, I'm quite sure a bird came out, flying strong, after you shot — do you think it was your bird, just possibly?" And pretty soon he decides it *might* have been, though he was right on it, and we may as well go along.

Some breeders advertise "perfectly trained grouse dogs — keen hunters, stanch on point, reliable retrievers" from a modest two hundred dollars up. These ads are put out by honest, reputable people, but they use a sort of code that the experienced buyer knows how to decipher.

Keen hunter means a dog not only keen about grouse, but anything that crosses his path, from field mice to deer. The keen part means once he has started hunting, it takes from one to three days to catch him.

Stanch on point means that if, when he gets the scent,

you attach a stout rope to his collar and tie him firmly to a tree, he will stay there until you flush the bird.

A *reliable retriever* will come in quickly when you shoot, pick up your bird, and if you reach him in time, will not eat it. While prying his jaws apart you should wear thick leather gloves.

The all-round thoroughly trained grouse dog for our style of shooting is about as rare as the whooping crane. The lucky owner of such a dog will tell you that all the money in New England wouldn't tempt him to sell. This is nearer the truth than anything else you're likely to hear from a grouse-hunter.

Long exposure to their human environment has produced in grouse dogs themselves an inherent capacity for lying. They can't talk, some owners to the contrary, but they manage very well in their own way. I will give but one of many examples. It concerns an extremely sly, crafty, clever tan-and-white setter bitch named Sue.

Through a friend of a friend, we were shooting one day with an unknown quantity whose name, we'll say gracefully, was Smith. He turned out to be a game hog — and worse, one of those who talk of grouse dogs as "broken" rather than trained. "Never make a pet out of a hunting dog," and all that.

Our Sue was unaccustomed to being yelled at, and she didn't like it. She would flash into a cover with an air that said, "Just leave me alone and I'll get you more shots than any other dog in the business," and the results usually proved she was right. Smith not only yelled at her. He shot a bird and picked it up before she could come in to look for it, thus cheating her out of life's proudest moment.

When he shot another bird, Sue got ahead of him. It was obviously dead and had dropped into a patch of thick brush. Sue dashed in out of sight for a minute and reappeared with no bird. We commanded her to hunt dead, and she went back in and sniffed over every inch of ground, but still no bird. Finally we all hunted for half an hour, but we never found it.

Later in the day the same thing happened again. We tried to apologize for Sue's duplicity but this time Smith got pretty mad. "That so-and-so dog of yours has buried my bird again! Why, if I owned a dog like that, I'd shoot her!"

To our great relief, and Sue's, Smith never asked to hunt with us again. And Sue never buried another bird in her life.

Literal-minded folk — the kind who, finding themselves with only a seventy-five-cent sherry, would never think of decanting it into an old Pedro Domecq bottle — may try grouse-shooting, but they never get far. Give them just one day like the one my wife and I ended last season with.

We started off at daybreak with a car full of dogs, lunch boxes, and heavy coats and blankets, hoping it would warm up while we drove thirty miles to the Goat-Man's Cover, one of our best. Instead it got colder, about fifteen above. The sun went under for keeps, and when we started hunting our eyes blurred with tears in the stinging wind.

I was crunching along down a snow-covered side-hill, trying to thaw my arthritic fingers inside my coat. My wife was working a young dog over in the cover somewhere to my left. After a while I heard her twenty-gauge, so muffled by the wind it sounded like a cork coming out of a bottle. A second later a grouse crossed ahead of me at about three hundred miles an hour. I got off both barrels well behind it.

"Did you get it?" she called. "Do you want the dog?"

"Heck, no. Keep on going, before we freeze to death."

"Well, why couldn't you hit it? I put it right out to you, didn't I? Apache needs to have a bird shot over him."

"All I could see was a gray streak," I said. "If you're so anxious to get Apache a bird, why didn't you hit it yourself?"

We found nothing more until midafternoon. Then, as we were circling back to the car to warm up, our old dog held five points in succession on grouse in open cover. We managed between us to miss all five. After that fiasco we were both too cold, disgusted, and disgruntled to hunt any longer, and we called it a day.

Some weeks later my wife was talking to a friend: ". . . and you should have been with us that last day. It was just heavenly! The air had that wonderful late-season tang, and the dogs all worked beautifully. We never had better shooting."

"How many birds did you get?"

"Oh, maybe not more than two or three, actually, but it was all such fun — the kind of day you live for, you know."

And the funny thing is, as I look back now, it *was* a wonderful day.

20

Confessions
of a Part-Time Squire

A STRANGER from the city phoned to ask about a piece
of land we planned to sell, and I arranged to meet him
down at the crossroads. "You can't miss me," he said, as
though we were meeting at Forty-second Street and
Broadway. "I'll be in my station wagon. Just look for a
white Country Squire." Without thinking I replied,
"That's fine. We don't have any color bars up in this
country, but as a matter of fact I'm a white country
squire myself."

Technically this was not quite true. Up here the real
English-style country squire requires a very substantial
private income or a rich wife. I practice the art only in
certain seasons: when skiing is good, during the spring
trout season, and in the fall shooting months. The rest of
the time, except for a little sailing, tennis or bird-watch-
ing in summer, I work.

But we do have quite a few neighbors who are full-time country squires. This part of New Hampshire seems to attract them, though it is not easy to fathom why. Our native country gentlemen of leisure had become almost extinct a generation or two back, and the incumbents of this happy way of life have moved up here from everywhere. It may be that they sense something of tradition, for we once had country squires who could hold their own in any company.

Sometime around 1880, one Louis Cabot bought up large holdings in the townships of Dublin, Harrisville, Nelson, Antrim, and Hancock. Farms of one hundred to five hundred acres with buildings more or less intact could be bought for a pittance in those days. The railroads had isolated the hill country, and farming had moved westward. The Cabot estate, most of it never accurately surveyed, at a conservative guess may have run to more than a hundred thousand acres. For a time we were pretty well surrounded by Cabot land, my grandfather having been one of the few natives silly enough to refuse all offers of the estate agents.

One day Mr. Cabot was touring the back roads, as was his wont on summer days, behind a fast team driven by his coachman. He passed a large open slope growing up to poplar whips, a promising situation for woodcock. Cabot was an upland game enthusiast and bought land with an eye for bird cover. On coming to a farmhouse, he stopped to inquire of an old man who was outside splitting wood.

"Looks like good woodcock country along here. Are there many birds around?"

"Plenty of 'em," the old man told him.

"Is that land across the road for sale, by any chance?"

"Dunno."

"Don't you own it?"

"Nope."

"Well, then, who does?"

"Rich old cuss from Boston, name o' Cabot."

Most people like to think comfortably that in the last fifty years or so we have made great strides in tolerance and broad-mindedness. But when it comes to leading the kind of life you want to live, up here in the country, I wonder. I can readily think of a dozen men, roughly contemporary with our grandfathers, who followed the happy lot of the country squire. And they were highly respected men who led exemplary lives. My father would say, "That Harry So-and-so, lives out to West Keene, never worked. Always had money . . ." This was not meant to imply that Harry was queer, or unintelligent, or a second-class citizen. It was, rather, a tribute to Harry's good sense.

By way of contrast, consider the neighbor we called on the other day. Though it was early for cocktails, he was already so potted he fell off the wharf when he was showing us his boat, and we had to fish him out. Now he is obviously a fine chap and has no reason at all to drink too much. No reason, that is, except that being a genuine country squire these days has proved too much for him. His neighbors all insist he is hopelessly eccentric and a real misfit, and even that he is not quite right in the head — just because he tries to lead a sensible life freed from the bonds of some active conventional occupation. Persecution has caught up with him.

Most country squires of today, because of this attitude of intolerance, haven't the nerve to accept the title. And they go to the most elaborate lengths to deceive the public. Some pretend to farm or sell real estate or analyze something. We know a chap who has been "writing a book" for half a lifetime. Another has an elaborately equipped small office building complete with secretary on the lawn of his extensive estate, so that he can "run his business" from the country. Then there is one poor fellow who for years has driven all the way to Boston each week. He spends a couple of days down there in a hotel and comes back full of wise talk about the financial world, a routine he fondly imagines we accept as proof he is really a working man.

In the very early 'thirties we had a wave, a real migration of young married couples moving to the country. These were the ones who still had a lot of money left after the Great Depression struck. There wasn't much doing then in the business world, so while their less fortunate fellows sold apples or went on WPA, these fledgling country squires and squiresses moved up here and showed us how to live.

At the time we must have known some twenty such couples, settled around here in elaborately rebuilt farmhouses or summer places. In about five years hardly any of them were still with us. It was a soft generation, perhaps, reared as it was on bathtub gin, F. Scott Fitzgerald and the Moral Rearmament movement. Somehow they all seemed to get the idea that being a country squire mainly involved throwing parties and swapping wives. Some became alcoholics, some committed suicide, some smashed themselves up in cars or planes, and one or two survived and went back into business.

The fact is, being a country squire — successfully — makes medicine or law look easy. It is the only field that leaves a man with no excuses. No excuse for not voting in every primary, getting put on every committee, entertaining visitors or house guests whenever they decide to drop in, helping a neighbor fix his plumbing or pacify his wife when she gets in a temper.

Anybody else can be sure of a quiet evening just by pleading a tough day at the office, or can escape some obnoxious local gathering by taking a business trip. Anybody else can say, "Gosh, Henry, ordinarily I'd give a few bucks — nobody knows better than I how much this town needs a bird sanctuary — but things are awfully tight in my line just now. Maybe next year."

A country squire must also keep in constant training, like a fighter or a ballet dancer. Why? Because all his friends expect him to look ten to fifteen years younger than his age. Or at least theirs. He must be ready, every time some old friend drops by: "Say, old boy, you don't look a day older. Must be hard as nails, but of course it's the life you lead up here!" And being hard as nails, he must be careful to stay vigorous up to ninety or so. Who ever heard of a country squire dying young? And when he does eventually pop off, the proper method is by being tossed from a spirited horse, or perhaps strangling himself in a tangle of fish line while landing a salmon.

Even so, just give me the rich wife or the bundle of Tel. & Tel. shares, and this will be the life for me. Some fellow who needs it can have my place in the work-a-day world. Let society look on me as it may, I will know how to spend every precious hour, so long as there are still fish in the waters, birds in the covers, and snow on the ski slopes.

21

The Unspoiled Country

WE have not told our neighbors, but our own private dream village is in a township several miles to the north. It is wild, rugged country. High wooded hills rise around dark tamarack swamps, and the streams are backed into little lakes at intervals by tireless work crews of beaver.

The village straggles along a wind-swept stretch of road where the last shade tree was long ago cut for stovewood. Houses are patched with tin, tar paper, and shingles of every shape and hue. One is a converted quonset, another an enlarged trailer. The store-post office has a false front giving it the look of a misplaced horse opera set.

The paint has peeled from the small church and its stumpy steeple will never be credited to Bulfinch. The second most prominent building is an unused hall, window panes smashed out, squatting forlornly in a patch of rank weeds. Behind it, against a backdrop of tall pines, is a white clapboarded outhouse; one of its twin doors has fallen off, revealing the vacant throne within.

The outhouse is a classic, but it is the only truly authentic architecture to be seen. The most undiscriminating couple from the city, looking for a "lovely old farmhouse" to remodel, would drive right on without even slowing down. But we have thought — secretly — of moving up to that township. It looks like one of the last strongholds against the infiltraters from Massachusetts and other southern states who have sent our taxes skyward.

In our town those of us who have always lived here get along very well, on the whole, with the new arrivals who fix up old farmhouses or build anew on old cellar holes. But the immigrants, young or old, and though they come from some New Hampshire city, or Boston, or New Canaan, Connecticut, bring with them one common trait that puzzles us no end. They arrive all excited about our unspoiled surroundings, eager to embrace our simple, natural ways of life. And before the natural finish on their new old-pine-paneling is dry, they begin to agitate for all the civic improvements they left at home.

First, of course, we should have a new school. Then this road or that should be paved with asphalt. We should have a new fire truck. We should have a broader insurance program. We should have an office for the selectmen, and stationery embossed with the name of the town.

A rare exception was the financial expert who bought an old farm here. He was against the town's becoming more indebted, against a new school instead of repairing the old, against asphalt roads and other expensive innovations. He is now considered a hopeless eccentric and doesn't speak any more at town meetings.

Sometimes we can still win. A newcomer in the village demanded street lights. He claimed that after dark motorists could drive right through the place and never know it was there. He was outvoted, and soon after left town.

A few years ago we did build a new school, but put the old one to good use as a wing. And we came out about ten thousand below the cost of a suburban-looking factory the "education" people tried to ram down our throats. They predicted disaster if we didn't provide, in addition to the ample new rooms we built, yet another in reserve. But so far we have had no population explosions up here, and it looks as though our building will serve for as long as the former one did — around a century.

I was chairman of the building committee, and by the time the school was finished several people among our four hundred population were on rather strained terms with several other people. Some of my relatives didn't speak to me for a year or so.

But what almost broke my spirit was the angry criticism of a lady from New York. She was not among the many townspeople who pitched in and helped build what turned out to be a thoroughly modern school of the highest standards. But when it was done, she came to inspect it, and then excoriated us for not having installed graduated sizes of toilet bowls. The committee, however, could not seem to understand why children whose homes provided but one size of toilet bowl — if indeed any at all — should be provided with special sizes at school.

Fortunately, the native-born in our town long ago became quite well integrated with the summer people. For had we not begun to practice intermarriage we would now be almost extinct. Today we can mingle freely in any gathering and an outsider would never spot us.

A Hungarian psychiatrist, looking for a vacation spot, lost his way and stopped at our house to ask directions. After some conversation, he inquired, "And how you peoples get along wiz natives in zis remote place? You find them friendly?"

My answer was automatic. "They're a damned tough lot," I told him. "Suspicious and unpredictable. You never know where you stand. We're beginning to make some progress with them, but it takes a lot of patience."

"So? You have been here for some time?"

"We've been right here since about seventeen-sixty," I said. He looked at me a little strangely, bade us good-by, and drove away.

When I was small, certain of our relatives still viewed newcomers with some reserve. About the way the Boer farmers accepted the English. The older generation knew, with the sureness of true instinct, that if you gave those city people an inch they would take a mile.

For a long time Ed Wilson was our town road agent. A New York lawyer who summered up beyond the village used to interrogate Ed frequently about the road work — when was he going to draw some more gravel, fill a mudhole, things of that sort. Ed was the kind who would not have cultivated the lawyer's favor even without the questioning.

One day the lawyer went for a walk and encountered the road agent and his crew. Ed was sitting down, holding drill, while one of the boys swung a sledge. When they stopped to rest, the lawyer greeted them pleasantly, and approaching Ed, went on, "And just what are you good men planning to do here, if I may inquire?"

"Well, I'll tell ye," Ed said promptly. "We're drillin' this here ledge that's blockin' the ditch. When we get deep enough, I'm goin' to fill the hole with dynamite. Then we'll touch her off, and anybody standin' around with nothin' better to do than ask damn fool questions will get blown straight to hell!"

Such independence of spirit on the part of town officials has in recent years almost disappeared. Now when the road agent wants to dig out a culvert or cut a little brush, he consults with the selectmen, who discuss it with the planning committee, who decide we had better hold an open meeting.

Nobody could have been more surprised than Old

Frank, our neighbor to the south, when we voted to remove the rock from the dead-end road just beyond his
house. He had complained at every town meeting for
forty years. True, it was a big cobblestone and you had
to dodge around it, but the road didn't go much farther
anyway, and no road agent ever paid it the slightest attention.

Sometime after the stone had been exhumed, I was
visiting with Old Frank, and spoke about the improve-
ment. "Well, I don't know," he mused. "Many a time,
Sunday night, I'd be settin' here by the kitchen window, and a car would go by. Somebody hadn't seen the
turnoff and think they was headed back to Boston. They
would go roarin' up past and then bang! After awhile,
they'd come creepin' back down, and next morning I'd
see a little trail of oil in the middle of the road . . . I
kind of miss that old rock."

People who have not lived up here keep right on
harrying us with that time-worn question about the
long winter evenings. And they envy our leisurely pace,
our escape from the complexity and strain of the urban
scene, our freedom to live as we please. The "country
writers" make a very good thing of catering to the il-
lusion.

A few of us do live pretty much as we please — but
not without a constant fight. Nowadays, the only sure
way to get a little uninterrupted peace and quiet is to go
to New York and spend a few days in a mid-town hotel.

A campaign to promote a big recreational state park

in our midst, a few years ago, revealed that even up here in the woods we were deep in the clutches of Madison Avenue boys. A few well-heeled hucksters had moved to New Hampshire to get away from it all. Before long we had "it all" too: publicity departments, promotion experts, regional associations, bales of shiny literature. Now they think the state should open an expensive New York office, and of course we will. We've got to sell New Hampshire, according to our live-wire governor and highly paid publicity people.

But in our little town we still like to do our own selling and choose our own customers. Wholesale advertising is something we have always managed very well without. We avoided starvation quite successfully long before such institutions as Planning & Development were invented. We built up an exclusive resort and real estate clientele — people who really did like our way of life, and were willing to pay for it.

Occasionally some dire threat from forces outside the town will make us unite in common cause. In our great Battle of the State Park all the citizens at town meeting — nearly a hundred — voted unanimously on the issue. (As one paper reported it, our first unanimous vote since the Civil War.) It lasted two years, and before it was over it seemed we were fighting practically all the rest of New Hampshire and part of Massachusetts too.

One warm summer afternoon I was privileged to accompany our selectmen to the land in question. Some weeks earlier we had learned that a legislative committee, Resources and Recreation, had been taken to view the area. They had reported favorably on a bill to buy the land. It was our darkest hour. But now the twenty members of Appropriations had insisted on making the same tour.

We had been caught napping when the first committee made its visit. They came by boat, and we suspected they were shown only what the State Park people wanted them to see. This time we were forewarned, and it seemed only common courtesy that we be on hand to welcome the delegation.

At the south end of the property, where we planned to intercept the legislators, we climbed a small ridge. It commanded a wide view of the lake. We found a comfortable log for a seat, in the shade of some tall spruces, and waited.

One could imagine the settlers of an earlier day sitting patiently perhaps on this very spot, waiting to ambush Indian war canoes. Pretty shrewd customers, our backwoods New Hampshire selectmen, I thought to myself. (Almost forgetting, in the excitement of the moment, that these three were recent arrivals from Connecticut, Rhode Island and Massachusetts.)

When two small outboard cruisers finally hove into sight we started down to meet them. But they kept on past and were some distance beyond the land they had come to look at before putting in to shore.

One of the selectmen then came up with an idea worthy of the late Kenneth Roberts. Why not stay out of sight for a while? We might find out just how this inspection tour — guided, as we knew it was, by a factotum of the enemy forces — was being conducted.

It worked out better than we could have anticipated. The guide was showing land that was not for sale, far more attractive ground than the park site itself. Rogers' Rangers followed them for some time, just near enough to hear what was said.

When it seemed quite sure there was no intention of leading the party onto the park site land — an impenetrable tangle of boulders and brambles — we stepped forth.

The legislators were genuinely glad to see us. They were interested only in an impartial survey and proceeded to question us in detail. We pointed out the boundaries and gave them all the facts we thought might be helpful. Altogether everybody had a very pleasant afternoon, except perhaps the man who had hoped to guide the tour without our expert assistance.

The Appropriations Committee turned in a recommendation that the park bill not be accepted. And the bill was finally defeated by an overwhelming vote.

The park fight was over, but the next year it was something else. Everybody loves our country, but nobody will let it alone. We have learned to keep up a twenty-four-hour alert.

If it were not for the fact that we seldom agree on the basic factors that make a country community spoiled or unspoiled, ways and means would be relatively easy.

"Zoning? Why, we moved our family all the way up here from New Jersey just to get away from that kind of thing!"

No zoning for our Jersey-style individualist, but he wants to raise the school appropriation by a couple of thousand. His eighth-grade son is going to grow up to be a scientist so we can win the rocket race. The nation's future is at stake. We must send our little Oppenheimer to a bigger school fifteen miles away where they have a cyclotron, or maybe a computer. Our three-room primary school still leans heavily toward Liberal Arts — philosophy, Greek, a course on the native dialect, that sort of thing.

It is the generally accepted idea that all native New Hampshire people spoil their villages, and people moving in from elsewhere unspoil them. As you drive up and down the state, from time to time you will come upon a village in which every building is immaculate. Houses are either white with green shutters or red with white shutters. White-painted buggy wheels and old coach lamps on posts grace the entrances. You will notice that all outbuildings — ells, sheds and barns — are as scrupulously maintained as the houses.

The country store, complete with cracker barrels and red-wheeled coffee mill, is kept by a former advertising man from Yonkers. Postmistress is a retired Radcliffe teacher.

To the practiced eye the story of such a wonderfully unspoiled hamlet can be guessed at a glance. The possibilities of the place were spotted by an heir of the Palmolive soap fortune, or Swift hams, or Budweiser. Probably a woman in late middle age.

Almost overnight the whole place was thoroughly and entirely "restored." The town hall and a few of the houses are reproductions, but you could never tell. The old native families have all mysteriously disappeared. Every carpenter and contractor for miles around retired and moved to Florida shortly after the restoration. Anybody interested in statistics will find a low birth rate, taxes considerably above average, and the highest per-dwelling consumption of fuel oil in the world.

We know an old resident of the upstate paper-mill town of Berlin who still understands little except his native Russian. He escaped from Riga in his youth and tried to reach Germany. Somehow he got on a ship bound for Boston, and eventually made his way to Berlin, New Hampshire. Nobody there could speak Russian, and he had been happily settled for over five years before he learned he was not in Berlin, Germany.

I got almost as lost as that in younger days while driving across Germany en route to study the Austrian ski schools. For years after I was reminded of that trip by the handsome octagonal brick chimney of the old woolen mill in Harrisville. Somewhere, in Frankfort I think it was, I had seen an eleventh-century cathedral with red brick columns of proportions that seemed identical. In our town, too, there was once an old brick mill with a beautiful chimney, but it has all been torn down. The skill and refinement of design that went into fashioning such monuments of handmade brick is a lost art. When the last of the old chimneyed factories has disappeared, then somebody will spend millions trying to create, in the manner of Williamsburg, a faithful reproduction.

Nobody seems to know why more and more people choose the woods of New Hampshire when they retire. The question was asked of one couple who moved here after some years in Florida and various Caribbean island paradises. Their answer was that they had tried just about everything else.

I do not know why they come, but once here they stay because they are never bored. They are much too busy keeping the country from being spoiled.

New school, library, town barn, fire station with two new trucks, black top on the back road to the village — and a new tax rate. The zoning committee will meet Tuesday night. Committee to repair the town hall, Thursday. Special town meeting some time next month.

Even so, home is still home. We probably would not leave even if the town should vote to buy helicopters to get the school children back to their TV sets more quickly.

But if you really want to get away, try that town a few miles north, the one with the outhouse in the center. It is more convenient than South America and the long trip up the Orinoco, looking for a village where the natives never worry about consolidated schools, civil defense appropriations, or zoning.

22

Year End

FOR us the year does not end on New Year's Eve. It has already ended on the last afternoon of November, when darkness has finally rubbed out any chance for a shot at a bird until the next October.

Judging from the letters we get every fall, most non-bird-hunters have a pretty clear picture of our upland sport: Dawdling over our third cups of coffee at breakfast, the setters lying patiently under the table, we decide to spend the day in some particularly inviting nearby area amid the scenic autumn foliage. Once afield, old Queenie soon stops in the middle of an open meadow, frozen on a solid point, one foot raised and tail straight as a ramrod. We saunter up ahead of the dog, and several birds sail gracefully into the air. And with the sure, easy marksmanship born of long experience, we knock down a brace. At the day's end we return home pleasantly relaxed, unload a bushel or so of birds and hang them up. Then we have a few drinks and sit down to a feast of roasted partridge and woodcock.

Well, once in a while the dogs do get stanch points — but not every day. Once in a while we find a bird, one that is uneducated or more likely just asleep, out in an open pasture or field. And on many a day we may empty a whole box of shells, and our marksmanship is naturally pretty keen. But birdshot will not penetrate through very many pine trees, nor will it overtake a bird that is flying a little faster than the shot is traveling.

Anyway, after a long, hard, exciting day in the woods, one good thing about fried chicken is that you do not have to pluck and clean it.

On those days when we come home with nothing in the old game box except some Baldwin apples or wild grapes, we are, to be sure, pleasantly relaxed. Tingling from the fresh air, gashed here and there from barbed wire, an eye closed from an encounter with a thornbush, and a leg gone stiff from having nearly wrenched it off sliding down a slippery ledge.

We who spend two whole months every autumn with guns and dogs, year after year, still face that Last Day with almost unbearable anticipation. Not that there always is a last day — sudden heavy snows may fall late in November, and you wake up some morning to find the season has just faded away.

This year things took a reverse twist. Right up to the end there had only been a day or two when we had used the folding lunch table and the little gas stove inside the station wagon. The last morning dawned clear and mild. It was like the best of late October shooting weather.

Last Day . . . last chance. Nothing must go wrong today. And the more so because of a long-standing date to finish the season with one of our best customers — the man for whom we trained Speck, handsomest and smartest pointer in the United States, if not the world, according to his owner.

While waiting for Fred, our gunner, we checked the gear. Spare clothes and boots, guns, water jug, lunch boxes, extra box of shells (optimistically) and other items that jammed the back of the wagon up to its roof.

Then the phone rang. It seemed we had once carelessly mentioned to Fred that we had been initiating our young nephew into the shooting world. Now Fred wanted to know if he could bring along a visiting grandson named Jerry, aged thirteen. "He's perfectly safe, I'm sure. Had lots of training on clay pigeons. But don't hesitate to say no, if you'd rather not take him."

We said we would be delighted. Perhaps an old hand like Fred, even in the case of his own grandson, would have made sure the youngster was not without some natural ability. At least we hoped so. In our time we have looked down the gun barrels of fledgling sportsmen, found their loaded weapons leaning precariously against car fenders, and dodged low shots aimed at woodcock flying in our direction.

Not that we haven't had similar adventures with adults. But that was before we started requiring our gunners to submit FBI clearances, aptitude test scores, and Dun & Bradstreet ratings.

Fred arrived well before nine with Jerry, the grandson, and Speck, the pointer, and we transferred them into our station wagon. Speck jumped eagerly into the big double dog-box in the rear, where Track, our little white setter bitch — Janet's favorite — was already ensconced in her half.

We planned to hunt Speck in the large covers where we would all march along in a wide formation. Track, a close-hunting precision artist, we would use on stands and little corners here and there where an exact line of flight must be anticipated in order to get a shot.

The night before we had argued over the potentials of a hundred covers, and rejected most of them. Finally we had agreed on the following itinerary: the Goat-Man's, the Black Horse, Suzy's, Across the River and into the Trees, Killer Run, Killer Annex, Freelove Cemetery, the Lithuanian's, Dead Hermit, Teacher's, Brick House Square, Cow Pasture (beloved of Janet — she once brought down three partridge there in as many minutes), Sheldon's Folly, and the Silver Spoon (so named because, in an ancient cellar hole there, we once found a fragile solid-silver teaspoon).

Killer Run is my own favorite cover, perhaps because years ago I got my first double on partridge there — or, as the English say, a left-and-right. It is a hellhole canyon for the dog handler, fighting through giant briars, gnarled apple and alder and thornbush, along a brook bed of slippery stones. But for the gunners high on the open banks it is paradise. Any bird started there means somebody gets a clear shot, and only once or twice in our lives have we failed to start one. It has been known to yield, along the few hundred feet of its length, seven or eight partridge with a bonus of a couple of woodcock.

It would take us almost an hour to drive to the Goat-Man's, but it seemed like a good place to begin because we had put up no less than nine partridge there a few days earlier. And from there on, the covers would be only a few minutes apart.

On the way we talked of other Last Days. I remembered the one, some fifteen years back, when we were out with Rollie Floyd, one of the best wing shots we have ever seen. It was at most 20° above zero, dark, a foot of snow, wind a howling gale. On a day like that nobody but a lunatic would go bird-hunting — a definition, however, that fitted both Rollie and my wife when it came to the thought of missing a day in the field.

We were hunting in the tall pines at the end of Killer Run, after failing to find a single bird anywhere else. Janet was in the center, and I heard her shout, "There's something that looks like a hawk sitting right over my head, 'way up at the very top of this pine!"

"Shoot it!" Rollie bellowed at her. Janet obediently aimed skyward and fired, and down came a large partridge. It was the only bird we saw that whole day.

Another memorable one-bird finish happened some

years later. There was even more snow, but it was not so cold — just wet and miserable, with every bush loaded and ready to dump down your neck and into your gun barrels.

There were four of us that time. There was Bill Clymer, who had shot with us for many years, and a young protégé of ours named Peter Denby, who was still in law school and would drive all night for a few hours' shooting.

The weather looked so impossible — raining on the snow — we had again decided only Killer Run might be worth a try. It took us an hour and a half to get there; and when we started hunting, the dog's bell at once filled with snow and was silent.

Janet and dog disappeared into a white jungle in the bottom of the run, while Peter took the high bank on the north side; opposite him, on the south side, I followed Bill. Halfway down the run ahead of us a partridge rose. It was much too long a shot, but Bill let off both barrels — the instant reaction of a veteran bird-hunter. He knew the only hope lay in turning the bird toward Peter, who was further ahead.

Sure enough, the bird veered toward the north bank, and Peter brought it down — barely — at about fifty yards. The dog did the rest.

We all trudged back to the car, soaked to the skin, but happy as only bird-hunters can be when the prospect of getting skunked is averted by a miracle. Then we drove home and Bill got out the special Irish whiskey

he reserves traditionally for those occasions when somebody has killed a bird.

These reminiscences were cut short, after we turned
off onto the dirt road leading to the Goat-Man's, when
somebody spotted a road-bird ahead. I tried to stop the
car at just the right range and Fred scrambled out,
hurriedly shoving shells into his gun. The bird was jumpy
and it flew before he could finish loading, but he snapped
off a shot into thick spruces as the partridge disappeared.

Shaking his head, he came back and Janet held out the
dime-box, laughing. Fred dropped a dime into the box.
"Got a whole pocketful with me, just in case," he
grinned.

We always hope to collect enough dimes in this manner to buy a bottle of champagne at the season's end.
One year Hank Roberts, after missing several road-
birds the day before, appeared with a heavy package
under his arm which he handed to us. "You may as well
have it right now, and get it over with," he said. It was
very good champagne, too.

Jerry proved to be a smart, husky boy with his grandfather's enthusiasm, quick reactions and good humor.
At the Goat-Man's, a circular, easy cover on level
ground, I guided him around the outside. Fred was in
the open field inside, with Janet running the dog between us.

The boy was as careful as could be expected of any
thirteen-year-old on his first adventure in brush shoot-

ing. Once he turned to speak to me and lowered his gun without breaking it, and I quickly pointed out this lapse of etiquette, using the voice of authority. From then on we had no trouble and I felt reasonably safe.

By lunchtime we had raised a dozen or so partridge. Jerry had fired both barrels twice, and once we thought he had dropped a bird. But after Speck had diligently hunted dead over a couple of acres, we decided the shot must have been just a little high.

Janet, Fred and I had each got off a few shots, but no damage had been done. I think each one of us secretly felt sure we could have hit a bird or two had we not been concerned with trying to get an easy setup for Jerry. But we would not have wanted it otherwise. Getting one's first partridge is a business of prime importance. Ask any bird-hunter, and he will recall every detail of his first partridge with more accuracy than his first paycheck, his first drink, or his first marriage.

Killer Run is at the bottom of a little valley surrounded by hills some people would call mountains. The road is narrow and grassy and all buildings on the old grown-up farms have long since fallen into their cellar holes. There is no inhabited dwelling for five miles in any direction. Just above where the Run begins there is a little sheltered field still mostly free of the steadily encroaching small pines. We ran the station wagon, in four-wheel drive, up into the field and got out our lunch.

On many a day earlier in the season we had eaten here, lying out on the grass in the warm sun. Today

we kept our coats on and sat on blankets against a sheltering stone wall, but it was still too nice to think of
eating in the car.

With the Last Day half gone and nothing yet in the
bag, it was natural that our thoughts should turn to
certain consoling aspects. Fred, looking ahead hopefully
to future seasons, remarked that bird-hunters he had
known seemed to be extraordinarily long-lived. He
claimed he knew one old gentleman in his nineties who
was still shooting.

This led to a rough count by Janet and myself of old
people with whom we had hunted, at one time or another, people in their seventies and even eighties. Right
off hand we could think of around sixteen. As we three
are all youngsters in the fifties, it was an encouraging
reflection.

We talked about Old Bob, who had shot for many
seasons with my brother Fran. It was Old Bob who
had insisted to Janet, when we were first married, that
she must have a more suitable gun. And he had made
her use a fine twenty-gauge of his own until we could
afford one, and given a rousing party to celebrate her
first partridge.

And it was Old Bob who had shot a woodcock directly in line with Fran's car, demolishing the windshield.
That was the season before he died, and he could walk
only a few steps. "I can buy you a new windshield any
day," he told my brother happily, "but I might never
have another chance like that at a woodcock!"

One day I was privileged to shoot with Old Bob — it was, I think, his sixty-third consecutive year of bird-hunting — and a friend of his, also over eighty. The two old gentlemen were stationed on a road while I worked the dog through an edge of alders. Across the road lay a wet marsh with cattails eight feet high. A woodcock flushed and there were a couple of shots.

When I emerged I could see only Old Bob. "Where's Ben?" I asked.

"Oh, he thought he might have hit that woodcock, even though I told him he never touched a feather," Old Bob said disgustedly. "And he's out there floundering around." He pointed to the marsh, where but for his bad heart and lameness he would have doubtless gone himself. "S'pose we'll just have to wait for him to come back — but I hope the damned old fool drowns!"

After lunch, hunting was slow. Even Killer Run produced only one bird, far ahead of Jerry and me. It had not lingered for Track to establish a point, and Jerry did not see it in time to shoot, and my own shot was late. With only an hour of light left, we drove up the steep lane leading to Sheldon's Folly.

The place had been christened by Bert Sheldon, who was with us when we discovered it. We had seen Bert, on another day, kill a partridge cleanly with a little twenty-eight-gauge gun at about eighty feet, when the bird crossed a narrow lane. But this time he had gotten partridge fever shooting at something like eight easy birds and missing them all.

Sheldon's Folly is what we call a three-dimensional cover, as contrasted to those on fairly level ground or on constant grades. It is long and narrow and runs horizontally across a steep slope, with heavy woods above and below; it takes perhaps ten minutes to walk its length. The middle part, more or less level, is largely open field dotted with apple trees, sumac, and juniper; upper and lower edges are bounded by stone walls along which it is possible to get outside shots.

We have found from long experimenting that this cover can best be hunted in two sections. An outside gun begins along the top edge, with the dog and handler just below, and when they reach the far end they swing back in the same way along the lower edge.

The third gun can take it easy, moving from one stand to another along the middle part and returning along the same route. Since there were four of us this time, it was decided that after placing Jerry on the first of these stands, I would return to the road and post myself at the end of the lower stone wall. Janet would run the dog and Fred would take the outside.

Without going into all the details of this chess-like maneuver, I will say only that the basic plan was necessary because Speck would not have known the cover well enough to avoid hunting right across it, whereas Track knew exactly the narrow route she was to follow. And as she will never hunt far from Janet, it devolved upon Janet to act as handler. And my own position was taken so that Jerry, for once, could be left to himself — if he followed instructions he could not go far wrong.

Figuring on a nice twenty-minute rest, I had just gotten down the hill to the end of the lower wall when two shots boomed out from the cover above. Then three blasts from Janet's whistle, the signal to come in.

I ran all the way back up the hill and arrived, thoroughly out of breath, to find Jerry, Janet, Fred, and Track, all in a huddle. With the deference we always show each other in the field, Janet yelled at me, "Where the devil have you been all this time? Didn't you hear me whistling? Jerry thinks he hit a bird, and it's up in that patch of pines!"

It seemed like a very long flight uphill for a bird that had been winged, so we laid out a careful plan of action. Fred, Janet and the dog would circle high above the pines and hunt down through. I would take a stand out in some fairly open gray birches below, and then Jerry — who to his great credit had remained where he had fired and marked the line of flight — would walk up on his bird.

Reaching my position in the birches, I blew my whistle, and presently heard Track's bell tinkling around in the pines. Then the bird jumped, and it came out flying low almost straight toward me. I turned to shoot after it passed and then decided there was no need; it was limping badly and would not go far. Track came down a second later like a white streak and caught the partridge almost as it landed, some fifty yards below.

Hearing me yelling "Dead bird!" the others came out of the pines and Track presented the bird to Janet, as she always does, and then lay down and rolled happily in the leaves. The expression on Jerry's face was something to remember.

We finished out the cover and there were no more birds in it, but nobody cared very much. For the rest of the afternoon birds were hard to find and we managed only a few wild shots.

When darkness had practically closed down, Janet insisted on one last try, a little stand with Fred out on the road. We groped our way through the brush and heard — it was too dark to see — a bird break out ahead toward Fred. And Fred saluted the season's last partridge with two shots that flashed red fire in the twilight, but it was an almost impossible chance, and he missed.

To a non-bird-hunter this may not sound like much of a day. But to us it had seemed like a pretty good one. And as for the bag — well, Janet and Fred and I had all had our lucky days, in the weeks past.

It is my firm belief that most people, even at our age, once in a while dream about how differently they would live if a little extra cash should fall their way — say a million or so. And thus it is with Janet and myself. But there is one time of year when we would just as soon leave things exactly as they are — bird season.

23

Hunting Hunters

SPORTSMEN from other states sometimes complain that New Hampshire deer behave in a singularly baffling manner. Whether or not this is true, there can be no doubt about the unpredictable and elusive nature of the deer laws. Actually, the wonder is that any New Hampshire laws make sense. This little state is far down the list in population, yet has one of the largest legislative bodies in the world: four hundred representatives and a twenty-four-member senate, with a corps of attendant officers such as councilmen, doorkeepers, and many others. We also have a governor.

Yankees are great for everybody's having a hand in government, and our system ensures it. Just about all of us get "sent to Concord" at some time during our lives, Concord being the capital and the home of the penitentiary and mental hospital. Several high officials have made the trip in two capacities, and one or two in all three.

By no means do all our citizens hunt deer, but every

single one of them has an idea for a new hunting law. At each session of the legislature, it takes a parliamentary wrangle to sift out all the deer bills and clear the decks for such minor items as education and budget.

At present we have an east-west line through the state, with one deer season above the line, another below it. There is some danger we may split in two, like Uruguay and Paraguay, over this line issue. But as all New Hampshire roads run only north and south — another of our unsolved mysteries — interdependence still holds us together.

Most people outside New England assume that the annual parade of cars carrying deer down the highways means that the cargoes were bagged in Vermont, New Hampshire, or Maine, whose publicity experts plug the idea. My own conclusion is that all these deer come from Canada, where they are bought in a large supermarket catering to hunters. Most of the animals are of Japanese origin, quick-frozen and exported to Quebec via the Panama Canal. This carrying of deer on car fenders has caused the mental breakdown of several cartoonists, unable to think of a new twist for the fall magazines. They have run through just about everything, from equipping the deer with tail fins to having the cartoonist lashed to the car with the editor driving.

It so happens that fewer deer have been killed recently in our neighborhood than in past years, but there is a definite increase in deer-hunters. There are also more partridge-hunters and fishermen and campers, and nobody knows where it will all end. We had to abandon one of our oldest bird covers last fall because of all the empty shells; our feet kept slipping out from under us.

Tracking, as we used to do it hour after hour, is no longer feasible. Today even in our wildest woods you cannot follow a deer more than a few minutes before several other hunters will cut in ahead. About half of them have no idea how to tell which way a deer is traveling, and they will likely as not be backtracking toward you. (I often find myself whistling or singing quite loudly while tracking.)

One day we saw a deer which had been tracked by so many hunters all going in different directions that after a while the deer itself didn't know which way it was going. Finally the bewildered animal just gave up and sat down.

Only about fifty years ago here in New Hampshire deer-hunting was no problem at all. A contributing factor may have been that there were no deer. They had been killed off by our forefathers, who objected to having all the vegetables nibbled out of their kitchen gardens and their apple trees chewed up every summer. With the advent of cheap canned goods this no longer mattered, and the ruminants known as Virginia white-tailed deer were reintroduced, with stringent protective laws.

Something similar happened in Vermont, but it is noticed by the curious that these two states — like as two peas except in the eyes of their inhabitants — always enact deer laws as divergent as possible. Over across the river, for example, they have a "buck law." Nobody can legally shoot a doe. We hear that this has resulted in runty stock. In fact, rabbit-hunters have been shooting a good many deer lately, mistaking them for hares. One Vermonter told us he didn't even bother to cut up his deer this year, just put the whole thing in the kettle and made a stew out of it.

My wife and I seldom find time to hunt deer these days, but we hunt deer-hunters more than ever. Years ago it was rare for a man to get lost in these parts; now it is a rare day when one doesn't. Personally I find hunting hunters the more rewarding sport. No bag limit, and a greater variety of quarry. Deer, by comparison to hunters, are quite easy to outguess. Also it is against the law to hunt deer after dark, but you can keep right on tracking hunters all night.

Recently we have been finding the lost hunters in our area to be in rather poor condition. They lack proper equipment, in spite of all that is written on that subject every year. Some were visibly undernourished.

Greenhorns would do well to emulate a veteran hunter of my boyhood days, Uncle Sim. Once, when he first took up hunting just after he was married, Uncle Sim managed to get lost. The neighbors did not find him until near midnight, somewhere over in the White Swamp. After that his wife never let him go out without the following equipment, in addition to his snowshoes, rifle, ammunition belt, and about five yards of bright cloth sewed on coat, pants, and hat: compass (navigating type), whistle, pocketknife, sheath knife, waterproof match case, newspaper for kindling, belt camp axe, sandwiches for two meals, week's emergency rations, Thermos of hot tea, flask of spirits, fifty-foot rope, flashlight, kerosene lantern, extra gloves, socks, first-aid kit, map of the county, and a package of toilet paper.

Such were the main items as I remember them. When his wife finished getting him loaded up for the day's hunt, he was not likely to travel far enough to get lost again. And there was the extra safety factor of the noise he made rattling and jangling through the brush.

Strange as it may seem, every season finds more and more hunters coming up here, eager to follow week-old deer tracks into strange territory equipped with nothing more than a rifle and some shells. They start off in zero weather, whistling happily, never leaving word in what general area they plan to hunt. Often their light shoes and clothing are about right for gathering blueberries in August.

Last season, after bringing in two exhausted specimens on two successive nights, we put up notices asking those wishing to be rescued on weekends to phone in advance for reservations. Even Red Ears, our little no-good white setter, had a rescue to his credit. One very black, cold night a young ex-Air Force man came crawling up to our house and rapped feebly on the front door. He was minus all survival equipment, as usual, and his flying boots were full of snow. When we got him thawed out enough to talk, he explained that for three or four hours he had been desperately working his way toward the sound of a dog's barking. This was Red Ears, whom we had never been able to cure of shrill and frequent yelping at nothing in particular.

Late in November, my wife and I were bird-shooting with a friend in a cover we had guaranteed to be virgin territory. It was in an uninhabited valley on a road that showed no sign of travel since Franklin Pierce was President. Janet and I took the dog through the cover, while Jim was posted on the road. At the end, when we reconvened, Jim said, "Maybe *you* think there's nobody in this country, but two characters just overtook me here the like of which you wouldn't believe."

On the way out in the jeep we saw what he meant. Trudging ahead were two figures, one large and stout, the other small and wiry, dressed all in Lincoln green. Their green hats sported feathers, giving them a jaunty air. Slung over their shoulders were quivers full of fine, knife-tipped shafts for the stout longbows they were carrying. I was just bethinking to ask these merry men the way to Nottingham when we remembered our newest law, which provided a week of deer-hunting for archers before the start of the gunpowder free-for-all December first.

Later we were to find that the arrangement would improve the deer-hunting considerably. All the deer, after being chased around for a week by the archers, are

well distributed and have caught their second wind by
the time the riflemen take over.

With ever-increasing armed hordes scrambling
through the thickets, it is inevitable that a few will snipe
at each other — though usually by mistake. Almost all
non-hunters work themselves into a perfect frenzy over
this every year. Letters and editorials demand that something be done.

All the noise is wasted effort. So long as deer abound
there can be no way to get rid of hunters. And so long
as deer-lovers abound there can be no way to get rid of
deer. Deer-lovers should be grateful that the hunters
shoot not them but each other, thus at least eliminating
some of the hunters. Then, too, every time a hunter
shoots a hunter, another deer is spared.

It has become the smart thing for the all-year-round
set — who now outnumber our "old natives" — to make
a great fuss over the deer season. They don't dare go for
a walk, they don't dare let the dog out. They might as
well be inside the stockade at the height of the Mohawk
massacres. All conversation revolves around the question of why licenses are issued without some sort of
examination, and their opinion that all deer-hunters are
(1) factory workers from Massachusetts who never shot
a gun before, or (2) ex-service boys whose military duty
has hardened them to a point of utter abandon with fire-
arms.

The non-hunters tell each other the same old stories at
every party: the hunter who tracked a sheep all day, the

hunter who shot the hog, the hunter who shot his mother-in-law, the hunter who was hauled into court and asked how he could have mistaken a horse for a deer and replied, "I didn't mistake it for a deer — I thought it was a cow."

Vainly deer-hunters may plead, "We too are lovers of nature," but they never get away with it. ("Anybody who would shoot a deer just *couldn't* feel for wild animals the way I do.") And let's not have any remarks about the deer-lovers' fur coats and doeskin gloves.

Living as we do in a large blank space on the map inhabited most of the time by only the deer and ourselves, we get a good look at the hunters pouring into our woods every fall. Even the ones who do not pour out again without some help from us are usually people we enjoy meeting, except for the two who built a fire on our boathouse floor and chopped a hole in the roof. And, unpopular conception though it be, we have long known deer-hunters are no more obnoxious than any other dedicated group. They are also just as intelligent as golfers, stamp collectors, or Democrats, in the main.

Most of our neighbors have now deteriorated into weekend hunters. But this is not the case with Stub Farnum, who will tell you — very willingly — all about every deer he has shot, legally and otherwise, over the past thirty years. ". . . I stood right by that old yeller birch, top o' Fox Ridge, studyin' the track, and I knew 'twas the old farrer doe 'cause of the way she drags that hind foot. Then I see somethin' move, over in the hemlocks, a good hundred yards. I held the old Savage right on it and waited, and pretty soon I see an ear twitch . . ."

One Saturday night Stub stopped by to tell us his latest exploits, obviously settling down for the evening. Four deer-hunters were spending the weekend with us. They were Air Force officers required to do constant long-range flying, a fact with implications unknown to Stub. He figured he had a good audience, but before he could get started one of the hunters remarked, "Last week I was up in the Chugach Range, hunting Alaska browns — man, what a country!" and another chimed in, "Yeah, I was up there a while back myself — but you ought to get out around Lake Chad sometime. Over there the other day, we took a trip after rhino. Got a couple. Talk about a real mean customer . . ." The other two men started arguing the relative thrills of knocking off a wild boar in Iran and stalking something called "tigre" in South America.

Before long Stub jumped up and headed for the door, muttering, "Got to get right home and put some wood on that fire, or it'll go out."

Any confirmed deer-hunter is drawn to the December woods as much by the prospect of glimpsing the unknown, the ever-present mysteries of the wilds, as by the main quarry. The hair-raising sight of a wildcat stalking its prey, perhaps — or an otter gliding silently along a frozen stream. There was, for example, Bert Whipple's encounter with a monkey over on the old lead mine road.

For forty years Bert always took a stand about half-way up Johnny Dick's hill every day of deer season. He would sit there on the stone wall with a quart of black-berry nectar (100 proof) in his pocket and wait for a deer to cross, and toward dark he would start back to the village. You can still see the monumental pile of bottles behind the wall, commemorating the spot where Bert used to sit.

When he saw the monkey, Bert was heading home-ward along the lead mine road where the treetops on the lower side — a sheer drop off — are about on eye level. He noticed something moving in the top of an oak tree about forty feet from where he stood. There could be no doubt about it, it was a monkey. They looked at each other a long time, and finally Bert went on home.

Nothing was heard about this until some three weeks later. Then a biologist came up for a weekend at his summer home near the village, and word got around he was looking for a monkey he had lost in October. When this news reached old Bert, he promptly announced he had seen that monkey all right, back in deer season, up on the lead mine road. The little cuss had set right up in the top of an oak and made faces at him for a good five minutes.

Somebody asked Bert, "Well, if you saw it, why didn't you say something about it?"

"You must take me for a plain fool," Bert answered. "What do you s'pose Dora would've done to me? No sir, I knew better'n to come home from deer-huntin' and tell Dora I'd seen a goddamn monkey!"

Far back north of us there lives in a weathered ruin, together with a hundred or so goats, a solitary but vigorous old native with the melodious name of Perley Swett. One year my wife and I found Perley's road posted with cardboard signs, not prohibiting hunting but demanding fifty cents per head for the privilege, "to defray loss of my goat shot by deer-hunters last year."

This seemed fair enough. We had no money with us, but when the old man came walking along the road on his way home with a sack of groceries, I told him we would bring him his dollar on another day. I had started along when my wife's youthful figure emerged from the woods near Perley, and I waited for some time while she chatted with him. Probably she was telling him he had a perfectly lovely house and how much she admired his goats.

When she finally joined me we heard Perley shouting after us. I went back a little to see what he wanted. "Women can hunt free!" he was yelling.

Among all the diverse types we run into during deer season, the young girl who periodically redesigns my wife's hair is easily the most spectacular. Whenever I stop to pick up my wife at her favorite beauty parlor down at the county seat, I have trouble getting her out of the place. The ladies are always in a huddle, and the exotic, perfume-laden air is filled with talk of .303's smacking into the shoulder of a big buck, or the doe that paunched out at two hundred pounds.

Just to fill in the picture, Joanne, the beautician, is a fragile-looking, startlingly beautiful honey-blonde who might have stepped right out of a New York model agency. Suddenly encountered five miles back in the Stoddard hills, clad in her insulated deer-hunting suit and carrying her Winchester three-forty-eight, she is almost as unlikely an apparition as Bert Whipple's monkey. And she swears there is nothing like a liberal dose of Chanel No. 5 to attract deer.

It all makes for a sort of holiday feeling with these people out roaming around, up on the mountain and down in the swamps and all over the place. Most of them are having a whale of a good time and getting nothing. Bang, bang, boom, boom, echoing through the hills — those early, cold, dark winter weeks would indeed be empty and lonesome without a deer season.

24

The Square Dance

UNTIL around 1930, square dancing had long been kept alive only in little backwoods places like this. Some people in our town think we started the great revival right here.

Anyway, when it did start, one of our local boys who had taken up "calling" soon found himself in demand from coast to coast. But he followed the modern trend, singing the calls and using any tunes that came to hand so long as he could sing to them.

When I was a small boy we always had several square dances during the slack time in winter. Old Wallace prompted, and played second violin too. There would be eight or ten in the band; old-timers who played strictly from the old scores, with the correct melodies for every figure of each dance. I was allowed to sit in with my piccolo after Mark Bailey, who had always occupied that chair, had died. In another decade most of the others had followed Mark, and the old band was no more.

217

In those days I never heard the term "fiddler" used except as an insult. Later Henry Ford "discovered" some old chap up in Maine (who couldn't play for sour apples) and the square dance revival began. "Old fiddlers" began to pop up everywhere from Unity Crossroads to Newark, New Jersey. And they are still with us.

But if in recent years there has been a truly authentic old-time square dance band anywhere in the land, I have never heard it. The dances have been revived but the music has not.

In the old days our dances were non-commercial. If the selectmen had tried to collect rent for the town hall they would have been lynched. The band played for fun, and we didn't have to fool with amusement taxes or Petrillo. Old Wallace, town moderator and a citizen of considerable stature, would have been outraged if somebody had tried to pay him for prompting.

Wallace's calls were spoken, or you might say shouted, like a train conductor announcing a station. The "singing caller" with his sickly blend of off-key warblings and idiotic rhymes had happily not been invented. Even young boys scrambled to see who could get old Mrs. Sullivan for a partner to make a "head couple." She was pretty fat, but she knew every note of the music and could steer anybody unerringly through the most intricate steps.

Walt Harris would park his old touring car by the door, a barrel of hard cider set up on the back seat. Between dances he would yell, "Come one, come all — a bird can't fly on one wing!" When he was well warmed up, he could whirl his partner "in the center" so high off the floor her feet would sail around over the heads of the others in the set.

It is strange that when square dancing became so exploited — movies, TV shows, books and articles — the old melodies still remained dead and buried. Today's fans, even those who go about the country attending "festivals" and affecting hillbilly costumes at dances, wouldn't even recognize many of the best jigs and reels we used to play. They caper around happily night after night, their toughened eardrums apparently immune to such incongruous and monotonous dirges as "Darling Nellie Gray" and "Hinky Dinky Parlez-Vous."

Among all the fiddlers on radio or recordings, never yet have I heard one who could accomplish all the notes of such old classics as Money Musk, Lady's Walpole Reel, Chorus Jig, or Durang's Hornpipe. Not as they were originally written. And when it comes to proper accent and expression, the way an old violinist taught us to play them long ago — well! I can still hear that old man, who had played in General Sherman's band in the Civil War and later led a famous orchestra, saying, "Now, in 'Devil's Dream' the first note in each of the first three measures must be accented, and in a rising crescendo, like this . . ."

The fact is, much of the best authentic square dance music is far from easy to play. I have seen first-class pro-

fessionals, even those of concert caliber, attempt it con-
fidently only to give up in despair. Something about the
rhythm and the repetition always throws them unless
they have grown up with the stuff.

As I look back over some forty years of playing for
square dances, sometimes professionally but mostly just
for fun, it is like thumbing through an album of carica-
tures. Square dance musicians are a strangely specialized
fraternity.

One fall day, out digging potatoes, I was visited by
old man Larkin, blacksmith and square dance impresario
from a nearby town. "Hear you've got a sax," he said.
"I'm shy one piece in the orchestry, and I wondered if
you'd help us out Saturday night?"

I explained that the saxophone had never been my
instrument; I had just inherited one from a friend, and
only tried it a few times. "Oh, that's all right," old
Larkin said. "Gertrude — she's the leader — she's
strictly a G-fiddler. You won't have no trouble."

A G-fiddler plays by ear, and only in the key of G.
Anything goes, so to speak, as long as you stick to that
key.

Larkin's hall was an ancient, sagging building behind
his house. But inside there was a pretty good floor, and
it was crowded. The platform for the band was big
enough, but we could hardly squeeze onto it. It was
piled high with rusty cookstoves, dismantled bedsteads,
stacks of sap buckets, old harnesses, a stuffed fox, and
hundreds of other discarded items. Overhead there was

an arch of brown and dusty dead branches, left from some long-forgotten Christmas party.

Old Larkin introduced me to the others — Gertrude, a tall rawboned woman; the pianist, also female, with four or five of her eleven children laid out asleep under the square piano; and the trap drummer, a fat man with one eye who also prompted. Larkin acted as floor manager in the old tradition.

"Shove your goddamn junk over, so this guy can set down," Gertrude said to the drummer, and, turning to me, "There's some fiddle music wrote out there on the piano, just in case we play somethin' you ain't heard before. 'Twon't be in the same key, but it may give you kind of an idea."

Gertrude took her job seriously, sawing away at a furious pace — at least twice as fast as I had ever heard dance music played before. It was good exercise trying to keep up, especially since she skipped all rests and never finished out the measure at the end of a strain.

The prompter was so enthusiastic about his drumming, flailing away at his various paraphernalia, that he would now and then forget to prompt. Gertrude would swear at him without slackening her speed, and remark at the end of the number, "The damn fool thinks he's one o' them jazz artists, whangin' on all them bells and things!"

Another unforgettable fiddler played for us briefly one winter when my wife and I were running dances. He was a tall, cadaverous-looking character whose nose almost met his chin. Our regular fiddler was sick or something, and the piano player had agreed to bring a substitute.

When the piano player arrived his old sedan was jammed with his fat wife and children, but there was no sign of the fiddler. Then it turned out he was locked inside the trunk, all curled up with his fiddle case and a great snarl of wiring. It was below zero and he didn't even have an overcoat.

We got him untangled and thawed him out, and he finally got himself all wired up and plugged in — he played an electrified fiddle. It made so much noise the rest of us could not be heard at all. This was just as well, because we never could tell what tunes he was trying to play anyway. Except for shifts from two-four to six-eight time, they all sounded exactly alike.

Well, it has all been great fun. And I would still rather sit in with a square dance band than with a chamber music ensemble. Playing "Finnegan's Wake" or "Pig-town Fling," even with a G-fiddler, satisfies me more than a Bach fugue in C minor. But if I ever have to play "Red River Valley" again I'm going to walk right out of the hall.

25

The Fireplace

DECEMBER is the fireplace month up here, with the un-accustomed cold, the evenings beginning around three in the afternoon, and all the holiday visitors and parties. When we talk about putting logs on the fire, we mean logs — five feet long. On cold nights we load up the fireplace with an oak or rock maple forelog so heavy it takes two of us to lug it inside.

At this time of year a six- or eight-cord pile of fire-place wood outside the back door looks like a small mountain. But even though after New Year's we only have an open fire occasionally, spending most evenings instead sitting in front of an open TV, along in March that big woodpile will have vanished.

And incidentally, fires are never banked in a house like ours. At least never on cold nights. When the fire gets low too much heat from the furnace gets sucked up that huge chimney. The trick is to pile on more wood and hope it will last until morning.

It is puzzling to us why fireplaces in modern houses,

even up here in this country of unlimited firewood, are built smaller and smaller. In a fine new house down the road the fireplace is just a little square hole in the wall with one of these mesh-screen curtains dangling across it. I would as soon sit in front of a couple of lighted candles.

Perhaps the less said about the first part of December, the better. For us it is a time of great sadness. The two months of happy bird-shooting have suddenly, abruptly ended. Even the dogs seem sort of let down and quiet.

In November it felt cold at fifteen or twenty above, but now the mercury drops down some nights to below zero. ("Five scratches below the hole," as Old Joe used to say.) Then we get a blizzard or two. All that quiet writing time we were looking forward to is spent winterizing the dog kennels, finishing putting up the storm windows, and doing all the things we meant to do in September.

Some morning about this time we will wake up to hear the house creaking and shaking like an old square-rigger. The driveway will be buried in grotesque ridges and peaks of powder snow, and the oil burner will be strangely quiet. The water will not run in the bathroom. Probably the telephone will not work either. Winter, glorious winter, has come to us here on our glorious mountaintop.

When we first moved up here we were intending to put in a wood-burning furnace. But it did not work out, because we wanted to rent the place occasionally and take a few trips. Wood demands somebody on hand at all times who knows how to stoke a fire. The wizards of modern technology are more interested in solid-fuel rockets for getting to the moon, or blowing everybody up, than in some efficient use of our most abundant natural combustible.

There was one old chap in a nearby town who claimed to have invented a more or less automatic wood-burning furnace. He built a great pit under his house and lowered whole tree trunks into it. The thing was controlled with various thermostats and drafts and blowers, and was supposed to run for a week before the logs had burned their way down to the bottom. Apparently there were certain problems, such as operating the derrick that was needed to hoist the logs into place. Anyway the idea never seemed to catch on.

New Hampshire is now almost entirely an oil-burning state. Even the poorest tar-paper shanties have a row of oil barrels outside instead of a woodpile. The oil stoves get overheated or blow up quite often, and every day in winter the local papers carry news of the results. "The two-room residence on Mink Hollow Road was totally destroyed. Mr. and Mrs. LaBounty and their thirteen children are residing temporarily in the homes of neighbors and friends."

The only market left for wood around here is the summer cottagers who burn it in their fireplaces in July and August.

My mother's wood-burning cookstove in the farm

kitchen must be one of the last in town. She still has her woodbox filled every morning with a carefully selected variety of split wood. White birch for quick heat, white maple for a little more lasting fire, rock maple and some red oak and ash for baking, and so on. "Mabel, bring in a couple of oak chunks — not too big, now — and a little of that fine-split birch. I'm going to make dough-nuts."

Our system up here on the hill is to keep two or three wood stoves going in very cold weather, in addition to the oil furnace. This keeps our oil bills from exceeding our total yearly income. But when we are both out shooting or off on a shopping trip, the oil burner keeps the place warm by itself.

I am forever amazed at the constant improvements wrought by the designers of household appliances. Stoves that look like refrigerators, refrigerators that look like washing machines, washing machines that look like tele-vision sets. We bought our furnace through a heating engineer who assured us it was the safest and most ad-vanced make in the country. Our road was pretty bad and it was hard to get hold of a plumber, so I put it together myself.

At first I thought I must have got the thing bottom side up. The smoke pipe came out at the base, with the burner mechanism on top. Finally I realized this clever arrangement was intentional. Any slight leak in any one of a hundred joints and couplings results in oil dripping down onto the hot stack. This at once warns the householder of the trouble, either by the fumes and soot that fill the house, or by burning the place down.

There is no doubt that oil burners have revolutionized life in such remote homes as ours. For weeks on end we live quite as comfortably as our city friends. And we never have to call a service man, with attendant delay and expense. For when our furnace quits it is always on the coldest winter night, with six-foot snowdrifts blocking the road. I have to fix it myself or freeze to death.

There may be some who would say we ought to have the furnace overhauled every summer. But they do not understand our way of life at all. We are much too busy in summer. Even if we were not, it would seem pretty silly to be spending time and money in a dark, clammy cellar when we could be off on a fishing trip. And anyway, the kind of person who worries in August about what is going to happen next January would never choose to live in a place like this to begin with.

December is a time when we ourselves often talk about what kind of people would want to live in a place like this year-round. And we wonder if we're not slightly nuts. Looking back on winter is wonderful, and the more rugged the winter has been the nicer it is to look back on.* But looking ahead is something else again.

* Our first year up here, the snow did not melt off until mid-May. The first hot weather hit us so hard we lay around for days sunning ourselves, in a sort of torpor, shedding the whole outer layer of our skins. Fortunately we had read a book about the Central Arctic Eskimos, so we knew this was perfectly natural.

When I was growing up on the farm it was pretty isolated, but it was not as wild as this mountaintop. And I always have a secret feeling, those first winter days when it looks as though the sun had gone behind the mountain for the final time, that maybe this winter will be the last. Maybe this time the place will catch fire some blizzardy night and that will be the end. Maybe the roof will blow off. Maybe we'll both get pneumonia or something and the phone wires will be down.

Janet, who grew up in Philadelphia and New York, has no such qualms. She dances for joy at the first sight of snowflakes wafting in out of the east. And when the snow is deep enough she roams the woods on skis or snowshoes, with the dogs, and often stays out so long after dark I am sure she must be lost, or down with a broken leg somewhere.

Looking back, the Dark Period in my life was a stretch of years, in my teens, when winters were almost solely taken up with working in the woods. This meant chopping some forty cords of wood and hauling it from somewhere back on the mountain, and then cutting logs and sledding them to Uncle Wilmer's water-power sawmill. Until the advent of skiing gave us a pleasanter occupation, December always meant the start of this drudgery, with constantly cold feet and miserable wet mittens, that looked endless to me.

Around that time Robert Frost's poetry began to be popular. There was a thing about chopping wood that made me so mad I have never quite appreciated Frost even to this day.

One good thing about this time of year was the skating on Tolman Pond. Though there are larger lakes all around, skaters have always gathered here because the water is protected by hills on all sides and freezes evenly with no spring holes or wind ripples. No surface ever equals the first natural window-glass ice of December.

But I should not talk about this only in the past tense. Our skating parties at the pond are active as ever. The pretty LaSourd girls swoop and spin, short skirts swirling gracefully, sure of themselves as a couple of Ice Follies stars. And the younger fry still play hockey and fox-and-geese and tickly-benders.

Tickly-benders, like swinging bendy birches, is one of those indigenous sports. The skaters form a circle which at one point passes close to the open water at the mouth of a brook, where the ice is thin as cardboard. The first skater gets up as much speed as possible, so as to coast over the thin spot with feet apart and weight evenly distributed. One by one the others follow.

You can feel the ice bend quite considerably as you skim over it. Everybody keeps going round and round until the ice is so weakened somebody goes through. This game has somewhat more appeal if the water is not over a couple of feet deep.

All the second half of our December is busy with the holidays, one way or another. Christmas here is not just a matter of a day or two. Janet starts turning the whole house upside down and inside out well ahead of time. Kitty and Helen will sleep in the kitchen bedroom — lug down another cot from the attic. Dot and Marsh will have the upstairs guest room. Uncle Buzz and any other extra men can bunk in Renn's room. And there is always the couch in the living room, if you can stop Sandy, the golden retriever, from sleeping on top of you.

It is a time when, until the last relatives and guests leave after New Year's, the TV set in the corner will gather dust. (Janet will not like that figure of speech.) Long cocktail hours around the fireplace, evenings of games or just gossip. When all hands have arrived, the table that serves for a bar will look reassuringly like one of the shelves down at the State Store. For a while, at least, we can greet all comers with "What will you have?" and really mean it.

My mother was not too pleased at first when we decided to have our Christmas dinners up here instead of at the farm. But it did not take her long to get used to the idea, and even to take a wild holiday fling with a small glass of sherry. After all, at ninety-odd managing dinner for twenty-five people would be quite a chore.

I suppose it is wonderful for a city family to be able to buy a Christmas tree, but there is something about taking money for one that goes against the grain with me. We always have plenty of spruce that needs thinning, and there is a swamp full of young balsams for those who prefer them. Several friends from nearby towns always drive up to cut their trees here. To me this is one of the best things about Christmas.

Janet has her own way of facing the long winter ahead. She starts talking about a trip we might take. Later on in the winter, of course, when we get a few of the worst bills paid and some money "comes in." (Comes in from where?) How about quail-shooting in South Carolina? Or visiting Mollie in the Everglades and doing some real fishing? Or maybe we ought to do something really different this time, like taking one of those cruises on a freighter to the West Coast.

What would we do with all the dogs? Oh, we'll figure something out. We'll just keep working on the idea . . .

I admit it would be nice to see something of the outside world once in a while. But the only thing about winter up here that really bothers me is the wind. And I don't mean just a stiff breeze. When we get a spell of wind up here it keeps you awake at night, dishes fall off the shelves, and Sandy creeps upstairs and tries to gnaw his way into our bedroom.

All night long the antenna on the roof — if it hasn't blown off into the woods some place — whines and screams like a siren. Once we saw a heavy oak table we had left out on the porch sailing away toward Harrisville village, four miles to the south. We have seen a light plane from Keene get just about over our east pinnacle and then start flying backwards until it was out of sight. When it blows like that an oil burner in every room wouldn't keep the drafts out. The only thing to do is turn on the electric bedclothes and crawl under.

But when it has been blowing for about a week and then stops, some winter night, there is nothing quite so wonderful. You can walk out to the woodshed in your pajamas, at zero, and not even feel a chill. Nowhere in the world is it so still and quiet. You can hear a hoot owl all the way over in the White Swamp. I have waked up in the night and it has been so quiet I could hear the interest accumulating on last year's unpaid taxes.

Among all the strangers who land up here every summer — people who got the wrong road and did not dare try to turn around, people looking for a lakeshore lot, fishermen, and other pilgrims — there has never yet been one who didn't come out with something like, "Say, you don't try to live up here all winter, do you?"

Having seen our road, they conclude there would be the constant danger of getting "snowed in." A fate worse than death — spending a few days unable to reach a supermarket. (Or a liquor store.) I am always tempted to make some offhand reply, such as: Well, we did have kind of a rough spell last March, when the snowplow broke down; had to eat a couple of the dogs, but we managed to pull through.

The fact is, getting snowed in is just about the last thing we have ever worried about up here. When it has been snowing hard all day and looks as though it would keep on all night, and nobody knows when the town plow will get around to attempt our hill, we just throw another log on the fire and have a drink. One thing sure, nobody is going to bother us until the road is plowed. And if the bottle-cupboard is bare, a pot of tea looks pretty good.

A few miles away, down the main road, a retired couple built a new house with every modern convenience known to man. They keep enough food on hand, with a well stocked Deepfreeze, to live like kings even if they didn't go outdoors for a month. And they spend the entire winter shoveling snow.

Any day you drive past the place you will see them out shoveling paths. They dig them very neatly all the way to the ground, and then coat the ground with sand. Paths to the garage, paths to the road, paths to the mailbox, paths everywhere. The house has five or six outside doors and a network of paths leads to all of them.

It looks as though those people must have some frightful allergy to snow, and any direct contact with the stuff would finish them off. And whenever it starts to snow, you can hear the phone ringing before half an inch has fallen — they will be calling the road agent to see why the plow hasn't come past their place yet.

I have not had a snow shovel in my hand for years. We just let it pile up. The wind keeps the back door clear and the others stay banked, sometimes all the way to the roof. Nothing keeps a house so warm and easy to heat. It would seem silly to dig away any of that free insulation.

Even so, except just after a fresh storm, I can walk all the way out to the dog kennels at night in my carpet slippers. The dogs, let out for their daily exercise, soon pack paths through the drifts; and these freeze hard enough to make good walking.

I suppose it would be unfair to nature-lovers if we should bring December to a close without some notice of our birds and beasts. And observing nature up here is after all one of our most unfailing excuses for avoiding work. The other day Janet insisted I walk through the woods about half a mile just to see a red weasel she had spotted up in an oak tree. She wanted me to explain what this ordinarily ground-inhabiting animal was trying to prove by acting like a squirrel. I dutifully observed the weasel, but hadn't the faintest idea what he was doing up in that tree.

I suppose if I were a real nature writer I would have stayed out there all day, figuring out what that weasel was up to, or at least inventing a good yarn to make my readers think I had.

Anyway, I have the wrong kind of name. I have a superstition about names, and a quick glance at our shelf of nature writers brings it out. I picture Edwin Way Teale winning his way with the teal toward Mobile Bay. And Ernest Thompson Seton earnestly scaling a Grand Teton; and good gray John Burroughs burrowing away among his furrows. Marjorie Kinnan Rawlings — beasts

and bugs, creepings, crawlings. Dallas Lore Sharpe —
lore, sharp . . .

By the end of December, wildlife around the house
here has pretty well shaken down for the winter. All the
waterfowl down on the lake have long since taken off for
the Everglades, and all other migratory birds have left
us. Hibernating animals have holed up. Jack rabbits have
finished turning snow-white and moved up from the
swamp, and on moonlit nights they play around just
outside the kitchen windows.

Some people do not like jays, but we feed a flock of
them every winter. They cheer us up. When the worst
wind and cold and snow has driven everything else to
take cover somewhere, they always hang around, happy
and bold as ever.

My latest observation of note has proved, just for the
record, that a large red fox can run at a speed of exactly
forty-four miles per hour. I clocked one, in the jeep, all
the way down the hill to Brickyard Brook. The snow-
banks were not very high and he could have jumped off
the road anywhere, but he probably wanted to show
that he could outrun the jeep.

It is also a good place up here to watch airplanes. As
they often pass below us, we can see what their top sides
look like. But I suppose this cannot properly be called
observing nature.

In any case, it seems that jets from Westover or Ports-
mouth must like to do their practice flying over this
region, doubtless because it looks so uninhabited. And

they do not always judge their altitude too carefully; some of the lightning rods on our roof are bent over almost horizontally.

And that just about covers December. From now on, until the first clacker-frogs start tuning up in the hollow and the first blue water opens down on Spoonwood, we will take each day as it comes along.

Fill up the kettle, and throw another log on that fire!

HERESY

THE SPANISH INQUISITION

PUBLIC PERSECUTIONS

Gerry Boehme

Cavendish
Square

New York

Published in 2017 by Cavendish Square Publishing, LLC
243 5th Avenue, Suite 136, New York, NY 10016

Copyright © 2017 by Cavendish Square Publishing, LLC

First Edition

Library of Congress Cataloging-in-Publication Data

Names: Boehme, Gerry, author.
Title: Heresy : the Spanish Inquisition / Gerry Boehme.
Description: New York : Cavendish Square Publishing, 2017. | Series: Public persecutions | Includes bibliographical references and index.
Identifiers: LCCN 2016033897 (print) | LCCN 2016034828 (ebook) | ISBN 9781502623294 (library bound) | ISBN 9781502623300 (E-book)
Subjects: LCSH: Inquisition–Spain–Juvenile literature.
Classification: LCC BX1735 .B67 2017 (print) | LCC BX1735 (ebook) | DDC 272/.20946–dc23
LC record available at https://lccn.loc.gov/2016033897

Editorial Director: David McNamara
Editor: Fletcher Doyle
Copy Editor: Nathan Heidelberger
Associate Art Director: Amy Greenan
Designer: Jessica Nevins
Production Coordinator: Karol Szymczuk
Photo Research: J8 Media

Contents

EXURG✚ PSALM. 73. TUAM. CAUSAM. JUDICA

Persecution on a Grand Scale

At first mention, the names King Ferdinand and Queen Isabella usually bring to mind images of Christopher Columbus and his famous voyage. With their support, Columbus set out across the Atlantic in 1492, eventually planting the Spanish flag in the New World. His successful landing marked the beginning of a colonial period that witnessed the rise and fall of a Spanish empire as well as the eventual founding of the United States.

Famous for their link to Columbus, Ferdinand and Isabella are equally **infamous** for the role they played in setting another historical event in motion. This time, however, their actions sparked one of the cruelest, longest, and most damaging persecutions in human history.

People of different faiths, races, or cultures have been harassed and oppressed since humans first inhabited the earth. Never in history, however, has persecution been so integrated

The emblem of the Spanish Inquisition included the Christian cross, symbols of mercy (*left*) and justice (*right*), and the motto "Arise, O Lord, and judge Thy cause."

into the fabric of daily life, organized so methodically, or lasted as many years as during the Spanish **Inquisition**.

While the British comedy group Monty Python famously poked fun at the Spanish Inquisition, in reality, few events in history inspire as much fear and dread. Simply uttering the phrase instantly conjures up images of terror, violence, and torture. Countless books, plays, and works of art relate harrowing tales of suspicion, fear, and deceit. Written accounts of that period, passed down through the centuries, portray a time of state and religious institutions running amok, their motives and actions driven by lies, deceptions, and systematic abuses of power.

Facts and Mysteries

Through the years, experts have been able provide a wealth of information to help describe the events of the Spanish Inquisition. We know that it began under the reign of King Ferdinand and Queen Isabella in 1478, and that it finally ended more than 350 years later, in 1834. We know that its stated purpose was to root out heresy—thoughts, words, and actions that disagreed with the Catholic faith. We know that it was not the first or the only inquisition; it followed other inquisitions that occurred across Europe well before the first proceedings began in Spain.

We also know that the Spanish Inquisition was conducted by the two most powerful institutions in Spain at the time, the royal crown and the Roman Catholic Church. We know that it was ingrained into every aspect of daily life and that it single-handedly repressed and expelled two great religions

Inquisitions often took the appearance of grand spectacles, including large crowds and ceremonies. This engraving represents a procession that took place during an inquisition in the city of Goa.

and cultures—Judaism and Islam—from lands they had both claimed as home for centuries.

However, there are still many things we do *not* know about the Spanish Inquisition. Despite centuries of study, historians still disagree on how many people suffered, how many **heretics** were burned at the stake, and whether the Inquisition **tribunals** were as savage as some say. Although the Vatican finally opened up its secret records in 1998, the Spanish Inquisition still presents a complicated and confusing picture.

Perhaps sorting through the confusion to understand the Inquisition's causes and effects can help us solve the issues that continue to drive persecution in our world today.

The Melting Pot of Iberia

Human history can be complicated. Great accomplishments and seismic events rarely happen for simple reasons. Watershed historical moments usually owe their existence to a complex web of circumstances, some sudden, some long developing, all of which come together at a certain point in time. Sometimes these circumstances cause a temporary change in attitudes or behavior that, in retrospect, contributes little to the overall path of history. Other events, however, interconnect in such a way as to cause a fundamental shift in human thought, leading to a new era and changing people's lives in an extraordinary way.

Historical Impact

The Spanish Inquisition stands out as one such event. Few if any other periods existed for so long, affected so many people, caused so much anguish and suffering, and influenced

The Grand Mosque of Cordoba, started in 784 and converted into a Roman Catholic cathedral in 1236, is still beautifully detailed.

the path of human history in such a significant way. Tactics first used by the Spanish Inquisition still provide a guide to follow for most modern-day persecutions, including the Holocaust, the internment of Japanese Americans during World War II, the Protestant-Catholic "troubles" of Northern Ireland, and today's struggles in the Middle East.

Just as important, the ghost of the Spanish Inquisition still haunts the world today, continuing to play a role in defining relationships among nations and religions. Learning about the Inquisition helps us to understand, at least in part, humanity's inability to free itself from the terrors of its past and move toward a future where all beliefs and cultures are equally accepted.

The history of the Spanish Inquisition contains its own tragedies, without a doubt, and it remains an ugly part of Europe's past. Its scale is truly mind-boggling. The Inquisition lasted more than 350 years. It drove entire ethnic groups and cultures from their homes and the only lives they ever knew. It forced Jews and Muslims to convert to Christianity or face expulsion or death. Families and friends turned on each other. People lived under constant surveillance, suspicion, and threat. Hundreds of thousands of people were arrested, interrogated, tortured, driven to poverty, punished, and sometimes even put to death by barbarous means.

However, some long-accepted "facts" about the actions and motivations of the Spanish Inquisition have recently been proven to be exaggerated, even false. Some people who disagreed with the Inquisition and its methods—as well as those who opposed the Catholic Church in general, or resisted

Spain as a European power—helped to spread misleading **propaganda** during and after the Inquisition for their own purposes. What we are left with is a complex, tortured time in history that is difficult to grasp without separating fact from fiction and truth from assumption.

As a start, it is important to go back nearly one thousand years before the Spanish Inquisition began. The conditions that helped create the Spanish Inquisition grew from a fertile mix of geography, religion, ethnic heritage, politics, and economics.

Heresy and Religion

It all started with Christianity's attempt to enforce the dominance of the Christian faith by rooting out those who questioned Christian beliefs or resisted the control of the Catholic Church. These people were "heretics" who, in the eyes of the Christian authorities, represented a grave danger to faith and order.

Over the years, the word "heresy" has taken on a life of its own. According to Merriam-Webster, "heresy" can mean an opinion or practice that is not true or does not agree with generally accepted or official beliefs. Heresy is most commonly associated with ideas and actions against a particular dominant religion.

Heresy has existed in every age. Obviously, the yardstick for determining what is heretical depends entirely on the judge's viewpoint and what the accepted or official position is at the time. Any group or individual who disagrees with another, more dominant group can be accused of heresy.

In Europe of the Middle Ages, Christianity dominated the lives of the people. It weaved itself into the fabric of daily life, politics, and economics. At that time, any belief or practice that went against the official position of the Catholic Church was considered heretical.

Inquisitions Existed Before

As the power of the Catholic Church increased in Europe, the Church began to view others who did not accept its beliefs or practices as a threat to its position of dominance. People of other faiths and cultures, including Jews, Muslims, and even other Christians, became targets to identify, attack, and destroy. In cooperation with the Christian European rulers of that time, the Catholic Church began a series of investigations—inquisitions—to root out and destroy those who practiced heresy. The goal was to stamp out the idea that anyone could oppose the official positions and actions of the Catholic Church and, by extension, the state.

For many centuries, the Catholic Church, in one form or another, conducted a series of inquisitions to stamp out any beliefs and practices it considered contrary to the true faith. Some were more extensive and cruel in their methods than others, but all helped establish a climate of fear and suspicion among the people living in Europe at the time. In many cases, these inquisitions were conducted by the Catholic Church with the full cooperation of the rulers of the kingdom. Other efforts took on a life of their own, as kings and queens used the power of the inquisition to exert their own control over their people and even the Catholic Church itself.

Of all the inquisitions, none has inspired more fear, more dread, and more misinformation than the one that began in Spain in the late 1400s. But how did it come about? What conditions had to exist to motivate the Catholic Church to persecute not only others, but its own converts? What motives could drive kings and queens to force their subjects to endure cruel trials, painful torture, and cruel punishments, including being burned alive at the stake? What forces could pit neighbor against neighbor, friend against friend, husband against wife, and sister against brother to accuse people of heresy and subject them to the cruel process of the Inquisition tribunal?

Spain Is Unique

The unique history and circumstances of Spain helped set the conditions that made the Spanish Inquisition possible.

In some ways, Spain was very much like its European neighbors—ruled by kings, mostly rural, and controlled by religion, particularly Christianity. But in other ways, Spain was very different than other European countries, especially due to its isolation and the influence of the Muslims and Jews who lived there. The importance of religion as an integral part of daily life, and the desire of Christian rulers to control the entire area of Spain, bred the conditions that led to the imposition of the Inquisition.

The Iberian Peninsula

Geography played a huge role in determining Spain's fate. The history of Spain, including all aspects of its development, has been influenced by its location on the Iberian Peninsula.

The Iberian Peninsula juts out from the southwestern tip of the continent of Europe. At its southern-most point, the

The Iberian Peninsula lies just off the North African coast and is separated from the rest of Europe by the Pyrenees mountain range. During the 1300s Iberia included Spanish Christian kingdoms as well as Portugal and the Muslim kingdom of Granada.

peninsula lies only 9 miles (14 kilometers) across the sea from the continent of Africa. The Pyrenees mountain range forms an effective land barrier in the northeast, separating the Iberian Peninsula from the rest of Europe. This was particularly effective in medieval times, making it difficult for invading armies and different cultures and ideas to cross the mountains to influence Spanish life and thought.

Spain and Portugal occupy most of the territory in today's Iberia. The peninsula also includes the tiny principality of Andorra, which is located in the high mountains of the Pyrenees between France and Spain, as well as the British territory of Gibraltar. Over the centuries, however, many different entities fought for control over the territory. The resulting clash of cultures, and their desires to dominate each other, set the tone for Spain's future.

Romans Arrive and Christianity Reigns

The country that we now call Spain was once part of the Roman Empire, a province known as Hispania.

Before the Romans arrived and for centuries before the birth of Jesus, African Iberians and Celts from northern Europe had been settling in Spain. For many years, two major empires of the western Mediterranean, the Romans and the Carthaginians, battled for control over the area. Eventually, the Romans conquered the eastern part of the peninsula, followed by the remainder of Iberia. Spain thrived under Roman rule as a prosperous part of the empire.

The Romans worshipped multiple gods, both before the birth of Jesus and for hundreds of years afterward. As Christians spread their teachings after Christ's death, the Romans considered this new religion to be a threat to the authority of the empire and to Rome itself. Christians at that time were, at best, discriminated against; at worst, they were actively persecuted. Regardless of how they were treated, the number of Christians continued to grow, and they spread their faith across the empire.

A major turning point in Christian history occurred when the Roman Emperor Constantine converted to Christianity. In 313, Constantine issued the **Edict** of Milan, which commanded official toleration of Christianity and other religions. While some historians believe that Constantine was sincere in his newfound Christian beliefs, others think that he adopted the faith to gain political power over his rivals and to take advantage of the growing number of Christians in the empire. No matter what the reason, his actions resulted in the end of the persecution of Christians and the beginning of Christendom.

While he advanced acceptance of Christians in the Roman Empire, Constantine did not make Christianity the official religion. That did not happen until the year 380, when Emperor Theodosius I became the first Roman emperor to decree that all citizens should be Christian.

At that time, there were many versions of Christianity, with a major point of disagreement being the nature of the relationship between God and Jesus. In 325, Emperor

Constantine had helped establish the Council of Nicaea, which established that Jesus (the Son) was equally divine to God (the Father) and condemned the teachings of other Christian sects. Theodosius decreed that only Christianity as defined by the Council of Nicaea was the true faith, and he persecuted all others.

Theodosius allowed most pagans to worship in peace. But he forcibly removed "heretic" bishops who followed other beliefs from Christian churches throughout the Eastern Empire (ruled from Constantinople). His enforcement of a "one, true" Christian faith set the groundwork for later persecutions that would be conducted by the Christian Church for more than one thousand years afterward.

Roman Empire Falls

Diocletian divided the Roman Empire for administrative purposes in 285, but the empire was still united. Theodosius was the last ruler to preside over a united Roman Empire. After his death, the empire split into western and eastern halves, with the eastern half being much stronger. The weaker Western Roman Empire included much of Italy, Spain, Gaul, Britain, and North Africa.

For centuries, great plagues and sicknesses killed many of Europe's inhabitants, wrecking the economy and making residents hesitant about traveling to other places where they might catch a sickness from strangers. Barbarian invasions made things worse, disrupting trade across the empire.

Christian Visigoths

After the fall of the Roman Empire, Hispania fell under the control of barbarian tribes known as the Visigoths, Germanic peoples who crossed over the Pyrenees and occupied Iberia. The Visigoths practiced a form of Christianity called Arian Christianity, which believed that Jesus was more than human but not quite divine. By the end of the sixth century, however, the Gothic rulers of Spain had converted from Arian Christianity to Catholicism and built a powerful Christian kingdom with its capital in the city of Toledo.

The Dark Age

While more than forty-six million people live in Spain today, only four million or five million people lived in the area during the later years of the Roman Empire.

The fall of the Roman Empire had a strong effect on Europe. While people living there were freed of Rome's oppression, they now suffered attacks from bands of conquerors and bandits. Perhaps more importantly, Rome had brought a sense of unification and organization to the European continent. When the empire fell, no single state or government united the people who lived there for the first time in hundreds of years.

Historians once commonly referred to this period of European history as the Dark Ages, due mainly to the belief that disunity, barbarian invasions, and constant warfare hurt the development of culture, arts, and sciences. Modern historians use the term "dark" simply to describe a time that we do not know very much about, since there is a lack of reliable information or written records that describe the period.

The Rise of the Christian Church

What is known about that period is that life could be hard. With no Roman Empire to dominate the government and culture, and with people increasingly turning to religion to fill the void and offer hope in their lives, the Catholic Church became the most powerful institution of the medieval period. Kings, queens, and other leaders derived much of their power from their alliances with, and their protection of, the Catholic Church. Ordinary people across Europe had to "tithe" 10 percent of their earnings each year to the Catholic Church, which, at the same time, was mostly exempt from taxation. These policies helped the Church to assemble a great deal of money and power.

Islam and the Crusades

As Christianity rose to a position of dominance in Europe, a very different situation existed in the Middle East, which contained the sacred Holy Lands.

The Holy Lands of the Middle East have been a source of conflict for thousands of years. Judaism, Christianity, and Islam all trace their roots back to this one place in the world, especially the city of Jerusalem. Jews consider the area to be their sacred homeland and the site of their most revered

For hundreds of years Christians and Muslims battled for control of the Holy Land during a series of wars known as the Crusades.

temple. Christians hold it to be the site where their savior, Jesus, preached and was crucified. Muslims believe that the area marks the spot where the prophet Muhammad ascended into heaven.

At the height of their empire, the Romans occupied the Middle East as they did much of the known world (this did not extend into eastern Asia). When the Roman occupation of the Middle East ended, Christians rose to become the dominant political and religious force. While there was always tension between Christians and Jews who lived there, a powerful new force was unleashed in the early 600s, when the prophet Muhammad introduced a new religion: Islam.

Inspiring strong passion among its followers, Islam grew quickly in both numbers and influence. After the prophet Muhammad's death in 632, Muslim armies conquered large parts of the Middle East, uniting them under the rule of a single **caliph**. At its height, the medieval Islamic world was more than three times bigger than all of Christendom. In the seventh century, Muslims seized control of the Holy City of Jerusalem and the surrounding area.

Losing control of the Holy Lands was unacceptable to the Christian kingdoms to the north. Over the next several hundred years, Christians from western Europe and the Byzantine Empire conducted a series of savage wars, known as "Crusades," to take back control of the region from the Muslims.

The first of the Crusades began in 1095, when armies of Christians from western Europe responded to Pope Urban II's plea to go to war against Muslim forces in the Holy Land. Though these wars were intended to return the Christian religion to dominance in these sacred lands, in reality they also were designed to regain political and economic control in these valuable territories.

Historians generally agree that the Crusades ended in 1291, when the Christians lost their last major stronghold in the Middle East. Though the Catholic Church continued its attempts to regain control of the Holy Land after that, support declined in western Europe as the people tired of the seemingly endless war, its costs, and the suffering it caused. The **Protestant Reformation** of the sixteenth century helped to end the Crusades once and for all as different Christian sects split from the Catholic Church, reducing the power of the pope.

The Crusades serve as a stark example of hundreds of years of conflict and tension among Christianity, Judaism, and Islam. The struggle was rooted as much in the desire for wealth and power as in the goal of enforcing religious beliefs. On the surface, the Crusades looked like a war between Christian Europe and the Muslim Middle East, with Judaism caught in the middle. In reality, however, the emotions and bias that drove the Crusades also greatly affected the relationships among Christians, Jews, and Muslims who lived in Europe.

In no place were those tensions so severe, the actions so divisive, or the effects so damaging, as in the lands of medieval Spain.

The Moor Conquest

Less than 10 miles (16 km) of ocean separate Spain from the Muslim country of Morocco in North Africa. In the year 711, a Muslim general named Tariq ibn Ziyad crossed the narrow passage, landing at the famous landmark that still bears his name—the Rock of Gibraltar (Jabal Tariq, or "Tariq's Mountain")—with about seven thousand warriors.

After defeating a much larger Visigoth army that had been sent to repel the invaders, Tariq went on to capture the capital city of Toledo. Within three years, most of today's Spanish peninsula had fallen under Muslim rule, and most Christians had been driven from the area.

The Muslims called their newly conquered territory al-Andalus, the "land of the vandals." Iberian Christians referred to their Muslim conquerors as *moros*, or **Moors**, based on the Latin name that the Romans had given to the peoples of North Africa (*mauri*, or *maurusci*). After the Muslims unsuccessfully tried to extend their territory beyond Spain, they settled into al-Andalus for the next few centuries. Over time, these Andalusians were able to develop their own culture. The Pyrenees separated them from the Christian kingdoms to the east, and the ocean, small as the barrier was, helped insulate Spain from more Muslim intervention.

When the Muslims arrived in Spain, the people already living there included Christians as well as Jews. There is evidence that Jews from the Near East had arrived in Spain by the second or third century CE, though some believe Jews had already been present in Spain for several centuries by then. Either way, Jews had lived and worshipped in Spain for hundreds of years before the Visigoths took control, and Spain hosted the largest Jewish community in the world in the thirteenth century.

After they conquered Spain, the Muslim rulers usually allowed the inhabitants to keep their possessions and their

Tariq ibn Ziyad, Muslim Conqueror of Spain

Muslim general Tariq ibn Ziyad served under North African governor Musa ibn Nusayr, who had conquered Morocco. When Spanish noblemen revolted against Roderic, the Visigoth king of Spain, they asked the Muslims based across the strait for help. The Muslims decided to take advantage of Spain's weakness and take it for themselves.

Tariq ibn Ziyad (also spelled Tarik ibn Zeyad) landed with seven thousand soldiers near present-day Gibraltar in May 711. According to legend, Tariq ibn Ziyad burned his ships, telling his soldiers to either conquer Spain or die with honor. After receiving five thousand more soldiers as reinforcements, Tariq advanced on the Spanish mainland, gaining valuable support from Spanish Jews, who had been persecuted by the Visigoths, and from Christians who opposed King Roderic.

The Visigoth king gathered what he thought

Tariq ibn Ziyad conquered the Iberian Peninsula.

was an overwhelming force, an army of one hundred thousand soldiers. He was so sure of victory that, it was said, he brought ropes to bind the captured Muslim soldiers and mules to haul the bounty. The two armies met in July 711. Even though they were badly outnumbered, the Muslims decisively defeated King Roderic's forces. Together with Musa, Tariq ibn Ziyad occupied more than two-thirds of the Iberian Peninsula over the next few years.

In 714, both Tariq and Musa were summoned home by their ruler, the caliph, where they were both accused of stealing funds and died in obscurity.

Tariq ibn Ziyad's invasion triggered a strong Muslim presence in Spain and played a major role in creating the conditions that eventually fueled the Spanish Inquisition.

religion in return for paying taxes and other forms of tribute to their new masters. In some ways, Jews living in the area benefited from the arrival of the Muslims. The Muslims often treated Jews better than Christians and sometimes left them in charge of towns as the Muslim armies moved to take over more territory. The Muslims felt less threatened by Jews than by Christians, since they were far fewer in number and were not as likely to revolt against their new rulers. The Muslims also felt that the Jews might be effective allies against the Christians, who had been prejudiced against them for so long.

The Golden Age of Cooperation

When the Muslims from North Africa conquered most of the Iberian Peninsula, they joined the Christians and Jews who already lived there. The result was a rich mix of culture and religion that, until then, had not been seen to such an extent. Three great religions of the world—all worshipping one God—collided.

Muslims, Jews, and Christians alike were confronted with vastly different ways of life and thinking. As each encountered the beliefs and customs of others who lived in their midst, they were led to reconsider many things that they had previously accepted based strictly on their faith. They were forced to think about whether their beliefs and practices were indeed the correct or only ones. They questioned their own assumptions.

Early Persecution

Past historians believed that Jews mostly lived freely and comfortably in Spain during this time. However, recent studies show that Jews in that period often experienced anti-Semitism and persecution. While Jews did manage to hold some political power in the Muslim government, Jews overall were considered to be legally inferior, and there were even some periodic outbursts of violence. Compared to their treatment in other parts of the world, however, Jews in Muslim Spain were generally better off.

Even before the Visigoths arrived, the Christian Roman Empire did not like the fact that Jews lived among Christians in Spain, and religious authorities tried to prevent mingling of the faiths by forbidding Christians from living in houses where Jews were present or even from eating with Jews.

The Visigoths treated Jews badly when they took over, forbidding Jews from marrying Christians and outlawing observance of Jewish holy days. They eventually forced the Jews to convert to Christianity or face exile or slavery.

One thing that served Jews well was that their devotion to studying the Torah led them to stress education and knowledge. The ability to read and write helped Jews to learn the culture and language of both Christians and Muslims. Since Jews constituted a small minority of the population, Muslim and Christian leaders did not feel threatened by their presence. Jews could sometimes work between the two larger groups and help promote communication and sharing.

Jews living in Christian Spain were often persecuted, attacked, or even killed in pogroms because of their different faith, practices, and culture.

For many years, Spain's monarchs had protected Jews, motivated more often than not by the generous tax revenue from the Jewish community and their importance in government and financial positions. However, that did not stop Christians from periodically rising against the Jewish population. When the Black Plague appeared in Europe in 1348, for example, it wiped out one-third of the total population within three years. When it ended as suddenly as it began, terrified Europeans looked for explanations; some blamed Jews for spreading a disease that they could not understand.

One of the worst **pogroms** in Spain took place in 1391, when mobs stormed a Jewish neighborhood in Seville and murdered thousands. Anti-Jewish riots soon spread to other cities, including Madrid and Córdoba.

Violence such as this led to the eventual decline of the Jewish population in Spain. Over the next century, many were murdered, while others left Spain. Some, however, decided to convert to Christianity, at least outwardly. These new converts were called "**Conversos**," or those who had converted. They were also called "New Christians." Jews who converted were then able to run businesses and take jobs that were previously forbidden to them.

Some Christians resented these new converts and the positions that they were able to assume. They claimed that Conversos still lived in Jewish neighborhoods and socialized mainly among themselves. They also felt that Conversos still practiced Judaism in secret, and that their improved status had come at the expense of "pure-blooded" or **Old Christians**. This started a new cycle of resentment.

Moor Weakness and Christian Reconquest

During the time that the Moors controlled the Iberian Peninsula, Christian rulers continued to hold on to a narrow strip of territory to the north. However, Christian kingdoms of this time continued to fight among themselves, even as they were dominated by the Moors, who controlled most of the territory.

Political infighting among the Moors led to a split of al-Andalus into many small kingdoms by the 1030s. The weakened state of al-Andalus allowed the Christians from the north to try to take back the land they had lost to the Muslims many centuries before.

The Christian advances were halted for a time as more Muslims came to Spain from North Africa and propped up the weakened Muslim kingdoms. Some of these new Muslims were more fanatical about their religion and less accepting of other faiths, leading to more resistance from the Jews and even more so from Christians that lived in the area and looked to merge with the Christian north. By the year 1265, Spanish Christians had managed to recapture much of the peninsula and reduce the former Islamic empire to the province of Granada, as well as some ports around Cádiz.

Despite the constant struggle between the Christian and Muslim forces, the next 150 years would turn out to be a time of relative calm. Christians made up about half of the population in Iberia, with the rest consisting of Jews and Moors.

The Christian Kingdoms

As the strength of Christianity grew, most of Christian Spain's six million people wound up owing allegiance to one of two kingdoms. The crown of Castile held about two-thirds of the Christian territory on the Iberian Peninsula and claimed about three-quarters of the Christian population. The crown of Aragon controlled the area east of Castile.

At that time, violent persecution led many Jews to convert to Christianity to maintain their own safety and their productive lives in Spain. By converting, Jews could not only escape eventual persecution but also be considered for the many offices and posts that were now being prohibited to Jews through new, more severe regulations. Many Conversos attained important positions in fifteenth-century Spain, including physicians, writers, and bankers. Two Converso bankers actually financed the first voyage of Christopher Columbus. Some Conversos even became nobles.

The Power of Religion in Medieval Times

In order to fully understand the strong feelings that motivated Christians to persecute Jews in Spain, or to grasp how jealousy, mistrust and misunderstanding influenced all relationships among Christians, Jews, and Muslims living in Iberia during the medieval period, one first has to understand the powerful role that religion played in the daily life of anyone living at that time.

During the Middle Ages, almost everyone in Spain, as well as most people who lived in Europe, were illiterate. People in general knew very little about the world. They hardly ever traveled very far outside their hometown. There was no way to learn about anything other than what their parents could tell them, which was very little. Mysterious diseases like the plague and terrible hardships like widespread famine occurred with little warning or explanation. Peasants lived in fear of local lords who controlled the land.

With no unified government to protect them, no real education to help them understand the world, and no way to be exposed to new ideas, people turned to religion to help them find value and hope in their lives.

For people of that time, religion was not just something you observed on a special day each week, a way that you worshipped a supreme being, or a framework to be used for moral guidance. Religion was life itself, embedded and intertwined with what you thought, where you lived and worked, and how you socialized with others. It filled the role of science and philosophy. It defined existence itself and became synonymous with whatever truth could be found in the world. Not only did it dominate a person's life; religion mapped out your path to salvation after death.

Any person who disagreed with the accepted religion or, even worse, proposed that it wasn't the one and only way to view the world, was accused of being a heretic, and his or her views were condemned as heresy, an attack on universal truth. Heresy had to be wiped out at all costs, and

During the Middle Ages, widespread plagues and diseases terrorized the population, leading to fear and mistrust of outsiders.

the heretic had to be either converted to the one, real faith, or struck down.

As leaders of the Catholic Church and rulers of kingdoms looked for ways to unite the people and turn them against their enemies, they seized on heresy as an opportunity to consolidate their own power and influence. The Catholic Church turned to a process called inquisitions to ensure that Christianity remained pure and that its influence remained unchallenged. Inquisitions became a common method to attack heresy and to ensure control of the common population.

Isabella and Ferdinand

In the early fifteenth century, two brothers and their descendants controlled the thrones of Castile and Aragon. A daughter named Isabella was born to the ruler of Castile in 1451. One year later, the ruler of Aragon welcomed a son, Ferdinand. In 1469, second cousins Ferdinand and Isabella married, thus uniting the two most powerful Christian kingdoms of Spain. Twenty-five years later, Queen Isabella and King Ferdinand would be proclaimed "Catholic Monarchs" by Pope Alexander VI. Together, they would complete the reconquest of Spain, explore the New World, and enforce the Catholic faith across the Spanish Empire.

The most powerful of all the inquisitions, the infamous Spanish Inquisition, began under the rule of King Ferdinand and Queen Isabella.

Isabella, Ferdinand, and the Seeds of the Inquisition

When Isabella of Castile and Ferdinand of Aragon married in 1469, their union triggered a chain of events that would lead to the eventual unification of Spain under one ruling power and one Christian faith.

At the time of their marriage, Isabella was next in line for the throne of Castile, held then by her brother. Ferdinand was heir to the Aragon throne. Isabella became Queen of Castile in 1474, while Ferdinand assumed his throne in 1479.

When Isabella and Ferdinand first united their two kingdoms and dreamed of asserting control over the entire peninsula, they faced many challenges. The land was filled with diverse cultures that had developed and thrived over many hundreds of years. Christians intermingled with Jews and Muslims, especially in the southern areas, including

Queen Isabella and King Ferdinand united Spain under one Christian kingdom and began the Spanish Inquisition to help solidify their authority.

Granada, that were still under Muslim control. Wealth and class also divided the Spaniards, with lords and nobles mixing with middle-class business owners, craftsmen, and peasant farmers.

Both Ferdinand and Isabella were devout Christians, and they believed that their faith could serve as the one common factor to bring everyone in the kingdom together. While armies and money helped Isabella and Ferdinand win control of their kingdom, the king and queen also harnessed the power of the Catholic Church to dominate the hearts and minds of their subjects and command unquestioned loyalty to the crown.

The Influence of the Church

Isabella and Ferdinand managed to combine the power of politics and religion, but the stage was set many years beforehand. As we have already seen, the Roman Catholic faith pervaded every aspect of social life. Christian Spaniards identified their country as one chosen by God, the kingdom with the most solid and pure Catholic religion. Christian victories over the Muslim territories reinforced their view of Spain being blessed by divine support.

The Catholic Church controlled great wealth, owned vast tracts of land, and wielded immense political power. It also held a unique position in that it was in some ways directly connected to the state, while in other ways totally independent. The crown nominated for Church approval most important religious officials, like archbishops and bishops, and members of the royal family often filled such positions. (This was termed the right of patronage.) However, the Catholic Church governed itself and was exempt from civil laws.

Despite the Catholic Church's influence, Spain remained a land of mixed heritages, cultures, and religions. Threatened by that diversity and what it could mean to the strength of the Catholic Church, popes had attempted many times in the past to identify and stamp out any thoughts or actions that resisted their control.

Inquisitions Prior to Spanish Inquisition

In the Catholic Church's view, anyone who did not conform with its established teachings was guilty of heresy, and Catholic authorities were determined to eliminate this severe sin. For centuries, heretics had been severely punished for resisting Christian principles and doctrine. Penalties could include anything from prayers, good works, and fines to death by hanging, beheading, or burning at the stake.

As Christian countries expanded their territory and influence into new lands, they encountered more and more nonbelievers who rejected Christianity. Looking for more powerful and uniform ways to root out and stop heresy, the Catholic Church created what might be considered to be its own legal system of courts and officials. These were called judicial tribunals; their purpose was to investigate each case of heresy and punish those who it found guilty.

These organized inquiries became known as inquisitions, describing a group of Catholic officials who were responsible for investigating heretics, getting them to confess their sins, deciding what punishment was proper, and having them ask for forgiveness so that their souls could be saved.

Early Church Attitudes

The idea of holding inquisitions to punish those who did not accept Christianity and forcing them to adopt the faith marked a very different approach compared to how the earliest Christians approached similar situations.

When the Christian Church was established by the apostles, it believed that the choice of faith should be based on a person's free will, and that acceptance of Christianity was a decision to be made according to a person's individual conscience. Apostles took the responsibility of preaching the faith so that everyone might have the opportunity to hear Christ's message, but it was then up to each person to either accept or reject it.

For the first three centuries of its existence, the Christian Church supported religious liberty and felt that religion should not be forced on others. In the eyes of the Christian Church, those who refused to accept Christianity would be punished spiritually; their decision to reject Christ's message of salvation would prevent them from being saved and entering heaven after death. Those who disputed Christian beliefs—heretics— could be cut off from the Christian Church but not punished in any other way. Christians felt that nonbelievers would suffer the consequences after death. Heretics were not persecuted by the early Christian Church, and they were most certainly not tortured or killed.

However, after the Roman Empire adopted Christianity as the state religion, some emperors significantly changed their approach toward non-Christians in their lands. Rather than leave the choice of religion to the responsibility of the person, these emperors felt that it was their duty as Christians to take responsibility for the souls of all their subjects as well as to manage their daily lives.

Emperors and kings of the Middle Ages considered heresy in much the same way as we think of treason in today's world. Heresy not only constituted a betrayal of religious faith; it represented a betrayal of government and society as well. Religious belief and loyalty to the king and state were considered one and the same.

In truth, the emperors realized that eliminating religious dissent would also help to prevent resistance in other areas as well, given how important religion was to every aspect of daily life. After Christianity was made the state religion of the Roman Empire in 381, emperors began to enact policies to seek out and punish heresy. Those found guilty could be subject to fines, to losing their possessions and property, to imprisonment, and even to death.

In 407, a law decreed for the first time that heretics were as dangerous to the state as those who resisted the authority of the emperor, and that anyone guilty of heresy should be punished the same as someone guilty of treason against the empire.

The Church as State

After the Roman Empire fell, western Europe transformed from a united land to a world of many different kingdoms that were growing but still poorly organized. The Catholic Church itself functioned as a monarchy in its own right. The papal state was located in central Italy. In many ways, the pope acted like a secular king and directly ruled over about one-third of Italy. In some ways, the papal state was the best organized of all the medieval monarchies.

While they ruled different kingdoms, medieval kings of the twelfth and thirteenth centuries followed in the footsteps of the Christian Roman emperors and assumed the role of protecting the Roman Catholic Church. While some Europeans practiced Judaism and Islam, most European kingdoms at that time adopted Roman Catholicism as the state religion. The major exception was the Muslim kingdom of Andalusia, which still controlled large areas of southern Spain. Similar to when the Roman Empire adopted Christianity, Catholicism and the state were closely linked in Europe's medieval kingdoms, and a heretical movement seen as a danger to Roman Catholicism also could be seen as a direct threat to the state.

During this time, the Catholic Church, for the most part, continued to take the position that faith should be spread primarily by persuasion, not violence. Those who resisted could be cut off from the Catholic Church and society, and perhaps even kept in confinement for the safety of others, but not executed. While some accused heretics were sentenced to death, these cases were usually attributed to the actions taken by secular rulers or even groups of fanatics among the population. Some Catholic authorities argued that Christianity did have the right to sentence heretics to death, but in reality, that action was rarely if ever taken by the Catholic Church itself.

That is, until Catharism appeared in the latter part of the twelfth century.

The Cathars

The Cathar heresy was a major challenge to the Roman Catholic Church. The Cathars believed that the material world was created by Satan and that it was corrupt. (The idea that the material world was bad and only the spiritual world was good had long been considered a heresy in orthodox Christianity.) Cathars rejected the entire Catholic organization, saying that the Catholic Church had become too concerned with the material world. They claimed that the Catholic Church was structured like a secular kingdom. It had its own bureaucracy, it owned property, and it collected taxes. In the Cathars' view, that meant that the institution was an instrument of Satan rather than of God.

The Cathars' claims came at a time when many other Europeans had also come to question some practices of the Catholic Church. Some felt that popes controlled too much political power and that Catholicism's organization had become corrupt. Perhaps the Catholic Church itself needed to be reformed or changed in order to move closer to its original founding principles. Claiming to be the only true

During the thirteenth century the Catholic Church considered Cathars to be heretics. Many were persecuted and even burned at the stake.

Christians, the Cathars developed an alternative religion and attracted many followers.

The Albigensian Crusade

The Roman Catholic Church viewed the growing opposition of the Cathars as a tremendous threat to its dominance in Europe. In response, in 1209, Pope Innocent III launched the Albigensian Crusade, named after the southwestern French town of Albi where many Cathars lived. Knights from northern and central France attacked the Cathars in a savage and bloody war. According to legend, when the Catholic forces attacked the city of Toulouse, soldiers told Catholic leader Simone de Montfort that they could not tell who in the city were Catholics and who were Cathars. Simon de Montfort is said to have replied, "Kill them all. The devil will know his own."

To justify the extreme and violent response in southwestern France, the Catholic Church likened the threat posed by the Cathars to the Crusades against Muslims in the Middle East. The Crusades were designed to win back the Holy Lands from Islam and re-establish Roman Catholicism among the people living there. Since the Cathars were spreading heresy, threatening the position of Catholicism and the people's loyalty, the Catholic Church felt that a crusade could justifiably be directed against them as well.

After successfully eliminating the Cathars, the Catholic Church insisted that more effort was required to make sure that heresy was rooted out in the minds and behavior of the people. It decided to conduct investigations to uncover and destroy heresy across Europe. These investigations came to be known as inquisitions.

Historians differ on when the first true Christian inquisition took place. Christian bishops had searched for heresy in their local districts for centuries. In 1184, Pope Lucius III and the Holy Roman emperor Frederick I had designed a method for the repression of heretics. They produced a document, "Ad abolendam," meaning "On abolition," a papal **bull** that prescribed penalties for heretical clerics and laymen. It also established a system of procedures to be followed by bishops who conducted inquisitions. It read in part:

To abolish the malignity of diverse heresies, which of late time are sprung up in most parts of the world, it is but fitting that the power committed to the Church should be awakened, that by the concurring assistance of the imperial strength, both the insolence and impertinence of the heretics, in their false designs, may be crushed, and the truth of catholic simplicity shining forth in the holy Church, may demonstrate her pure and free from the execrableness of their false doctrines.

The Albigensian Crusade is considered by many experts to be the first organized inquisition conducted on a grand scale, with the full support of the papal state behind it. "Ad abolendam" is sometimes called the charter of the inquisition because it helped set the tone and format for the future. The Catholic Church now had a procedure that proved successful and that could be used as a model for attacking heresy in other places.

Next Medieval Inquisitions

In 1231, Pope Gregory IX continued the process, appointing "inquisitors of historical depravity" who were directed by the Vatican. Inquisitions now became a regular occurrence in Europe.

An inquisitorial tribunal was established on April 20, 1233, when Pope Gregory IX issued a bull that assigned a religious order of friars named Dominicans to root out heresy. The Dominicans were chosen for the job because their founder, St. Dominic, had played a major role in the effort against the Cathars. Anyone who had been baptized into the Catholic faith was included, but non-Christians (including Jews and Muslims) were not, since they were still not officially considered to be heretics under the official definition at that time.

Spanish priest St. Dominic founded the Dominican order (the Order of Preachers) to spread the Christian Gospel and to combat heresy.

During the thirteenth century, the inquisition became much more formalized in its methods and practices. Highly trained Dominicans took over the institution, creating courts that some believe represented the best legal practices in Europe. Even so, the prisoner was assumed to be guilty and denied defense counsel. The names of witnesses against the accused were kept secret, meaning that the accused could not confront them face-to-face.

In 1252, Pope Innocent IV officially approved the use of torture to force accused heretics to admit heresy. Since financial support for the inquisition itself came from money and property that was confiscated from heretics who were found guilty, the deck was stacked against those accused.

As royal authority grew during the fourteenth century and beyond, control over the inquisition slipped out of papal hands and into those of kings. Instead of one inquisition, there were now many. Despite the prospect of abuse, monarchs like those in Spain and France generally did their best to make certain that their inquisitions remained both efficient and relatively merciful in comparison to the secular courts of the time.

Isabella Begins the Spanish Inquisition

Queen Isabella was a devout Catholic. She believed that true Christians should not just talk about their faith; they needed to practice its principles in their daily lives. Isabella was critical of officials in the Catholic hierarchy who acted contrary to the faith, like priests who did not remain celibate and who used money collected from the faithful for their own personal purposes.

In response to Isabella's criticisms, as well as to protect their own positions and that of the Catholic Church, some members of the Catholic hierarchy tried to convince Isabella that those who were baptized into Christianity from other faiths, such as the converted Jews called Conversos, constituted a greater threat to the faith than bad clerics. They claimed that New Christians secretly clung to their Jewish beliefs, thereby mocking the Christian faith and weakening it from within. Some merchants and court advisors joined in and made the same complaint. They were jealous of Conversos who held important jobs and owned businesses, and they wanted to protect their own wealth and position.

In 1477, three years after she assumed her throne, Queen Isabella visited the city of Seville. While there, she heard a Dominican prior, Alonso de Hojeda, preach about the wickedness of Jews and their betrayal of Christianity by being baptized but not really believing in or practicing the faith. The archbishop of Seville, Pedro González de Mendoza, and the Dominican prior of Segovia took the same position. They accused Conversos of secretly practicing Judaism and argued that the problem could only be solved by a full-time inquisition.

Alarmed by what they heard, Queen Isabella and King Ferdinand petitioned Pope Sixtus IV in 1478 to endorse an inquisition for Castile. On November 1, 1478, Pope Sixtus IV appointed several priests to be inquisitors. Their mission?

The 1933 film *The Wandering Jew* depicted a scene from the early Spanish Inquisition. Jews and Conversos became the Inquisition's first victims.

Target Conversos who were secretly practicing Judaism. This command marked the official start of the Spanish Inquisition.

This Inquisition Was Different

The first Spanish inquisitors, operating in Seville, proved so strict and cruel that Sixtus IV tried to intervene. However, the Spanish crown now had in its possession a weapon too precious to give up, and it rejected the efforts of the pope to limit the powers of the Spanish Inquisition. In 1483, Isabella and Ferdinand convinced the pope to name a grand inquisitor (inquisitor general) for Castile.

While Pope Sixtus IV's original intent was to establish an inquisition only in Queen Isabella's kingdom of Castile, King Ferdinand wanted the same for his kingdom of Aragon. During that same year, Aragon, Valencia, and Catalonia were placed under the power of the Spanish Inquisition. Ferdinand also took steps to make sure that he was in control of the Inquisition, not the pope. In 1486, he reminded the inquisitors that:

> Although you and the others enjoy the title of inquisitor, it is I and the queen who have appointed you, and without our support you can do very little.

Under pressure from Ferdinand and Isabella, the pope relinquished control of the Spanish Inquisition to the crown, and it became an instrument of the state, even though members of the Catholic Church functioned as its officers.

The Spanish Inquisition was much different in its aims and scope than previous versions. While previous inquisitions generally tried to uncover all kinds of heresy, Castile's inquisitors focused almost exclusively on uncovering false converts from Judaism. The Spanish Inquisition was also much better organized than previous investigations.

For the first time, an inquisition operated under royal rather than papal control, relatively free of the checks and balances that papal authorities were able to employ in the past. Isabella and Ferdinand sought to use the Spanish

Six Reasons for the Inquisition

Why did Queen Isabella and King Ferdinand support the Spanish Inquisition so passionately? Given the situation in Spain and their goal to unite Iberia, they had a number of motives. Isabella and Ferdinand wanted to:

1. Live their faith

Isabella in particular was a devout Catholic. The monarchs believed that one of their roles as the rulers of Christian Spain was to spread and protect the faith.

2. Establish political and religious unity

Isabella and Ferdinand were trying to consolidate their control over Spain, and they knew how important religion was in the daily life of their subjects. They saw that other European kingdoms were divided into different religious sects, and their rulers had been forced to compromise with groups holding different beliefs to effectively rule their kingdoms. Ferdinand and Isabella felt that their best chance to unite Spain under their control was to force all of its inhabitants to either adopt Christianity or leave the country.

3. Combine religious and political might

The Inquisition provided Isabella and Ferdinand with more control of religious affairs without the interference of the pope. At the same time, Ferdinand and Isabella wanted to create an efficient state organization. They believed that religious unity could help support a more centralized political authority.

4. Weaken local political opposition

To strengthen their kingdom and to establish centralized rule, Isabella and Ferdinand knew that they needed to weaken anyone who had local influence. By linking political opposition to religious heresy through the Inquisition, Isabella and Ferdinand could force allegiance to Christianity, to the state, and to them.

5. Eliminate the powerful Converso minority

Many influential families and business leaders were Conversos. Targeting them through the Inquisition could reduce their status and wealth and force them to bend to the will of the crown.

6. Increase wealth

Those who were found guilty by the Inquisition often faced fines or had their money and property confiscated. The Inquisition and the crown took this money to use for their own purposes.

Inquisition to support their regime and most especially to increase their royal power.

Another important difference was financial support. Previous inquisitions depended on the Catholic Church or the king and queen for funding. The Spanish Inquisition, on the other hand, supported itself by levying fines and penalties against those it found guilty. The fact that its income depended on finding people guilty in order to levy fines constituted an inherent conflict of interest; the Inquisition would need to persecute more and more victims and collect more and more money in order to survive.

1492: A Big Year

Most people think of 1492 as the year famous explorer Christopher Columbus departed for the new world under the sponsorship of Spain. With his three ships—the *Niña*, the *Pinta*, and the *Santa Maria*—Columbus set sail to the west on August 3 in the hope that he would discover a passage to the Far East and the riches it would provide. He instead made a much greater discovery, first landing at the island of San Salvador in the Bahamas and setting in motion the European settlement of the New World.

The year 1492 bore witness to two other important events, however. Both took place well before Columbus sailed west, and both would mark watershed moments, affecting the entire course of the Spanish Inquisition.

On January 2, 1492, the army under King Ferdinand and Queen Isabella entered the Muslim city of Granada and merged it into the crown of Castile, finally exerting their control over all of Spain. Granada was the final piece of Muslim-held territory in Iberia. Its ruler, King Boabdil, chose to surrender rather than see all of his people slaughtered.

Just three months later, Isabella and Ferdinand took another remarkable step to consolidate their power in Spain. On March 31, 1492, the king and queen issued the Alhambra Decree (also known as the Edict of Expulsion), which ordered Jews living in their kingdom to convert to Christianity or leave Spain. In just a three-month period, Ferdinand and Isabella managed to lead Christianity to total dominance over the two other major religions that had coexisted in Spain for more than seven centuries.

The Jewish Expulsion

The first grand inquisitor in Spain was the Dominican Tomás de Torquemada. At Torquemada's urging, Ferdinand and Isabella became convinced that they must remove all heretics and non-Christians from their land in order to purge it of pagan influences and firmly establish the Christian faith. The Alhambra Decree gave Spanish or Sephardic Jews the choice of exile or baptism, and only three months to decide. Sephardic is the Hebrew word for Spain.

Queen Isabella and King Ferdinand gave Jews a choice: convert to Christianity or leave Spain. Many Jews were forced to leave the only homes they ever knew, such as the people shown in this eighteenth-century print.

Ferdinand and Isabella justified their edict to expel from Spain all Jews that would not convert to Christianity and faithfully follow its practices by saying that they had tried other, less drastic measures to have Jews follow the Christian faith. Among the methods they considered to be less drastic were separation from other faiths, arrests, torture, imprisonment, expulsion from cities where they thought the influence of these nonbelievers was strongest, and even execution.

After Ferdinand and Isabella proclaimed that Jews had to convert to Christianity or leave Spain, thousands of Jews boarded leaky, crowded ships in 1492 and sailed into uncertain exile. In a quirk of fate, this was the same time that Christopher Columbus was preparing to set out on his first expedition from Spain. As he watched the Jewish refugees sail away from the port, Columbus described the scene in his written log as a "fleet of misery and woe."

In her book *Strange Gods: A Secular History of Conversion*, author Susan Jacoby wrote that the decision to force Jews to convert to Christianity or leave Spain was not just about anti-Semitism or hatred of Jews. "The very presence of [uncooperative] religious Jews in Christian Spain might induce Conversos to revert to the faith of their forefathers … Conversos could not be counted on to embrace Catholicism fully as long as faithful Jews were around … to remind them of the old ways and to seduce them from the True Faith."

In their edict, Ferdinand and Isabella claimed they had been too soft hearted in the past and now had to take stronger measures. Part of the edict read:

Notwithstanding that we were informed of the great part of this before now and we knew that the true remedy for all these injuries and inconveniences was to prohibit all interaction between the said Jews and Christians [Conversos] and banish them from all our kingdoms, we desire to content ourselves by commanding them to leave all cities, towns, and villages of Andalusia where it appears that they have done the greatest injury, believing that that would be sufficient so that those of other cities, towns, and villages of our kingdoms and lordships would cease to do and commit the aforesaid acts. And since we are informed that neither that step nor the passing of sentence against the said Jews who have been most guilty of the said crimes and delicts against our holy Catholic faith have been sufficient as a complete remedy … because every day it is found and appears that the said Jews increase in continuing their evil and wicked purpose wherever they live and congregate, and so that there will not be any place where they further offend our holy faith, and corrupt those whom God has until now most desired to preserve, as well as those who had fallen but amended and returned to Holy Mother Church, the which according to the weakness of our humanity and by diabolical astuteness and suggestion that continually wages war against us may easily occur unless the principal cause of it be removed, which is to banish the said Jews from our kingdom.

No one really knows the actual number of Jews who left Spain. Historians of the past estimated very high figures, some saying from three hundred thousand to eight hundred thousand Jews departed. Current estimates show much lower impact. Historian Henry Kamen believes that, of a population of approximately eighty thousand Jews, about one-half, or forty thousand, made the painful decision to leave. Some emigrated to Portugal, from which they were expelled in 1497. Others made their way to Morocco, other European kingdoms, North Africa, and the Ottoman Empire.

Those who remained converted at least in name and joined the ranks of the Conversos. Many of those continued to practice their Jewish faith in secret while hoping to escape the wrath of the Inquisition.

Muslims and the Moriscos

While the Spanish inquisitors of that time paid more attention to Jews and Conversos, they also had their sights trained on Muslims and **Moriscos** (Moors who had been baptized as Christians). Most historians agree that fewer Moriscos were placed on trial for heresy, and many fewer were punished or put to death, than Conversos. That does not mean, however, that persecution of Muslim residents in Spain was less than harsh, cruel, and relentless.

When he gave up his kingdom to Ferdinand and Isabella, Muslim ruler Boabdil hoped that the new Christian monarchs would keep a promise they made to allow Muslims to continue to practice their religion. Ferdinand and Isabella did keep their word, but only for a short time. By 1500, the rulers

Muslim leader Boabdil surrendered the kingdom of Granada to the forces of Isabella and Ferdinand in 1492. Christianity now ruled over all of Spain.

decided that all Muslims living in Castile had to agree to be baptized or leave. They also banned the use of the Arabic language and wearing traditional clothing.

Inquisitor Francisco, Cardinal Jiménez de Cisneros, pursued the suppression of Muslims with the same zeal that Torquemada had directed at Jews. Even so, many Muslims in the early 1500s were largely left alone as the inquisition concentrated more on the persecution and banishment of Jews.

The situation changed for the worse in the latter part of that century, however. Spain was fighting wars with Muslim Turkey as well as several Protestant European countries. Spain's ruler and the Catholic Church began to view Moriscos as enemies living in their own country, a kind of **fifth column** that could weaken Spain from within by allying with its enemies.

While Moriscos in Spain were commonly viewed as a threat, many people within the Catholic Church and the crown disagreed on how to handle the situation. Some believed that, since Moriscos had been baptized as Christians, they should be treated as loyal members of the faith. Others felt that Moriscos only portrayed themselves as Christians in public while privately remaining loyal to their Islamic religion, culture, and customs.

Eventually the latter view won out. On April 9, 1609, King Philip III signed an order to expel Moriscos from Spain, about 117 years after Jews had similarly been ordered to leave the country. In total, about three hundred thousand Moriscos left.

Sad Consequences

Many of those expelled from Spain, both Jews and Muslims, found life to be hard after they departed. Jewish communities in Europe and North Africa treated Spanish Jews with contempt, questioning their loyalty to the faith while living in Spain and knowing that many had become Conversos. The same thing happened to Spanish Muslims, who were badly treated by established Muslim communities in their new homelands.

The expulsions also caused negative effects in the Spain they left behind. Local economies suffered in places where Jews and Muslims made up large populations. Tax returns fell and agricultural production dropped. Many businesses closed as Jewish and Muslim owners were forced to leave, and fewer goods were purchased as these same Jews and Muslims had been good customers in the past.

New Targets

The expulsion of Jews and Muslims from Spain obviously reduced the number of potential heretics that could be accused by the Inquisition. Inquisitors managed to find other targets, however. When the Protestant Reformation began to sweep across Europe after 1530, the Spanish Inquisition was called upon to protect the faith from the threat of these new, heretical Protestant ideas.

Though they were few in number, Spanish Protestants were accused, tried, and eliminated. Foreigners suspected of promoting Protestant faiths within Spain met similar fates. Even prominent Roman Catholics who opposed the Inquisition were victimized. Saint Ignatius of Loyola (the founder of the Jesuits) was twice arrested on suspicion of heresy, and the archbishop of Toledo, the Dominican Bartolomé de Carranza, was imprisoned for almost seventeen years.

The total impact of the Spanish Inquisition is mind boggling. Within about one hundred years, the Inquisition enabled the monarchy and the Catholic Church to virtually erase from Spain two great cultures, societies that coexisted with Christianity on the Iberian Peninsula for many centuries.

And that does not even begin to describe the levels of human suffering and misery that define the true cost of the Spanish Inquisition.

Fear, Suffering, and Death

To fully grasp the scope of the Spanish Inquisition, it's important to consider its sheer size and the length of time it existed.

In his book *Inquisition: The Reign of Fear*, author Toby Green writes: "From 1478 to the mid-18th century the Inquisition was the most powerful institution in Spain and its colonies in the Canaries, Latin American and the Philippines. In neighboring Portugal and Portugal's colonies in Africa, Asia and Brazil, the Inquisition was preeminent for 250 years from 1536 onwards. This means that the Inquisition was a significant force in four continents for more than three centuries."

The Inquisition targeted everyone who could be considered critical of the Christian faith. Its victims included entire classes of people who practiced other religions, especially Jews, Muslims, and Protestants. It also pursued individuals unlucky enough to have made one remark, or even one joke, that

Condemned heretics were forced to dress in a special garment called a sanbenito and show their shame in public during the auto de fé of the Spanish Inquisition.

offended a Christian or appeared to violate any Christian belief or practice. Strangely, the evil weight of the Spanish Inquisition fell mostly on those who had already been baptized—Christians, particularly those who had converted from Judaism (Conversos) or Islam (Moriscos).

Conflict Between Church and State

We have already seen that Christianity and the crown were considered to be one and the same in medieval Spain, and that the Spanish government ran the inquisition, not the Catholic Church. This situation led to a major dispute between the papacy and the Inquisition over the jurisdiction of bishops.

According to Catholic rules at the time, bishops could only be tried by Rome. When the Inquisition decided to place bishops themselves under investigation, the pope was forced to choose between resisting, using his authority as leader of the Catholic Church, or yielding to the state and the inquisitors. The pope knew that the Catholic Church depended on royal authority for its own power and support, however, so he bowed to the Inquisition's demands.

Beginnings

When the Inquisition began in 1478, its headquarters were established in the city of Seville. Many Conversos who lived there feared that they would be accused of heresy, so they decided to leave the city. Unfortunately, the act of fleeing was, in itself, often enough to convince inquisitors of their guilt. Why flee if you were not guilty?

The Inquisition commanded nobles who controlled nearby lands to capture any Conversos they found and bring them to the prison in Seville. If they refused, the nobles could be arrested themselves for aiding heretics, so they usually followed the Inquisition's orders.

On February 6, 1481, the first ceremony of the Inquisition took place in Seville. Six Conversos, who happened also to be leading citizens of the city, were charged with heresy. They were forced to walk barefoot from the prison to the cathedral to hear Mass. They were then sentenced to death, marched out of town, and burned at the stake. Other victims

Those accused of heresy were imprisoned, tried, and tortured in cold, dark chambers with no contact from family or friends.

soon followed. Eventually, there were so many burnings that a huge stone platform (called the quemadero, or burning place) was built outside the city.

The Inquisition grew rapidly, and over the next few years tribunals were formed in all the major cities of Castile. At first, some towns and cities resisted the call for the Inquisition in their area, but they eventually bowed to the demands of the King Ferdinand and Queen Isabella, often under threat of attack.

The Targets

Conversos

By the time that Isabella and Ferdinand expelled the Jews from Spain in 1492, many had already converted to Christianity. When the edict was announced, some Jews wanted to remain in Spain and decided to convert. Historian Henry Kamen estimates that perhaps forty thousand Jews converted at that time, which he believes was roughly half of the remaining Jewish population.

Unfortunately, their decision to accept baptism into the Christian faith did not protect Jews who converted— Conversos—from the Inquisition's wrath. Persecuting Conversos became the primary focus of the early Spanish Inquisition. All Conversos were subject to being accused of heresy, including those who had converted long before the expulsion decree and Conversos who were born as Christians but had descended from one-time Jews. All were viewed with suspicion.

Moriscos

As the Inquisition gained strength and momentum, it expanded its persecution of Conversos to include the other large group of Christian converts, Moriscos. Officially, all Muslims (Moors) in Christian Spain had been converted to Christianity by 1526. These Moriscos lived mainly in the recently conquered kingdom of Granada, as well as in Aragon and Valencia. Like certain Conversos, some Moriscos continued to practice their former religion in private.

In the first half of the sixteenth century, Moriscos remained a powerful political and economic class. They were not actively persecuted by the Inquisition, which was more concerned with the threat of converted Jews. However, in the second half of the century, the situation changed. A Morisco revolt against Christian Spain was put down in 1570, but the rebellion fanned the flames of suspicion. Spanish Christians questioned the Moriscos' loyalty to Christianity and to Spain. The Inquisition targeted more Moriscos and the persecution intensified until Moriscos were expelled from Spain between 1609 and 1614. After that, few Moriscos remained in Spain to be accused of heresy.

Protestants

In the sixteenth century, the Catholic Church was challenged by reformers like Martin Luther and John Calvin. They opposed certain Catholic doctrines and practices and even questioned the authority of the pope. This period, known as the Protestant Reformation, shook northern and central Catholic Europe to its very core. These revolutionary ideas caused people to question their basic beliefs and their loyalty to their religion and their kings. Wars and persecutions followed, and the Catholic Church responded with force.

Due to Spain's relative isolation on the Iberian Peninsula, the Reformation did not affect it nearly as much as it did the rest of Europe. Nonetheless, Protestant reformers suffered under the Inquisition during the later sixteenth century. The first trials against Protestants took place between 1558 and 1562 in two communities of Protestants in Spain. Several large trials were held, some of which were presided over by members of the royal family. While the Reformation movement in Spain was small to begin with, the Inquisition's actions mostly put an end to Spanish Protestantism.

Highly Organized

So how did the Inquisition conduct its business? Who was in charge, and what other important positions were there to fill?

The Grand Inquisitor

The Spanish Inquisition began as two separate efforts, in Castile and Aragon. In 1488, these two inquisitions were united under one structure and one master inquisitor. The grand inquisitor, also called the inquisitor general, acted as the head of the Spanish Inquisition.

Although the grand inquisitor was named by the crown, his selection had to be approved by the pope. The grand inquisitor had the power to name other Inquisition officials, however, and these positions were filled in cooperation with the government. That arrangement placed real control of the Inquisition in the hands of the royal government rather than the Catholic Church.

The inquisitor general was the only public office whose authority stretched beyond Spain to all its possessions, including those in the New World. A Dominican friar, Tomás de Torquemada, served as the first grand inquisitor for the Spanish Inquisition. He controlled all of the tribunals in the two regions, and he set the rules of procedure. According to James Anderson, author of *Daily Life During the Spanish Inquisition*, Torquemada was "admired by some but feared by all."

The Suprema

The inquisitor general presided over the Council of the Supreme and General Inquisition (generally known as the **Suprema**). In the beginning, the Suprema had six members. That number changed over time, but it was never higher than ten. As the Inquisition grew, the authority of the Suprema grew at the expense of the inquisitor general.

The Suprema met every morning except on holidays, and for two hours in the afternoon on Tuesdays, Thursdays and Saturdays. Morning sessions focused on heresies related to faith, while afternoons were dedicated to other crimes, such as sexual offences, witchcraft, and other offenses not related to heresy.

The Grand Inquisitor

In 1483 Tomás de Torquemada became the first grand inquisitor of the Spanish Inquisition.

Torquemada was born in 1420 in Castile, the nephew of a well-known Dominican cardinal and theologian who was actually a descendant of a Converso. Torquemada joined the Dominican order himself in 1452 and rose to serve as prior of the monastery of Santa Cruz at Segovia for twenty-two years. Torquemada served as both confessor and advisor to Queen Isabella from the time she was a child.

In August 1483, he was appointed grand inquisitor of the Spanish Inquisition for Castile and León, and on October 17,

Grand Inquisitor Tomás de Torquemada prays with King Ferdinand II and Queen Isabella. His cruel practices continue to provide a lasting example of the savagery of the Spanish Inquisition.

his powers were expanded to Aragon, Catalonia, Valencia, and Majorca. Torquemada reorganized the Spanish Inquisition and also wrote guides for inquisitors to follow. Nothing could take place without his approval. He controlled priests and bishops, and targeted some of them as heretics.

While Torquemada lived simply and was considered to be pious in private life, his behavior as grand inquisitor was harsh and even fanatical. He believed that Jews, Muslims, Conversos, and Moriscos who lived in Spain threatened both Christianity and the state. He convinced King Ferdinand and Queen Isabella to persecute these groups and expel them from Spain.

Toward the end of his life, Torquemada's cruelty caused so many complaints that Pope Alexander VI appointed four assistant inquisitors to control him. Torquemada died in 1498, but his name lives on, linked forever with the horror, cruelty, and blind hatred of the Spanish Inquisition.

Tribunals

Fourteen local tribunals were established under the jurisdiction of the Suprema. In the beginning, the tribunals traveled anywhere they were needed to attack heresy. Later they based themselves at fixed locations. Each tribunal had two inquisitors and a prosecutor. One inquisitor, the alguacil, was responsible for detaining, jailing, and physically torturing the defendant. Inquisitors were officials of the Catholic Church and were trained in law and theology.

Spanish artist Francisco de Goya (1746–1828) painted this scene depicting a tribunal of the Spanish Inquisition.

Familiars

Each tribunal included a police force, called familiars. These were laymen who often dressed in black with the white cross of St. Dominic on their chest. They could carry weapons and had several jobs, including apprehending the accused and protecting the inquisitors. They also functioned as informants and spies. It was an honor to be a familiar, and nobles often held the job.

Since familiars were laymen, the secular courts first claimed jurisdiction over familiars who may have committed crimes of their own. In 1518, however, the king at that time, Carlos I, sided with the Inquisition and gave it legal control over the familiars. That decision gave the Inquisition even more power and led to even worse behavior by some familiars, knowing that they were likely to be treated more favorably by their masters than by the secular courts.

Notaries and Commissaries

A notary kept records of proceedings, interrogations, and confessions for the tribunals. Records were necessary so that heretics who **reconciled** with the Catholic Church, but who later relapsed, could be identified and retried.

Members of the rural clergy called commissaries were usually parish priests who worked with the Holy Office and supplied information about suspects. As a rule, these men were not well educated, but their cooperation helped the Inquisition to reach out of the main cities and into the rural areas.

Finances

For the most part, the Spanish Inquisition relied on the crown for its financial support, but that money actually came from the Inquisition itself. Victims were often fined and their property confiscated. The money and property went first to the crown, which shared some with the Catholic Church. The crown then paid the salaries and expenses of the inquisitors. The fines could be for any amount the inquisitors decided.

Such an arrangement was obviously ripe for abuse. The need to generate their own financial support often motivated the tribunals to target people who had more money and property to seize. The desire to make money often influenced the decisions that the tribunals made in terms of who to persecute and what penalty they would pay. An anonymous letter to the king in 1538 stated that if inquisitors did not burn people, they did not eat.

Search for Victims

The coming of the Inquisition to a town was designed to cause fear. According to Henry Kamen, one author at the time wrote that "we must remember that the main purpose of the trial and execution is not to save the soul of the accused but to achieve the public good and put fear into others."

When a tribunal was opened, a proclamation called an "Edict of Grace" would be issued, usually read to the congregation after Sunday Mass. The proclamation called for those who thought they might be guilty of heresy, or who knew someone who was, to come forward in the next thirty to forty days (a period of grace) to ask for forgiveness. In return for coming forward, they could be spared from severe punishment. They would also have to show sincere repentance, often by accusing others of heresy.

Most accusations of heresy came from ordinary people, usually neighbors or acquaintances, or even business rivals. Some thought it was their sacred duty to inform on heretics, while others made accusations based on personal hatred, grudges, jealousy, or greed. The identities of those who made accusations were hidden from the defendants, which helped to instill fear and mistrust in the minds of all.

If someone was accused by two witnesses, he or she was assumed to be guilty unless clear proof of innocence could be presented. The problem, however, was that those accused were not told what the specific charges were against them. That made it difficult to defend themselves or even to confess.

At first, the Spanish Inquisition allowed defendants to choose their own lawyers, which was different than other medieval inquisitions. However, the policy later changed, and the tribunal actually chose the defense lawyer. Just as unfair was the fact that the defendant and the attorney could not talk privately. Inquisitors attended every meeting, and a notary wrote everything down. Defendants soon realized that the odds were stacked against them. All were advised to confess, and few managed to be judged innocent.

Immediate Prison

Unlike today, the Spanish Inquisition imprisoned the accused as soon as they were arrested. No contact with the outside world was allowed, even with family members. Prisons were usually located close to the tribunal, often in the same building. The cells were dark, damp, and dirty, often overrun with insects and rats.

Prisoners were forbidden to speak and were often chained. Sometimes a device call the *pie de amigo*, which resembled an iron fork, was used to prevent the prisoner from bending or turning his or her neck. The more the prisoner suffered, the better the chance that he or she would confess. As an additional act of cruelty, the Inquisition often confiscated victims' money and property in order to pay for their own imprisonment, heaping further indignity and hardship on the accused and their families.

Prisoners could remain in their cells for months or even years without coming to trial, or even knowing what they were charged with. This led some prisoners to confess to crimes for which they were not even accused, which the inquisitors welcomed.

Trial and Interrogation

Instead of trials like we have today, the inquisitorial process consisted of a series of hearings in which both the denouncers and the accused gave testimony. The accused could defend themselves by either finding witnesses to support their side or presenting evidence to the court that the witnesses against them could not be trusted. Most of the hearing consisted of the prosecutor interrogating the defendant. Again, the notaries wrote everything down.

If the accused did not confess quickly, the interrogation could go on for hours. If there was still no resolution, the prisoner was returned to his/her cell and brought back for another hearing. In the meantime, inquisitors studied their notes for evidence they could use later.

The "Question"

Were people really tortured during the Spanish Inquisition? The answer is yes. However, historians disagree how much torture was used and how extreme the methods were.

In the United States, people charged with a crime are assumed innocent until proven guilty, and the use of torture to collect information or to gain a confession is usually condemned. Yet even today, cases do come to light where torture is considered to be permissible. Some people in the United States believe that torture should be used against accused terrorists, either to apprehend those who have killed innocent people or to stop those who plan to do so in the future.

In medieval times, however, it was fairly common for kingdoms and even local secular authorities to use torture to get information. While the Catholic Church had previously forbidden the use of torture in church-related proceedings, Pope Innocent IV officially approved the use of torture to obtain the truth from suspects in 1252. From then on, papal tribunals included torture in their arsenal as they pursued cases of heresy across Europe and the New World.

Surprising to us in today's world, the medieval Catholic Church did not think that there was anything "unchristian" about torture if it was the only way to obtain a confession. It was thought that torture could lead to confession, and confession could lead to a request for forgiveness, and that might save the person's soul. In other words, the end justified the means.

During the Spanish Inquisition, if the accused still refused to confess after more interrogations, the next thing he or she had to face was "the Question," which really meant a trip to the torture chamber. Here the accused was stripped of his or her clothes (although undergarments were sometimes allowed out of modesty) and subjected to cruel instruments and procedures that were designed to force a confession.

While torture was intended to convince the accused to confess rather than as a form of punishment, the reason for their suffering made little difference to the victims. Inquisitors did not actually torture their victims themselves, but they did attend the sessions so they could hear confessions when the pain became unbearable. As usual, a notary was always present to write everything down. A doctor was usually present as well, waiting to step in if any life-threatening situations occurred.

No defendant was excluded from being tortured. Pregnant women were allowed to sit while enduring their suffering, but everyone—male and female, young or old, healthy or sick—all could be subjected to "the Question."

The Tools of Horror

Three methods of torture were commonly used by the Inquisition. They included the *garrucha*, the *toca*, and the *potro*.

The garrucha, or strappado, involved suspending the accused from the ceiling by a pulley, with weights tied to the ankles. The victim was then subjected to a series of sharp lifts and drops, the arms and legs suffering violent pulls and sometimes dislocation.

The toca, also called *tortura del agua*, was similar to what we call waterboarding today. The torturer placed a cloth into the victim's mouth and then poured water through it, which created a feeling of drowning for the accused.

The potro, more popularly known as the rack, is perhaps the most infamous device used by the inquisitors. It consisted of a bedlike open frame suspended above the ground. The victim's ankles and wrists were secured by ropes that passed around axles near the top and bottom of the rack. When the axles were turned slowly by poles, the victim's hip, knee, shoulder, and elbow joints would be painfully stretched and eventually torn from their sockets.

Almost Always Guilty

After the process was completed, the inquisitors met with a representative of the bishop and with the *consultores*, experts in theology or canon law, in a process called the *consulta de fe*. They would review the evidence and then vote on the verdict and the sentence, which had to be unanimous. If they disagreed, they had to inform the Suprema. Once decided, the accused had to face the sentence and the penalty.

It was rare for someone accused of heresy to be found not guilty and released. It did occasionally happen, though, if the inquisitors became convinced that the person had only

Living in Fear

Living during the time of the Spanish Inquisition must have been truly terrifying. People at first were encouraged to come to the tribunal voluntarily so that they could confess their heresies. Then they also were forced to inform on their families, friends, and neighbors.

Stories were told of inquisitors sneaking up to houses at night, on horses with padded hooves, so they could listen at doors and windows for sounds of heresy coming from inside. Children feared these demons of the dark, who came to snatch people away and burn them alive.

Those accused of heresy could be immediately imprisoned and cut off from everyone and everything they knew. Without even knowing the charges, they faced both physical and psychological torture, pressured to confess with little hope of rescue or relief.

Notaries of the inquisition kept meticulous notes on all tribunal sessions. In one account, a woman in Toledo was interrogated on the rack for heresy, accused because she did not eat pork:

She was told to tell what she had done, for she was tortured because she had not

Anyone arrested and imprisoned by the Inquisition was likely to be judged guilty even if they were innocent of heresy.

done so, and another turn of the cord was ordered. She cried, "Loosen me, Señores!, and tell me what I have to say: I do not know what I have done, O Lord have mercy on me, a sinner!" … More turns were ordered, and as they were given she cried, "Oh! Oh! Loosen me for I don't know what I have to say."

People lived under a constant state of anxiety, suspicion, and peril. Even worse, it soon became clear that members of certain classes, like Conversos and Moriscos, were more likely to be accused, whether they were guilty or not.

Author Henry Kamen described what it was like to be a Converso during this time:

Between fear and humiliation, many Conversos lived in constant dread. "I was concerned because the Inquisition was coming," a tanner in Segovia said. "I would rather see all the Muslims of Granada enter this city," a resident of Cuenca exclaimed in 1491, "than the Holy Office of the Inquisition, which takes away life and honour."

While many defendants confessed whether they were guilty or not, others decided to go to their death rather than confess to lies or to betray their own beliefs. Don Carlos de Sesa, chief magistrate of the town of Toro, was accused of spreading Protestant ideas in 1559 and sentenced to be burned. He wrote:

In Jesus Christ alone do I hope, him alone I trust and adore, and placing my unworthy hand in his sacred side I go through the virtue of his blood to enjoy the promises that he made to his chosen.

been accused due to a personal grudge or malice by the person making the charge. Even so, such defendants had to swear that they would never tell anyone about the case or anything they experienced—nothing at all—or else they could be severely punished.

Even if the defendant was not acquitted, the process could be suspended. Perhaps the tribunal realized that a mistake had been made or that an accusation had been false. The defendant could be released without the tribunal admitting any problems with the process. The accused would still be under suspicion, however, and he or she lived with the threat of being arrested again at any time.

However, most defendants were convicted of heresy.

Auto de fé

Once condemned, the guilty had to appear at a ceremony called the **auto de fé**, the "act of faith." The Inquisition considered the auto de fé to be a religious act, intended to motivate the guilty person to ask for forgiveness and reconcile with the faith. While some could be held in private, autos de fé were usually held in a public square after the Inquisition trial ended. The accusations, verdicts, and penalties were announced, and the event often included Mass and public prayer.

At first, the autos de fé were simple events. In time, however, they became solemn ceremonies featuring large crowds and an almost circus-like atmosphere, staged to garner the greatest possible reaction from the crowd. The guilty were forced to walk in a procession to the local church and the sentences were read out. Then, barefoot and exposed to the weather, they were paraded through the streets while holding unlit candles, often weeping as they were publicly shamed.

Sometimes the auto de fé procession would include marchers who carried long green poles, dangling **effigies** of people who were absent but had been convicted of heresy. Other marchers might display the bones and rotting bodies of people who had been condemned after they died, then removed from their graves to be paraded for the crowd.

Artists of the time often chose to portray the spectacle of the auto de fé on their canvases. It has been said that during the sixteenth and seventeenth centuries, attendance at an auto de fé could rival the attendance at popular bullfights.

Punishment

Punishment for those found guilty of heresy ranged from the mild to the severe, depending upon the offense and how easily the convicted person confessed.

The defendant could be given penance. Considered guilty, he had to publicly renounce his crimes and accept his punishment. The defendant could also be reconciled, which might include a public ceremony in which the condemned was forgiven and accepted back into the Catholic Church. The guilty could be sentenced to prayer or fasting. Public displays could include wearing a penitential garment for a certain length of time, possibly even for the rest of their lives.

Other punishments were much more harsh. Offenders could be fined and their possessions and property could be confiscated. They might have to go on a sacred pilgrimage to a holy site. More severe punishment included whipping, imprisonment, banishment, and even being sentenced to the **galleys**.

The most serious punishment, of course, was death, which could be carried out by hanging or, more often, by being burned at the stake. Death was usually applied to heretics who refused to repent and those who had previously been tried by the inquisition but then relapsed into heresy. Those sentenced to death were executed in public. If the condemned person repented before the sentence was carried out, he could be granted a more humane death and be strangled before his body was burned. If he still refused to express remorse and ask for reconciliation, he would be burned alive.

People who escaped a summons from the Inquisition could still be tried for heresy, even though they were absent. In these cases, or if the defendant died before the verdict, the condemned were burned in effigy.

Why Burning?

Why were most victims who were sentenced to death burned instead of executed in a more humane way? First, those convicted of heresy who could not be reconciled were turned over to secular authorities. Priests were forbidden to shed blood, and the layman who performed the execution had to do so "bloodlessly." Burning, as it turns out, was thought to be the most reliable way to kill someone while ensuring that no blood be spilled. Plus, it was thought that punishment for the crime of heresy should be similar to the fires of hell.

Contrary to popular belief, witches were not a common target for the Spanish Inquisition. While parts of Europe were consumed with great witch-hunts during the sixteenth century, Spain for the most part did not follow along. The Inquisition was much more concerned with heresy than with witchcraft, usually leaving accusations of witchcraft and sorcery to be handled by the secular courts.

Efforts at Censorship

In addition to persecuting those accused of heresy, the Spanish Inquisition also worked hard to prevent heretical ideas from spreading in Spain. The less that people were exposed to ideas that contradicted Catholic teachings, the less likely they would be to stray from the righteous path.

Censorship was a key element of the Spanish Inquisition. Not only did the tribunals silence the sounds and hide any sights of heresy, they banned books, pamphlets, or any other form of communication that could spread dangerous thoughts. The Inquisition produced indexes, or lists, of books that were forbidden due to content that contradicted accepted Christian thought and teachings. The indexes included a great number of books of all types, although special attention was dedicated to religious works and, in particular, unapproved translations of the Bible.

The books of famous authors and great works of Spanish literature were included in the indexes, including writers like Dante, Machiavelli, and Thomas More. A number of religious writers who were later considered to be saints by the Catholic

Church were banned by the inquisition. It publicly burned any heretical books that it could find.

In the beginning, any book listed in the index was totally forbidden, even if only a section, or even one line, was deemed as heresy. Enforcement of this rule became a problem, however, especially since the works were forbidden to everyone, including priests, which resulted in a less educated and knowledgeable clergy. After a while, the Inquisition modified its policy to allow certain officials to delete or mark out offending material from books and then make them available to others.

Propaganda: A Powerful Tool

Censorship wasn't the only technique that the Spanish Inquisition used to control the thoughts and minds of the people. To maintain its influence, the tribunals and the state also effectively harnessed the power of propaganda, spreading information that supported their own beliefs and intentions. The public edicts, proclamations, and even the autos de fé were all carefully orchestrated by the inquisition to demonize other religions, different cultures, and opposing ways of thinking, all designed to turn the masses against the enemies of the Catholic Church and the state.

As the Spanish Inquisition continued for century after century, however, its opponents also learned to use propaganda to motivate others to resist.

When the tribunals started to persecute Spanish Protestants in the mid-sixteenth century, European Protestants spread the idea that the Inquisition represented the "true, dark and cruel nature" of the Spanish people. During the **Age of Enlightenment** that followed the Protestant revolution, activists, politicians, and even artists turned the Spanish Inquisition into a symbol of religious intolerance. One of the first to write about this theme was the British writer John Foxe, who dedicated an entire chapter of his book *The Book of Martyrs* to the Spanish Inquisition.

Writers and artists opposed to the Spanish Inquisition contributed to a movement that eventually became known as the "Black Legend," a term used to describe propaganda that portrayed an intensely negative image of Spain and Spaniards. They accused Spain of cruelty and intolerance while describing the horror and menace of the Spanish Inquisition. The Dutch and English, political rivals of Spain, were particularly focused on spreading stories of the Black Legend to gain political power for themselves. Their task was made easier by an invention that changed the world.

The Printing Press: Agent of Change

During medieval times, books were painstakingly written and copied by hand. People had little access to information and most could not even read. This played into the inquisitors' hands.

Right from the beginning, the inquisitors relied on their ability to control information to keep residents uninformed, preventing them from being exposed to ideas that contradicted the actions of the tribunals. However, the invention of the printing press changed the situation significantly. Different points of view could now spread quickly and easily, making it hard for the government and the religious establishment to maintain their domination. If knowledge was power, the dispersion of knowledge from the privileged few to the masses shifted the balance of that power away from the ruling class and toward the people.

In time, more and more books and pamphlets appeared that accused Spain and the Inquisition of committing heinous acts in the name of the crown and the Catholic Church. Authors wrote of "hooded fiends" who tortured their victims in unimaginable ways, pushing Spain into an age of darkness and evil. Thus began what can truly be called a war of propaganda, where the battle was fought not with weapons on the field, but rather through books and paintings that grappled for the minds and hearts of the common person.

Portugal and the New World

The kingdom of Portugal established its own inquisition in 1536. When it started, many Jews living there fled to Europe or the New World. Some hoped that the wide expanse of the Atlantic Ocean might offer them refuge and relief. Unfortunately, that was not to be the case.

The Inquisition also followed accused heretics to the New World. A full-scale Inquisition was launched in Mexico City in 1569, and some Conversos fled to what is now Santa Fe, New Mexico. Historical records show that the Inquisition followed into those areas as well to prosecute Jews and Protestants, and even Native Americans who had converted to Christianity but then returned to their traditional practices.

The Spanish Inquisition Ends

As Spain's former empire weakened, more of the continent's wealth and power shifted to other European countries, especially France and England. When the French invaded the Iberian Peninsula in 1807, French emperor Napoléon Bonaparte occupied Spain and installed his older brother Joseph as king of Spain in 1808. Joseph ended the Spanish Inquisition, deeming it a threat to civil society. It was reinstated for a short time when Spain managed to depose Joseph in 1814, but by then the people had no real appetite for the Inquisition anymore. Tribunals were rare from then on until the Spanish Inquisition was finally abolished by royal decree in July 1834.

Most Spaniards rejoiced when the Inquisition finally came to an end after causing so much pain and suffering.

Inquisition Fact Sheet

When did the Spanish Inquisition begin? The Spanish Inquisition, also known as the Tribunal del Santo Oficio de la Inquisición, was officially established by a papal bull, *Exigit Sincere Devotionis*. It was issued by Pope Sixtus IV on November 1, 1478.

Was it the only inquisition? No. Inquisitions were conducted in many other countries both before and after the Spanish Inquisition. But the Spanish Inquisition lasted far longer and claimed more victims than any other.

Who started it? The inquisition was requested by the sovereigns of Spain, Queen Isabella of Castile and King Ferdinand of Aragon, in order to consolidate their kingdoms and form a power base in Spain.

Who was in charge? Unlike past European inquisitions, where the Catholic Church was the ultimate authority over the prosecution of heretics, the Spanish Inquisition operated under the civil authority of the Spanish monarchy.

Who were the targets? Anyone suspected of heresy could be persecuted by the Inquisition. The first primary targets were Jews and those who converted to Christianity (Conversos). Attention then shifted to those practicing Islam and Moors who were baptized (Moriscos). The Inquisition later pursued Protestants and even Roman Catholics who objected to its methods.

How many victims did the Inquisitions claim?
Historians disagree on the number of victims. While estimates once ranged up to three hundred thousand people found guilty and more than thirty thousand put to death, more recent studies claim that about forty thousand were convicted and perhaps two thousand were executed.

Was it just in Spain? The Spanish Inquisition was not just limited to Spain, but also spread to Spanish-controlled colonies in the New World, including Mexico, as well as to other countries like Portugal.

When did it end? The Spanish Inquisition lasted for 356 years and was finally abolished in 1834.

The Toll

The last execution attributed to the Spanish Inquisition took place in Valencia in 1826. Cayetano Ripoll was a teacher and deist who was accused of supporting ideas like freedom of religion and speech and teaching his students about them. Ripoll was held prisoner for two years and then sentenced to death. Rather than burn him alive, the inquisitors decided to use a more "humane" method and instead hanged him on June 26. It is said that Ripoll's last words were, "I die reconciled to God and man."

It is clear that Spanish people, and Spain as a whole, paid a heavy price during the three and one-half centuries of the Spanish Inquisition. Thousands of people were persecuted, tried, and punished. Spaniards of all regions and faiths lived in constant fear of being exposed or being falsely accused of heresy.

That being said, the true magnitude of the numbers behind the Spanish Inquisition continues to be the subject of passionate debate. Recent revelations and the discoveries of documents previously unseen have caused many historians to revise their opinions on exactly how many trials and executions really took place over the Inquisition's cruel history. Some historians still believe that the number of victims killed ranged from thirty thousand to as many as three hundred thousand. Others, however, believe that the final toll of the inquisition has been exaggerated.

Juan Antonio Llorente served as the general secretary of the Inquisition from 1789 to 1801. He had direct access to tribunal records and wrote what is considered to be the first history of the Spanish Inquisition. Llorente said that the Inquisition investigated a total of 341,021 people, and that at least 10 percent (31,912) were executed.

Some experts believe that Llorente was biased and that his calculations were not accurate. Historian Henry Charles Lea published his own book, *History of the Inquisition of Spain, Vol. 1*, in 1888. Lea believed that high figures like Llorente's were overstated and not based on careful study.

Today's historians have recently been able to examine real documents compiled by the Inquisition. The archives of the Suprema, which are stored by the National Historical Archive of Spain, say that just over forty-nine thousand judgments were made, and that less than 2 percent (fewer than one thousand people) were burned at the stake.

However, these documents only include tribunals that occurred up until the year 1560. They also do not include records from many local tribunals. To fully comprehend the magnitude of the Spanish Inquisition, it would be necessary to examine the local archives. However, most of those records have been lost to the devastation of war, the ravages of time, or other events.

Historian and author Henry Kamen wrote a well-respected study of the Spanish Inquisition in 1965. In 1997, after conducting more than thirty years of additional research, he published a revised history. Kamen now estimates that approximately two thousand people in total were executed, a majority of the victims being Conversos of Jewish origin.

Regardless of the true number of victims, whether two thousand or three hundred thousand, the reality remains horrifying. For any single person subjected to the brutality of the Inquisition, the toll in terms of pain and suffering was immeasurable.

The Will to Resist

J ust think of how difficult it must have been to resist the onslaught of the Spanish Inquisition.

The tribunals were operated under the authority of the two most powerful institutions in people's lives at the time—the state and the Catholic Church. They channeled four of the most powerful emotions felt by men and women: faith, fear, greed, and patriotism. They capitalized on the many unique circumstances that defined Spain at that time, including its relative isolation from Europe; its melting pot of ethnicity, religion, and culture; and its link to the Catholic faith of its Roman ancestors.

The Spanish Inquisition challenged its citizens to either cooperate with the tribunals or forsake all their bonds with Spain and the people around them: their beliefs, their relationships, their religion, and their country. Even worse, even the slightest hint of resistance would likely exact a terrible

The autos de fé of the Spanish Inquisition were intended to excite and entertain the crowds to strengthen their support of the crown and the church.

price, anything from painful punishment to a horrible death and the threat of eternal damnation.

Given those circumstances, is it any wonder that most people in Spain cooperated with the Spanish Inquisition? They had little education or knowledge of the world. They had been raised to accept without question the demands of their religion and their rulers. They were easily convinced that heresy represented a significant threat to their own well-being as well as their faith. They felt they had no real power to change their lives. Many were jealous of those with better positions and more money, or simply fearful of those who had different backgrounds or ways of living.

Even if some Spaniards remained unconvinced that the tribunals were justified, they tried to appear supportive for fear of being targeted themselves. Some may have believed that if they could avoid the storm, it would eventually pass and life would get better.

Little did they know that the storm would last for more than 350 years.

Move, Submit, or Fight

Some Spaniards did resist the Inquisition's scourge. Brave souls refused to confess to false charges or to give up their non-Christian faiths. Many Jews and Muslims chose to leave Spain rather than convert to Christianity. Some Conversos and Moriscos also moved out of Spain, even though they had converted, rather than face accusations of not following their adopted faith.

Others took more direct action. Certain groups, cities, and regions actively fought the actions of the inquisitors with noncooperation and sometimes even violence. Even some members of the Catholic hierarchy tried to rein in the power of the inquisitors, believing that the tribunals had either usurped the Catholic Church's authority or committed criminal actions of their own.

When the Inquisition first began, some towns and cities strongly resisted the tribunals sent to their area. For hundreds of years, they had lived in an open, tolerant society based on acceptance of other cultures, and they were used to handling their own affairs locally. They resented the presence of inquisitors, sent from afar, who intended to change their comfortable way of life and enforce a set of rules that seemed foreign to them.

Establishing the new tribunals in Ferdinand's kingdom of Aragon was particularly difficult.

The Pope Objects

When King Ferdinand tried to extend the Spanish Inquisition from his wife Queen Isabella's kingdom of Castile to his own kingdom of Aragon, Pope Sixtus IV initially refused to support Ferdinand's request. In fact, he tried to halt the Inquisition already taking place in Castile.

On April 18, 1482, he wrote to the bishops of Spain, accusing the inquisitors of being motivated by greed and of using questionable witnesses against the accused:

In Aragon, Valencia, Mallorca, and Catalonia the Inquisition has for some time been moved not by zeal for the faith and the salvation of souls but by lust for wealth ... Many true and faithful Christians, because of the testimony of enemies, rivals, slaves, and other low people—and still less appropriate—without tests of any kind, have been locked up in secular prisons, tortured and condemned like relapsed heretics, deprived of their goods and properties, and given over to the secular arm to be executed, at great danger to their souls, setting a pernicious example, and causing disgust to many.

Pope Sixtus ordered the bishops to actively participate in all future tribunals and to make sure that the inquisitors followed the rules of justice. The accused should have lawyers and the right to appeal their case to Rome. The pope also issued a new papal bull that specifically forbade extending the inquisition to Aragon.

Up until that time, the pope's commands would have been obeyed without question, but in Spain the power of the crown was growing at the expense of the Catholic Church. Upon hearing of Sixtus's letter to the bishops and the bull, an angry King Ferdinand wrote to Sixtus, accusing him of being bribed with Converso gold. Interestingly, some historians believe that Ferdinand's charge may have been true.

Due to continued pressure from Ferdinand, the pope eventually suspended his previous bull. In 1483, he issued a new one, naming Tomás de Torquemada as inquisitor general of Aragon and Valencia in addition to Castile.

When Pope Sixtus IV died, other popes continued to try to take control of the inquisitorial process. They argued that the Inquisition by nature was a religious undertaking and that continued abuses by the tribunals were hurting its reputation. These objections had little effect, however, and the Inquisition continued to grow under the power of the crown.

Resistance and Defeat

Public opposition continued in Aragon. The most striking case took place in the city of Teruel in 1484. Two inquisitors were sent to establish a tribunal but local magistrates refused to let them enter the city. The inquisitors excommunicated the city's leaders, but Teruel's clergy convinced the pope to reverse that decree. King Ferdinand then decided to assert his control by massing troops from both Aragon and Castile to force Teruel to accept the inquisitors. Faced with such a threat, Teruel had no choice but to obey.

Other cities also tried to resist the Inquisition. Some worried that attacks on Conversos and Moriscos would hurt the local economy, since many of the converted owned businesses and controlled large amounts of wealth. Others preferred to manage their own affairs and resented the crown's efforts to take control of local governments. Still others believed that the Inquisition contradicted good Christian practices by not allowing everyone to use their own free will to choose their faith.

Pope Sixtus IV: Second Thoughts

Of all those closely associated with the Spanish Inquisition, perhaps no one person presents such a complicated and contradictory picture of both support and resistance than the pope who helped start it all, Pope Sixtus IV.

Sixtus IV was born Francesco della Rovere in Genoa, Italy, in 1414. A Franciscan priest, he served as a teacher and was named minister general of his order in 1464. He was appointed a cardinal in 1467 by Pope Paul II, and after Paul's death, he was elected pope in 1471.

For much of his term as pope, Sixtus concentrated on expanding Italian politics and expanding the power of the papacy. He also supported the arts, however, and built or restored many Roman churches. The Sistine Chapel, built from 1473 to 1481 during his time as pope, is named after him.

In 1478, Pope Sixtus yielded to Queen Isabella's request and authorized an inquisition for her home kingdom of Castile in Spain. However, he soon learned of terrible abuses by the first inquisitors and tried to take control of their actions.

Sixtus also knew that he depended on Spain's power and wealth for support.

Pope Sixtus IV lost control of the Inquisition.

When Ferdinand and Isabella objected to his resistance, he not only yielded control, he authorized its expansion into other kingdoms, allowing the Spanish Inquisition to begin its savage reign. While he continued to object to its excesses, Sixtus never took steps to halt the Inquisition. Pope Sixtus IV died in Rome in 1484.

These protests, from Aragon and other areas, continued to be directed at the tribunals through the mid-1500s. In 1506 a Córdoba mob stormed the fortress where the Inquisition kept prisoners and freed them all. Two other uprisings occurred in Spain in 1591. However, with support from the crown and the Old Christian majority, the tribunals persevered and became more powerful.

An Assassination Backfires

When the Spanish Inquisition began, many Conversos grew fearful as they realized they represented the primary targets, and they used their contacts and economic power to oppose it. Unable to find support in Spain, they turned to Rome in hope that the papacy would withdraw support from the tribunals. Pope Sixtus IV agreed at first, but under pressure from King Ferdinand, he finally authorized the spread of tribunals throughout Spain. Other popes also tried to defend Conversos against the Inquisition, but with little success.

Seeing their position continuing to weaken, some Conversos gave in to desperation and plotted to assassinate an inquisitor. In September of 1485, men hired by Conversos attacked and killed inquisitor Pedro Arbués while he prayed

The assassination of inquisitor Pedro Arbués by Conversos led to more persecution.

in Saragossa Cathedral. Instead of helping the Converso cause, the murder turned the entire city against them. Arbués was declared a saint, the conspirators were hunted down, and persecutions of Conversos increased. Over the next few decades, upwards of 90 percent of all accused were Conversos of Jewish origin.

The Morisco War

After the Spanish defeat of Granada and the fall of al-Andalus in 1492, the Moriscos realized that they would have to compromise their religion and customs in order to survive in Christian Spain. They still managed to live in relative peace for more than two generations, until local Catholic councils in Spain decided that the same Inquisition policies for Conversos should be applied to Moriscos.

The tension exploded on Christmas Eve of 1568, when a savage war between Muslims and Christians began in Granada. Both sides committed horrible atrocities, but the Christian military won out, and thousands of Moriscos died. Despite the rebellion's defeat, Christian Spain still feared the Moriscos' very presence, and in 1609, Spain expelled all Moriscos from the country.

Protestants

Roman Catholic Spain considered the Protestant Reformation to be a very real, yet very different, threat than what it had faced previously.

Jews and Muslims practiced their own religion, but they did not actively recruit Catholics to their way of life. Conversos and Moriscos might doubt their adopted Christian faith, but at least they had been baptized and claimed to be faithful. Protestants, on the other hand, called themselves Christians

English Protestant Nicholas Burton was tortured and put to death in 1560.

while questioning many of the religion's basic beliefs and practices. The Protestant movement was disrupting the rest of Europe, and the Inquisition had no intention of letting that happen in Spain.

In 1557, the Jeronymite monks of the San Isidro monastery near Seville had become, in the words of the inquisitors, a "hotbed of Lutheranism." Two friars from the monastery began to spread ideas about the Protestant Reformation while questioning the traditional positions of Catholicism. The Inquisition moved in and arrested eight friars; the prior and four priests were tried, convicted, and burned.

In all, eighty-eight cases of Protestantism were punished by the Inquisition in 1559, including eighteen burnings, effectively ending Protestantism in Spain.

Protest in Art

While it was extremely dangerous for anyone to publicly criticize the Spanish Inquisition, many still tried. Artists and writers, in particular, expressed their objections, though very carefully. The first writings to question the Inquisition and to praise the ideas of free choice began to appear in the mid-1700s. The newspaper *El Censor* published protests against the activities of the Holy Office and other writers pleaded for freedom of expression. Many artists of the time painted scenes that depicted the cruelty and suffering caused by the tribunals.

While many did oppose the Spanish Inquisition over its history, most efforts were doomed due to the sheer might born of the union between church and state. Despite all internal resistance, the Inquisition's final collapse would come only after an invasion and, even more important, due to rising indifference and disgust among Spaniards themselves.

Aftereffects

How and why did the Spanish Inquisition end?

The French abolished the Inquisition in 1808 after they occupied Spain. Traditionalists in Spain pressured King Ferdinand VII to restore it in 1814, but by then it was fairly inactive. Progressive opposition won out a second time in 1820, and the Inquisition was again abolished. Finally, on July 15, 1834, Queen Isabella II issued the final decree of suppression. The Spanish Inquisition was finally over, although by that time the decree was just a formality.

Queen Isabella started the Spanish Inquisition way back in 1478. Ironically, almost 360 years later, it was ended by her namesake, Isabella II, who once and for all rid Spain of its cruel practices.

While history may tell us that the French invasion, the Protestant Reformation, or the Age of Enlightenment helped to end the tribunals, two other powerful forces played perhaps an even more important role.

The Spanish Inquisition finally ended under the reign of Queen Isabella II.

A shift in popular attitudes, combined with simple economics, finally put a halt to the Spanish Inquisition.

Losing Interest

After more than three centuries of terror and misery, the people of Spain simply started to lose interest. By the end of the seventeenth century, the pageantry of the auto de fé no longer held the same appeal for the masses. People became indifferent to the all-day event.

This change of opinion was certainly influenced by what Spaniards heard about themselves from other countries. As Spain stubbornly held on to its Inquisition, the kingdom was ridiculed throughout the rest of Europe. French philosophers like Voltaire portrayed Spain as a relic of the Middle Ages— authoritarian, intolerant, ignorant, and barbaric. Writers, philosophers, and artists railed against the cruelty and unfairness of the inquisition, as well as its accompanying censorship that cracked down on different ideas and new ways of thinking. As independent thought and religious tolerance continued to spread across Europe, popular support for inquisitions, both Catholic and Protestant, withered.

Putting the historical times in perspective, the last execution by the Spanish Inquisition occurred fifty years *after* the signing of the American Declaration of Independence. Unlike some European governments that still believed it was possible to stamp out heresy and control their people through religion, one of America's guiding principles preached just the opposite: separate the church from the state and permit all citizens to practice religion in their own way. As different

Protestant denominations continued to multiply in northern Europe, and as Europeans learned more about the United States and its beliefs, inquisitors and their supporters were forced to realize that the rise of new religions and ways of thinking was unstoppable.

Fewer Victims Meant Less Money

In a manner of speaking, the tribunals also became victims of their own success. They did such a good job of eliminating heretics that it was difficult for inquisitors to find more people to persecute. Fewer victims meant fewer penalties, and that meant there was less money and property to be confiscated to pay for the rising costs of the Inquisition.

With less wealth and fewer people to persecute, the Suprema began to lose its influence. Spain's war with France weakened the Inquisition even further. The government sold off some Inquisition assets, such as property, to finance the war, and many agents of the tribunals were summoned to serve in the army, ending their life of privilege beyond the government's control.

Echoes of the Black Legend

Eventually, the Spanish Inquisition collapsed under its own weight. Now came the time for the era to be put to rest and the judgments of history to begin.

As time passed, many records of the Inquisition were lost or destroyed by Joseph Bonaparte and others. As propaganda in favor of the tribunals mixed with propaganda

Painters and writers who opposed Spain and the Catholic Church exaggerated the real horrors for their own purposes.

promoting the Black Legend, it became increasingly difficult for historians to determine with any certainty what exactly happened or did not happen during the Spanish Inquisition.

Some of the researchers approached the subject with predetermined opinions and biases, committed to presenting a particular point of view rather than to consider all the facts. Perhaps they wanted to defend Spain and the Catholic Church, or they wanted to speak out for the victims who were unjustly targeted and punished. Maybe they simply wanted to attack Spain and the Catholic Church for political or religious reasons. No matter what their intent, authors and artists found plenty of material they could use to support whatever point of view they set out to portray. Their efforts served to further darken the already muddy waters surrounding the conduct of the tribunals.

History Revised

Fortunately, recent discoveries and the release of new information sources have made it easier for historians to construct a much more accurate and honest account of what actually occurred during the nearly 360 years of the Spanish Inquisition. The past 40 years, in particular, have witnessed the development of what is called a revisionist school of Inquisition history, a controversial area where the aim is to re-examine the traditional history of the tribunals.

Two extensively detailed books—*Inquisition*, written by Edward Peters in 1988, and *The Spanish Inquisition: A Historical Revision*, written in 1997 by Henry Kamen—strived to use newer sources to more accurately portray what really happened during those times.

Kamen's book is especially noteworthy. He had previously written a well-respected history of the Spanish Inquisition back in the 1960s. New information had become available since he wrote it, however, and he felt the responsibility to examine his earlier conclusions. What he discovered led him to publish a major revision, and call it as such, more than thirty-five years later. In the preface to his revision, Kamen writes, "Very much [in his previous book] has been superseded by subsequent research. Thanks to the quality of work over these years by specialists, it is now possible to get a far more reliable image of the Holy Office of the Inquisition. In many key respects, consequently, I have been obliged to change my views."

Vatican Opens the Archives

In 1962, Pope John XXIII summoned about two thousand bishops for the Second Vatican Council. The council acknowledged many "unhappy chapters of Christianity's past relations with other religions," noting "past quarrels and hostilities," and "urged all … to strive sincerely for mutual understanding." Since that time, even more information about Catholic Church inquisitions has come to light.

Perhaps most importantly, the Vatican finally opened up its own private archives for historical investigation. In 1998, Pope John Paul II granted access to the archives of the Holy Office (the modern successor to the inquisitions), which were previously shrouded in mystery and hidden from public view, and invited thirty scholars from around the world to attend a three-day symposium. The discussion would concentrate on the historical background of all the persecutions that began back in the thirteenth century and continued until the Spanish Inquisition ended in 1834.

The symposium came about due to the efforts of one man that began nearly twenty years earlier. Carlo Ginzburg, a distinguished Italian historian, wrote a letter to the newly elected Pope John Paul II asking "as a Jew, an atheist and a historian" that the Vatican open its long-sealed archives on the Inquisition. "I told the pope it was absurd not to submit this archive to examination by scholars," said Ginzburg. After much discussion and debate over many years, the pope ultimately agreed to Ginzburg's request.

Pope John Paul II spoke to those who attended the symposium, promising the Catholic Church's willingness to admit to its own shortcomings, but "only after the historians have established the truth of the facts." Records stored by the Inquisition itself could be impartially examined for the first time in history. After the symposium ended, the Vatican went further and allowed qualified researchers of any religious belief to examine the archives. More former "facts" have now been revised, and a much clearer picture of the Inquisition has come into view

The new policies reflected a broader pattern of honest self-examination by the Catholic Church that Pope John Paul II supported during the later years of his papacy. He called for an examination of conscience so the Catholic Church could ask forgiveness for the sins of its past before it entered its third millennium. Referring to the new approach, Reverend Georges Cottier, president of the Vatican's theological commission for the year 2000, said that the Catholic Church "cannot pass into the new millennium without urging its sons to purify themselves, through penitence, of its errors, its infidelities and its incoherences."

A Shocking Conclusion

In June 2004, the Vatican published a new study, nearly eight hundred pages in length, about the Inquisition. The study's conclusion surprised, even shocked, many who read it. After examining the evidence, the study said, the tribunals were not as brutal as previously believed. One headline at the time read, "Vatican Downsizes Inquisition."

According to the study, the number of victims who were actually killed or tortured into confessing during the Inquisition was far fewer than previously thought. In fact, the study's editor, Professor Agostino Borromeo, claimed that, in Spain, only 1.8 percent of those investigated by the notorious Spanish Inquisition were executed. This meant that many of the thousands of executions previously blamed on the Catholic

When the Vatican opened its secret archives in 1998, it revealed records and documents about the Spanish Inquisition that had been hidden for centuries.

Church may in fact have been carried out by non-Inquisition tribunals, or did not occur at all.

Regardless of its conclusions, when the report was published, Pope John Paul II apologized once more for the inquisitors' excesses, expressing sorrow for "the errors committed in the service of the truth by the recourse to non-Christian methods."

The Debate Continues

Despite all the new research and discoveries, experts still disagree about what really happened during the Spanish Inquisition, why it started, and how it stayed so strong for so long.

Some still argue that the tribunals were not formed to destroy diversity or oppress minorities. They insist that the

Catholic Church was only trying to prevent unjust executions by the state and to provide fair trials for accused heretics, using lawful procedures and knowledgeable judges. The state believed that heretics were traitors to God and the king and therefore deserved death, they say, and the Inquisition provided an alternative for heretics to escape death and return to the community.

Others believe that the Spanish Inquisition arose due to cold-hearted, calculated planning by the royal crown and the Catholic Church to gain power. The king, queen, and pope worked together to extend and improve the practices of previous inquisitions in order to conquer and unite the Iberian Peninsula under one dominant Christian state.

Perhaps there is some truth on all sides. What is clear is that the Spanish Inquisition thrived due to one other key element: the support of the people. Huge throngs attended the autos de fé. With some notable exceptions, most regions either actively participated in persecuting heretics, or at least passively accepted the tribunals. Furthermore, the Spanish Inquisition finally collapsed only when popular support vanished.

Needs of the Times

Like other aspects of the Spanish Inquisition, experts disagree on why Spaniards backed it so strongly. Some cite loyalty to faith, the Catholic Church, and the crown. Others blame fear, ignorance, and bias. Historian Henry Kamen presents another rationale: "the needs of the times." Crisis times demand crisis measures, he writes. The clash of cultures, faith, and language in medieval Spain led to civil war and chaos, and the Inquisition was constructed as a "crisis instrument" to be used only temporarily as an emergency measure, until the crisis passed.

However, once the Spanish Inquisition was established as a joint state and religious institution, it took on a life of its own. It made its own rules, appointed its own leaders, and survived on its own income. It spread its own propaganda and invented its own messages of crisis.

The same elements that powered the Spanish Inquisition appear in virtually all persecutions throughout history. First, identify a person or group as an imminent threat: Christians in pagan Rome; heretics in medieval Spain; Jews in post–World War I Germany; Japanese Americans in California just after Pearl Harbor; Muslims in today's United States. Next, use fear to overpower reason, and spread emotional propaganda to raise concerns to crisis levels. Finally, direct government and other organizations to respond to the looming emergency.

Using the powerful tools of politics, religion, and propaganda, the leaders of the Spanish Inquisition managed to create what can be called the first effective police state in Europe. No one could be trusted. Loyalty to the state and the Catholic Church was all that mattered, superseding love for family, empathy for others, and acting according to conscience.

Outside of its scale and length, the Spanish Inquisition in many ways was not much different than other mass, state-sponsored persecutions that have occurred throughout history and, unfortunately, remain with us today. The capacity for religions, governments, organizations, and even individual

Righting a Wrong

The expulsion of Jews is one of the darkest stains on the history of Spain. The country moved to make reparations for it more than five hundred years later.

In 2015, the country passed a law that said that anyone who could prove they were descendants of Sephardic Jews and could show a "special link" to Spain could apply for citizenship in their ancestral country. The law, which was to be in force for three years, also stated that these people would not have to give up their current citizenship. These descendants do not have to be Jewish.

According to an article in the *Los Angeles Times*, there are as many as 3.5 million Jews who can claim Spanish lineage and there are about 50,000 observant Jews currently living in Spain.

The special links could include rabbinical certification of Spanish ancestry, or knowledge and use of a Spanish dialect used by Sephardim called Ladino.

people to persecute those who are different, or who disagree, remains an evil side of humanity that continues to rear its ugly head year after year, in country after country. Fear, suspicion, and greed continue to pit one group against another, their passions inflamed by those who use misleading propaganda for their own ends. The targets can be large or small. An inquisition impulse can quietly take root in the very systems of government and civil society that shape our lives.

Haunted by the Past

A case can be made that many of today's religious animosities trace their roots back to the Crusades of the Middle East and the Inquisition of medieval Spain, where Muslims still remember the carnage of the Christian conquest and the Inquisition that followed. But that hides the fact that, at one time, Christians, Muslims, and Jews lived side by side, all contributing to a rich economy and culture.

In truth, Spain is a very different country today than it was back in medieval times. Support for religious diversity was included in the country's first democratic constitution in 1978, and some consider Spain to be one of the most tolerant countries in Europe. Many Muslim immigrants have moved to Spain, and Islam is once again a large presence there. Even so, anti-Muslim and Jewish sentiments remain in Spain, and Catholics still want to protect their leading position.

At the end of the preface for his revised history, Kamen writes, "Like its predecessor, my book is fundamentally a

'state of the question' paper and therefore still open to discussion."

Today, nearly twenty years after that book was published and the Vatican records were unsealed, the true scale and effects the Spanish Inquisition, and solutions to the persecutions of today, still remain open to discussion.

A statue of Jewish Philosopher Moses Maimonides stands today in Cordoba, Spain. Maimonides lived under Muslim rule when Muslims and Jews worked together.

711: Moors invade Iberian Peninsula.

October 25,1085: Christians recapture Toledo.

1231: Pope Gregory IX authorizes Dominicans to examine Cathar and other Christian heretics in southern France and Italy, known as the "medieval inquisitions."

1236–1248: Cities in Muslim Andalusia recaptured by Christians, including Córdoba (1236) and Seville (1248).

1391: Riots target Jews across Spain; many Jews are forced to convert to Christianity.

1449: Riots target Conversos in Toledo, and they are banned from holding official positions in the city.

October 18,1469: Isabella marries Ferdinand II of Aragon.

March 1, 1476: Isabella becomes Queen of Castile after her forces win the Battle of Toro.

November 1, 1478: Pope Sixtus IV issues a papal bull authorizing the Spanish Inquisition at the request of Ferdinand and Isabella, the Catholic monarchs of Spain.

January 20, 1479: Ferdinand II becomes king of Aragon; Isabella and Ferdinand begin joint rule.

September 27,1480: First Spanish Inquisition tribunal becomes active in Seville; converts from Judaism (Conversos) suspected of remaining loyal to their ancestral religion are targeted.

February 6, 1481: First autos de fé held in Seville.

1483: Jews expelled from Andalusia; the Supreme Council of the Spanish Inquisition (Suprema) established to supervise all tribunals.

1484: Torquemada writes first instructions for the operation of the Spanish Inquisition.

September 17, 1485: Inquisitor Pedro de Arbués is assassinated in Aragon.

1488: The inquisitional tribunals of Aragon and Castile are unified.

1492: Jews expelled from Spain; Christians capture last Muslim cities in Spain; Columbus leaves Spain on first voyage to the New World.

December 5, 1496: Jews expelled from Portugal.

February 12, 1502: Muslims who wouldn't convert expelled from Granada.

November 26, 1504: Queen Isabella dies.

January 23, 1516: King Ferdinand dies.

November 1525: Royal decree orders Muslims to convert to Christianity or be expelled from Aragon and Valencia.

October 17, 1528: First auto de fé in the New World; two Conversos burned in Mexico City.

May 23, 1536: Papacy allows Portuguese Inquisition, first with reduced powers; full powers granted in 1547.

July 21,1542: Pope Paul III establishes the Roman Inquisition.

1559: Pope Paul IV's Pauline Index lists forbidden books; the pope authorizes inquisitional jurisdiction over bishops; trials of prominent Spanish Protestants in Valladolid and Seville; focus of Spanish Inquisition shifts to Protestantism.

January 1, 1567: Laws clamp down on Moriscos.

1569–1571: Spanish Inquisition establishes tribunals in Mexico and Peru.

1580: Spain and Portugal unite under Philip II.

April 9, 1609: Expulsion of Moriscos from Spain begins.

February 13, 1668: Spain recognizes Portugal's independence.

June 15, 1808: Joseph Bonaparte declared king of Spain; Spanish Inquisition soon halted.

July 21, 1814: Spanish Inquisition restored by Ferdinand VII; continued debates over its existence leads him to pass a decree suppressing the Inquisition in 1820.

1821: Official abolition of the inquisition in Portugal.

July 26, 1826: Last death sentence by the Inquisition for heresy.

July 15, 1834: Law abolishing the Spanish Inquisition is formally passed in Spain.

June 29, 1908: Roman Inquisition becomes the Holy Office.

December 7, 1965: Pope Paul VI reorganizes Holy Office, renames it Congregation of the Doctrine of the Faith.

June 14, 1966: Index of Forbidden Books abolished.

January 22, 1998: Pope John Paul II opens Vatican's historical archives on inquisitions

March 12, 2000: Pope John Paul II admits during Jubilee that the Catholic Church had been intolerant in its "use of violence in the service of truth" and asks forgiveness.

GLOSSARY

Age of Enlightenment Also called the Age of Reason, a time in eighteenth century Europe known for advancing progressive ideas about science, religion, politics, and society.

auto de fé "Act of Faith," usually public, at which the sentences against those tried by the Spanish Inquisition were announced. In Portuguese, the term is written auto da fé.

bull A special kind of patent or charter issued by a pope. It is named after the seal (bulla) that is appended to the end to authenticate it.

caliph The chief civil and spiritual ruler of Islam.

Conversos People who converted from Judaism to Christianity; used primarily to describe Jewish converts; also refers to their descendants.

edict An official order given by a government or by a person in power. During the Inquisition, it was a declaration of faith read in public by inquisitors at the beginning of proceedings.

effigy An image or figure representing a person, absent or dead; at an auto de fé, an effigy for an absent or dead heretic might be paraded and burned.

fifth column People in a country who help or work for its enemies.

galleys Open-oared boats or ships, known for cruel treatment of slaves and criminals condemned to row under the whip, usually until death.

heretics Those who disagree with established religious doctrines, especially baptized Roman Catholics who abandon official Catholic teachings.

infamous Well known for something evil or shameful.

inquisition An investigation or inquiry, often associated with the medieval Christian Church investigations of heresy.

Moors Muslims who lived in Spain after the Islamic conquest of 711.

Moriscos People who converted from Islam to Christianity.

Old Christian A "pure" Catholic who had no Jewish or Muslim ancestors.

pogrom An organized massacre of helpless people; specifically a massacre of Jews.

propaganda Information that is biased or misleading, usually used by one group against another.

Protestant Reformation A major sixteenth-century European movement that intended to reform the beliefs and practices of the Roman Catholic Church.

reconcile People prosecuted by the Inquisition could "reconcile" and be received back into the Christian Church after punishment.

Suprema Supreme Central Council of the Spanish Inquisition.

tribunal A court of justice.

Books

Green, Toby. *Inquisition: The Reign of Fear.* New York: Thomas Dunne Books, 2007.

Kamen, Henry. *The Spanish Inquisition: A Historical Revision.* New Haven, CT: Yale University Press, 1998.

Lowney, Christopher. *A Vanished World: Medieval Spain's Golden Age of Enlightenment.* New York: Free Press, 2005.

Websites

Spanish Inquisition—New World Encyclopedia

http://www.newworldencyclopedia.org/entry/Spanish_Inquisition
This site provides a long look at the Spanish Inquisition, and also includes a list of sources and links to articles on the history of Spain.

Spanish Inquisition: Spanish History 1478–1834 —Encyclopædia Britannica

http://www.britannica.com/topic/Spanish-Inquisition
A precise history of the Spanish Inquisition and links to other articles related to the subject can be found at this excellent reference.

Online Articles

"Vatican Is Investigating the Inquisition, in Secret"

New York Times, October 31, 1998
http://www.nytimes.com/1998/10/31/world/
vatican-is-investigating-the-inquisition-in-secret.html

SELECTED BIBLIOGRAPHY

Books

Anderson, James M. *Daily Life During the Spanish Inquisition.* Westport, CT: Greenwood Press, 2002.

Carr, Matthew. *Blood and Faith: The Purging of Muslim Spain.* London: C. Hurst & Company Ltd., 2009.

Jacoby, Susan. *Strange Gods: A Secular History of Conversion.* New York: Pantheon Books, 2016.

Kamen, Henry. *Empire: How Spain Became A World Power, 1492–1763.* New York: Harper Collins, 2003.

Murphy, Cullen. *God's Jury: The Inquisition and the Making of the Modern World.* New York: Houghton Mifflin Harcourt, 2012.

Reston, James, Jr. *Dogs of God: Columbus, the Inquisition, and the Defeat of the Moors.* New York: Doubleday, 2005.

Online Articles

Arie, Sophie. "Historians Say Inquisition Wasn't That Bad." *Guardian,* June 15, 2004. http://www.theguardian.com/world/2004/jun/16/artsandhumanities.internationaleducationnews.

"Christian-Jewish Relations: The Inquisition." Jewish Virtual Library. Accessed June 6, 2016. http://www.jewishvirtuallibrary.org/jsource/History/Inquisition.html.

Cohen, Mark. R. "The 'Golden Age' of Jewish-Muslim Relations: Myth and Reality." Princeton University Press. Accessed June 22, 2016. http://press.princeton.edu/chapters/p10098.pdf.

Editors of Encyclopædia Britannica. "Sixtus IV." Encyclopædia Britannica Online. Accessed June 22, 2016. https://www.britannica.com/biography/Sixtus-IV.

Gascoigne, Bamber. "History of Spain." History World. Accessed June 10, 2016. http://www.historyworld.net/wrldhis/PlainTextHistories.asp?groupid=1741&HistoryID=ab50&gtrack=pthc.

Haliczer, Stephen. "The Cathar Heresy." PBS. Accessed June 12, 2016. http://www-tc.pbs.org/inquisition/pdf/TheCatharHeresy.pdf.

History.com Staff. "Middle Ages." History.com. Accessed June 5, 2016. http://www.history.com/topics/middle-ages.

Hundley, Tom. "Hoping to Heal, Vatican Revisits the Inquisition." *Chicago Tribune*, November 9, 1998. http://articles.chicagotribune.com/1998-11-09/news/9811090166_1_inquisition-vatican-carlo-ginzburg.

Lockwood, Robert P. "Secrets of the Spanish Inquisition Revealed." Catholic.com. Accessed May 30, 2016. http://www.catholic.com/magazine/articles/secrets-of-the-spanish-inquisition-revealed.

Madden, Thomas F. "The Real Inquisition." *National Review*, June 18, 2004. http://www.nationalreview.com/article/211193/real-inquisition-thomas-f-madden.

McDonald, James. "Cathars and Cathar Beliefs in the Languedoc." Cathar.info. Accessed June 13, 2016. http://www.cathar.info.

New World Encyclopedia contributors. "Spanish Inquisition." New World Encyclopedia. Accessed May 24, 2016. http://www.newworldencyclopedia.org/p/index.php?title=Spanish_Inquisition&oldid=991350.

Rice, Ellen. "The Myth of the Spanish Inquisition." Catholic Education Resource Center. Accessed May 24, 2016. http://www.catholiceducation.org/en/culture/history/the-myth-of-the-spanish-inquisition.html.

Ryan, Edward A. "Spanish Inquisition." Encyclopædia Britannica Online. Accessed June 13, 2016. http://www.britannica.com/topic/Spanish-Inquisition.

Stanley, Alessandra. "Vatican Is Investigating the Inquisition, in Secret." *New York Times*, October 31, 1998. http://www.nytimes.com/1998/10/31/world/vatican-is-investigating-the-inquisition-in-secret.html.

Wilkes, Jonny. "In a Nutshell: Spanish Inquisition." History Extra, January 15, 2016. http://www.historyextra.com/article/international-history/nutshell-spanish-inquisition.

INDEX

Gerry Boehme is a published author, editor, speaker, and business consultant who was born in New York City. He loves to travel and to learn about new things. He especially enjoys talking with people who have different backgrounds and opinions.

Gerry has written books for students dealing with many subjects, including dangerous drugs and famous people who have made a difference in other people's lives. He has also published many articles dealing with media, advertising, and new technology, and he has been featured as a speaker at business conferences across the United States as well as in the United Kingdom, Australia, and the Republic of Korea.

Gerry graduated from The Newhouse School at Syracuse University and now lives on Long Island, New York, with his wife and two children.